# Henry and Edsel

## The Creation of the Ford Empire

### Richard Bak

WILEY

John Wiley & Sons, Inc.

*For Denise Marie Maher,*
*my little Irish sweetheart*
*from the old neighborhood in Detroit*

This book is printed on acid-free paper. ∞

Copyright © 2003 by Richard Bak. All rights reserved

Published by John Wiley & Sons, Inc., Hoboken, New Jersey
Published simultaneously in Canada

Frank Marquart, *An Auto Worker's Journal: The UAW from Crusade to One-Party Union*. University Park: Pennsylvania State University Press, 1975, pp. 5–9. Copyright © 1975 by The Pennsylvania State University. Reproduced by permission of the publisher.

Excerpts of oral histories from the Walter Reuther Archives of Labor History and Urban Affairs, Wayne State University. Used with permission.

Excerpts of "Reminiscences" from the Collections of Henry Ford Museum & Greenfield Village, Benson Ford Research Center. Used with permission.

No part of this publication may be reproduced, stored in a retrieval system, or transmitted in any form or by any means, electronic, mechanical, photocopying, recording, scanning, or otherwise, except as permitted under Section 107 or 108 of the 1976 United States Copyright Act, without either the prior written permission of the Publisher, or authorization through payment of the appropriate per-copy fee to the Copyright Clearance Center, 222 Rosewood Drive, Danvers, MA 01923, (978) 750-8400, fax (978) 750-4470, or on the web at www.copyright.com. Requests to the Publisher for permission should be addressed to the Permissions Department, John Wiley & Sons, Inc., 111 River Street, Hoboken, NJ 07030, (201) 748-6011, fax (201) 748-6008, email: permcoordinator@wiley.com.

Limit of Liability/Disclaimer of Warranty: While the publisher and the author have used their best efforts in preparing this book, they make no representations or warranties with respect to the accuracy or completeness of the contents of this book and specifically disclaim any implied warranties of merchantability or fitness for a particular purpose. No warranty may be created or extended by sales representatives or written sales materials. The advice and strategies contained herein may not be suitable for your situation. You should consult with a professional where appropriate. Neither the publisher nor the author shall be liable for any loss of profit or any other commercial damages, including but not limited to special, incidental, consequential, or other damages.

For general information about our other products and services, please contact our Customer Care Department within the United States at (800) 762-2974, outside the United States at (317) 527-3993 or fax (317) 572-4002.

Wiley also publishes its books in a variety of electronic formats. Some content that appears in print may not be available in electronic books. For more information about Wiley products, visit our web site at www.wiley.com.

Library of Congress Cataloging-in-Publication Data:

Bak, Richard, date.
    Henry and Edsel : the creation of the Ford Empire / Richard Bak.
        p.   cm.
    Includes bibliographical references and index.
    ISBN 0-471-23487-7 (Cloth : alk. paper)
    1. Ford, Henry, 1863–1947. 2. Ford, Edsel, 1893–1943. 3. Industrialists—United States—Biography. 4. Automobile industry and trade—United States—History. 5. Ford Motor Company—History. I. Title.

HD9710.U52F655 2003
338.7'6292'092273—dc21                                    2003004786

10 9 8 7 6 5 4 3 2 1

# Contents

∽o∾

# Acknowledgments

Many individuals and institutions contributed to the making of this book, and it is my pleasure to acknowledge their help. The staffs of the Benson Ford Research Center at Henry Ford Museum & Greenfield Village, the Walter Reuther Archives of Labor History and Urban Affairs at Wayne State University, the Burton Historical Collection of the Detroit Public Library, the Edsel and Eleanor Ford House, Albert Kahn Associates, and the Detroit Institute of Arts located written and visual materials. Judy Platt at the Federal Reserve Library in Philadelphia translated the Fords' immense wealth of eighty years ago into current dollars. Dick Folsom and Mike Skinner of the Henry Ford Heritage Association provided several useful leads. Al Bardelli, Mark Beltaire, Lucienne Bloch, Paul Boatin, Ford R. Bryan, Rosalie Kahn Butzel, Henry Dominguez, Linda Downs, Richard Earl Jr., George Ebling Jr., Virginia Ebling, Edsel Ford II, Doug Fraser, Bill Hackett, Bill Kahn, Bill May, Tim O'Callaghan, Bruce Simpson, and Dominick Vettraino offered insights and anecdotes. Bill Dow and Aric Karpinski assisted in portions of the research. Through it all, Hana Umlauf Lane at John Wiley & Sons remained a remarkably patient and supportive editor, enduring the hiccups in the production of this manuscript with an equanimity that would have startled Henry Ford's head-cracking factory boss, "Cast Iron" Charlie Sorenson. My sincere thanks go out to all.

# 1

⣥⦾⣥

# Farmboy, Tinkerer

*When we had mechanical or "wind up" toys given to us at Christmas, we always said, "Don't let Henry see them! He just takes them apart!"*

—Margaret Ford Ruddiman

W hile the Ford Motor Company officially traces its origins to June 16, 1903, when the world's second-largest automaker was incorporated with $28,000 scraped together from a grab bag of investors, the year 1847 can be said to mark the true hardscrabble beginnings of the Henry Ford story. That year, his father, William Ford, crossed the Atlantic from Ireland in one of the notorious "coffin ships" that over the course of a decade deposited more than a million of his countrymen in harbors up and down the eastern seaboard—and more than a few unfortunate souls into the sea en route.

Only the most gullible child believed the New World was a land of lemonade lakes and seven-pound potatoes. But even if the United States failed to live up to its utopian billing, the notion of America as the last best hope never shined brighter to ordinary folks looking for the space and freedom to better their daily predicament. Outposts of opportunity seemed to be everywhere in 1847, for foreigners and native-born alike. Gold was discovered in California, touching off a stampede of prospectors, sutlers, saloonkeepers, card sharks, and prostitutes. American troops invaded Mexico and quickly occupied the capital, opening up land north of the Rio Grande to disorderly settlement by discharged "doughboys" and the assorted misfits, adventurers, and desperadoes that filled the West. The Mormons, led by Brigham Young, steered their oxcarts into the valley of the Great Salt Lake in Utah. In the wilds of Oregon and Minnesota, other pioneers—many of them European immigrants—stubbornly planted seeds and their dead children in the same soil. In villages and on tenant farms throughout the Old World, tens of thousands of men, women, and children readied bundles for their own transatlantic voyage, while ten times that number dreamed of one day escaping themselves.

Nowhere did "America fever" rage greater than in Ireland, where a potato famine exacerbated the grinding poverty in which most had been living under British rule for generations. In 1847 alone, 100,000 of the Emerald Isle's population squeezed their way into the cramped, damp, disease-ridden holds of ships bound for the United States. Among this multitude was a twenty-one-year-old carpenter from County Cork named William Ford.

William traveled in a group of Protestant emigrants that included his father, John; his mother, Thomasine, who died aboard ship; six brothers and sisters; and several other relatives. Their destination was Dearborn, Michigan, where two uncles had settled fifteen years earlier. The farming community, incorporated as the village of Dearbornville in 1838, was located eight miles west of Detroit and was the site of a federal arsenal. A plank road, today's Michigan Avenue, connected the village with Detroit and extended all the way through the wilderness to Chicago.

The Chicago road underscored the growing importance of Michigan. The former territory, teeming with natural beauty and resources, had become a state in 1837. With the opening of the Erie Canal and the development of the steamboat, the vacant lands of the interior were now within reach of thousands of newcomers. Detroit, a somnolent river community of just 2,200 souls in the early 1830s, suddenly became a major port of entry, shedding its character as a former French trading post in the process. Like many ports, it became as much a destination in itself as a jumping-off point. In 1847 the "gateway to the West" was home to nearly 20,000 people, making it one of the largest and fastest growing urban centers in the country. Within a dozen years the population would swell to 46,000, with roughly half its citizens foreign-born, the majority of them Irish.

After a bone-jarring journey of several weeks, the weary band of Fords trudged into Dearborn one day in 1847. Either they liked what

they saw or they were too tired to travel any farther, for most of the
party ultimately decided to stay put. John Ford immediately borrowed
$350 to purchase eighty acres of land in Greenfield, the township adja-
cent to Dearborn. Over time, trees were cleared, fields were laid out, a
main house and outbuildings were built, trade was established, the debt
was serviced, and life fell into its comforting cyclical patterns.

William, who appears resolute and clear-eyed in his few surviving
photographs, worked as a carpenter for the Michigan Central Railroad
and helped around the farm when he could. In 1858, after eleven years
of scrimping and saving, he bought half of his father's acreage for $600.
He then set about finding a wife. He had recently met a young woman
named Mary Litogot, a dark-haired orphan of Belgian descent who had
been adopted by Patrick and Margaret O'Hern. The O'Herns were a
charitable, childless couple for whom William had done some carpen-
try work. Mary, fourteen years William's junior, waited until she had
finished school before accepting his proposal of marriage.

William Ford and Mary Litogot exchanged vows on April 25, 1861,
just as the first drum rolls of the Civil War were sounded. While many
local men soon marched off to fight (including Mary's two brothers, one
of whom was killed and the other wounded at the battle of Fredericks-
burg), William, too old for effective soldiering, concentrated on growing his farm and a family.

Successful farming hinged to a great degree on the number of children—ideally, several strapping sons—that were available to work the
land and mind the endless chores. To that end, William and Mary immediately started a family. After their first child, a boy, died in delivery,
Mary soon announced she was pregnant again. Early on the morning
of July 30, 1863, a midwife named Granny Holmes helped Mary give
birth to a healthy boy in an upstairs bedroom. The baby was named
Henry, after William's brother, who had caught gold fever and, after his
dreams of riches literally failed to pan out, settled in California.

Henry Ford's birth came within a month of Union victories at
Gettysburg and Vicksburg, which turned the tide of the war. When the
fighting ended two years later, Henry was joined by a brother, John.
Over the next several years four more children followed: Margaret
(1867), Jane (1869), William (1871), and Robert (1873). All grew up
inside the spacious, substantial-looking frame house that William built
on his in-laws' property at what is now Ford Road and Greenfield in
Dearborn. Today a splendid, sprawling retirement community—Henry

Ford Village—covers the site, while the original white-painted two-story house has long since been moved to Greenfield Village, the museum-park located nearby.

Thanks to its geographic advantages, Detroit boomed as a shipping and manufacturing center in the years following the Civil War. Paints, pills, boats, cigars, stoves, shoes, seeds, railroad cars, brass fittings—all helped the city and the surrounding region grow in population and importance. "Detroit will resolve into one of the greatest industrial islands on earth," predicted steel tycoon Eber Brock Ward, the city's first millionaire. "With immense supplies of iron and copper to the north, coal to the south, the Detroit River in front and canals on either end, the city cannot miss."

Mirroring this prosperity was William Ford, who became a man of substance in the community. Sidney Olson would write, "William Ford was a churchwarden who married people, a justice of the peace, a solid figure in town councils, a man who read every day not only the county paper but also a New York newspaper and who all his life never ceased to marvel that a famine-driven Irish immigrant boy could find himself the owner of honest acres in a free land." That kind of man would come to find fault with his firstborn, who grew up not sharing his old-fashioned views about an eldest son's duties to land and family.

✧

One autumn day in 1913, Henry Ford—by now a fifty-year-old captain of industry himself—rummaged around in the attic of his mind and, on the pages of one of the "jot books" he often carried with him, recorded the particulars of his first memory.

> The first thing that I remember in my life is my Father taking my brother John and myself to see a bird's nest under a large oak log twenty rods East of our Home and my birth place, John was so young that he could not walk Father carried Him I being two years older could run along with them this must have been about the year of 1866 in June I remember the nest with 4 eggs and also the bird and hearing it sing I have always remembered the song and in later years found that it was a song sparrow, I remember the log layed in the field for a good many years this field was pasture there was a mill clost to the log where the cows used to drink now 1913 there is slight depression where the well was and the field is a nice meadow now.

Henry's appreciation for the natural world, especially for birds, was genuine and lasted a lifetime. But for all his bucolic recollections of his rural upbringing, the fact is that he grew up hating the drudgery involved in living close to the land. There were cows to milk, potatoes to dig, fruit to pick, chickens to tend, stalls to clean, horses to harness, wheat and corn to harvest, wood to chop, kindling boxes to fill, buckets of water to haul—the list of chores went on and on. Of course, disenchanted farmboys in the 1870s were not a new phenomenon. Preachers and parents and editorial writers had been moaning about the "dissipation" and "lost vigor" of American youth since well before the Civil War, their concern growing more strident as labor- and time-saving mechanical devices became increasingly prevalent in daily life. One measure of the furious pace of technological change in the last part of the nineteenth century is the number of patents granted inventors. Between 1860 and 1900, a forty-year period that roughly parallels Henry Ford's formative years, some 640,000 patents were issued—an eighteen-fold increase over the mere 36,000 registered with the U.S. Patent Office in the previous seventy years. During the Civil War, William Ford had invested in a McCormick reaper and, like thousands of other farmers around the country, realized an immediate gain in productivity and a corresponding rise in personal wealth.

When it came to removing all of the monotony and hard work from daily life, however, the industrial age wasn't moving fast enough to suit young Henry Ford. His overall impression of the family farm, he admitted years later, "is that, considering the results, there was too much work on the place."

Henry's relationship with his mother was considerably closer than the one he had with his father, although Mary Litogot Ford could be a formidable disciplinarian in her own way. One time, for example, Henry was caught in a lie, and as punishment his mother ignored him for an entire day.

"Shame cuts more deeply than a whip," he remembered. "For a day I was treated with contempt. There was no smiling or glossing over my shortcomings. I learned from her that wrong-doing carries its own punishment. There is no escape."

Mary Ford was firm, evenhanded, and at the same time encouraging and optimistic. She praised her eldest child, who loved nothing better than exploring the innards of a piece of machinery, as "a born mechanic" while reminding him, when he grumbled over a task, that "'I don't want to' gets a fellow nowhere."

Young Henry Ford. This first portrait of the future industrialist was made sometime in late 1865 or early 1866, when he was two and a half years old.

"Life will give you many unpleasant tasks to do," she told him. "Your duty will be hard and disagreeable and painful to you at times, but you must do it. You may have pity on others, but you must not pity yourself." Henry would remember his mother as being "of that rarest type, one who so loved her children that she did not care whether they loved her. What I mean by this is that she would do whatever she considered necessary for our welfare even if she thereby lost our good will."

As was the case with most children then, Henry attended school sporadically. Formal learning, though highly coveted in theory, always took a back seat to the practical demands of farmwork. Henry first stepped into a classroom when he was seven years old, sharing a desk at the Scotch Settlement School (the same one-room schoolhouse his mother had attended) with a bright, dark-haired boy named Edsel Ruddiman. Edsel became Henry's best pal and they engaged in the usual juvenile high-jinks and pastimes: playing ball, catching frogs, annoying girls, swimming, skating, and carving their initials into desks. They wrote notes to each other in class using a secret alphabet. "I remember distinctly one time Miss Proctor kept us there on the back seat in the corner and gave us a lecture on being better boys," Henry recalled as an adult. "I am afraid she labored in vain to reform two such hard cases as we were."

Helping to correct a youngster's sometimes wobbly walk along the straight and narrow path was William Holmes McGuffey, the Ohio educator whose *Eclectic Readers* had long been standard fare in Midwestern schoolhouses. The series of books, originally released between 1836 and 1857, were more than anthologies of selections from English and American literature. They were compilations of simple, easily understood morality plays, in which virtue was immediately rewarded and vice was just as quickly punished. As this selection from one of his *Readers* demonstrates, McGuffey drove home his lessons with all the subtlety of a blacksmith striking an anvil.

Look, look, is not this Frank Brown? What can be the matter with him?

The poor boy is dead. He was on his way to school, when a bad boy met him, and said:

"Come, Frank, go with me to the pond." "O no," said Frank, "I can not; I must go to school."

But the bad boy told him it was not time to go to school. So Frank went with him to the pond.

Do you see the bad boy? He stands by the side of the man.

Frank fell into the pond, and the bad boy could not help him out.

He cried, "Help, help!" A man heard him, and ran to the pond. But when he got there, poor Frank was dead.

What will his parents do when he is taken home dead?

Do not stop to play on your way to school. Do not play with bad boys. They will lead you into harm.

*McGuffey's Eclectic Readers* had a profound effect on generations of schoolchildren, perhaps none so famous as Henry Ford. Taking his lead from McGuffey—and his mother—Henry tended to reduce life's complexities into simple questions of black and white, good versus evil, passing off aphorisms and homespun remedies as profundity. The notebooks he carried around as an adult are filled with such entries as "Anybody can complain" and "Don't find fault—find a remedy."

One March day in 1876, Mary Ford died of a fever, several days after giving birth to a stillborn child. She was only thirty-seven years old and Henry twelve when she passed away. Already a person comfortable with long stretches of solitude at a workbench or under a shade tree, he became even more quiet and withdrawn, later describing the suddenly motherless house as being "like a watch without a main-spring." For the rest of his days he would worship the memory of his mother, elevating her to near sainthood status. "She taught us what the modern family needs to learn—the art of being happy with each other . . . that if we couldn't be happy here in this house we'd never be happy anywhere else," he recollected.

At the same time he harbored a grudge against his father. He seemed to hold him at least partially responsible for his mother's death, as Mary Ford, already worn down from the grind of daily housekeeping and eight previous pregnancies, died before her time while dutifully bearing yet another of William Ford's progeny. Alcohol also was a point of quiet contention. Drinking, which often brought a good man low, was a vice that Henry hated. His father's tippling would inform all of Henry's future views on the subject, from his approval of the various temperance movements to his disapprobation of his own son's indulgence in an occasional cocktail.

After his mother's death, Henry became wary of revealing too much of himself to others, even close friends and family members. "It is not necessary to expose your inner self to anyone," he once explained as a young man. Deep inside his callused heart, he may very well have considered himself more of a Litogot than a Ford. Once, very late in his life, Henry pointed out his birthplace to one of his mother's cousins. "You see that home?" he said. "That's my mother's home. My father just walked into that place. That belonged to my mother."

∽○∾

The Centennial Exposition, the great fair commemorating the centenary of the Declaration of Independence, opened in Philadelphia a few weeks after Mary Ford's death. William Ford and several traveling companions made the arduous trip from Dearborn to Pennsylvania, returning home with brochures, catalogs, and a greater appreciation of a young, vibrant nation flexing its industrial and technological muscle.

Henry, who had "wheels in his head," ate up the detailed literature and anecdotal accounts of what his father had seen: lathes, band saws, locomotives, and a two-story-high steam engine, the world's largest, as well as several different versions of the internal combustion engine. For as long as anybody could remember, he had demonstrated a passionate interest in—and a remarkable aptitude for—all things mechanical, taking apart watches, windup toys, and farm machinery to see how they operated and then reassembling them with nary a part left over. "Every clock in the Ford home shuddered when it saw him coming," quipped one contemporary. William responded to Henry's fascination with gadgetry by giving the boy unfettered access to his workshop and placing him in charge of the upkeep and repair of all the farm machinery.

"Father was quick to recognize Henry's ability in making new things," wrote Henry's sister, Margaret. "He was very understanding of Henry's demands for new tools for the shop and ours was one of the best equipped in the neighborhood."

That same year, 1876, Henry got his first glimpse of a self-propelled steam engine—an epiphanic moment. He was riding in a wagon with his father on one of their regular trips into Detroit when they came across the huge iron contraption noisily making its way down the dirt road. "I had seen plenty of these engines hauled around by horses," he recalled, "but this one had a chain that made a connection between the engine and the rear wheels of the wagon-like frame on which the boiler was mounted." The engineer on this machine stood on a platform behind the boiler, feeding it coal, operating the throttle and steering the unwieldy beast as best he could.

It was at once clumsy, primitive—and the very embodiment of Yankee ingenuity. While William reined in the startled horses, Henry jumped down from the wagon to interrogate the engineer. How fast did the engine run? (Two hundred turns a minute.) How much fuel did it require? (A lot.) How fast did it go? (Not very.) And on and on. When Henry returned home, he immediately set about replicating the marvel he had seen, employing a five-gallon oil can as his boiler. It would be his first of countless experiments in building a practical machine capable of moving under its own power.

∽o∾

In the fall of 1879, sixteen-year-old Henry Ford left school and the farm and took his first job in the city: a highly paid ($1.10 a day) apprenticeship with the Michigan Car Company, a manufacturer of railroad boxcars and one of Detroit's largest employers. He lasted just one week. His mistake was being *too* good of a tinkerer, for after solving a mechanical problem that had stumped older employees, his embarrassed foreman fired him. He left with a valuable lesson, one that

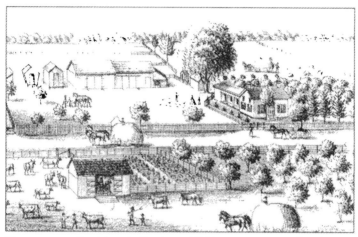

The prosperous Ford farm in Dearborn, Michigan, as it appeared in the 1876 *Illustrated Atlas of Wayne County*.

reinforced his growing suspicious nature: "I learned then not to tell all you know."

William Ford was not happy with his son's decision to leave the homestead for the factory, but he did not stand in his way, figuring, perhaps, that a taste of life in the dirty, hectic confines of the city would hasten his son's permanent return to the open rural spaces of Dearborn. In fact, he helped set him up in his next job, a position with the James Flower & Brothers Machine Shop. The dilapidated two-story shop was owned and operated by three aging Scotch brothers who occasionally bought fruit and vegetables from the Fords. For $2.50 a week, a meager salary even in those times, Henry worked ten hours a day, Monday through Saturday. He started on a milling machine, shaping hexagons on brass valves.

"They put Henry in with me, and he and I got chummy right away," recalled a young co-worker, Frederick Strauss. "Henry was to do the same work that I did. He didn't sweep the floor. I did that because I was more of a worker than he was. He never was a good worker, but he was a good fellow."

It was a valuable learning experience for Henry, though he had to moonlight as a watch repairman at Robert Magill's jewelry shop to cover the $3.50 weekly expense of lodging at a nearby boardinghouse. The Flowers' foundry "manufactured everything in the line of brass and iron—globe and gate valves, gongs, steam-whistles, fire hydrants, and valves for water pipes," said Strauss. "There was a great variety of

Mary Litogot Ford,
Henry's mother.

work. Some of the castings of the iron bodies of the large gate valves weighed a ton or more. They made so many different articles that they had to have all kinds of machines, large and small lathes and drill presses. . . . They had more machines than workmen in that shop."

Henry spent nine months at Flowers' before moving on to the Detroit Dry Dock Engine Works for $2 a week. When he wasn't soaking up mechanical arcana about the varied collection of machines in use at the sprawling shipbuilding firm, he was spending his day off skipping stones on the Detroit River and discussing grandiose projects with his friend. "Henry was always wanting to make things," said Strauss. One week it was an eight-day clock, the next it was a boat. "Every Sunday we started something and never finished it," Strauss remembered.

A wonderful anecdote survives from the two years he spent at Detroit Dry Dock. One day Henry was straining to push a wheelbarrow up a steep gangway when Frank A. Kirby, the rich and locally famous construction engineer who had started the company, stopped what he was doing long enough to offer some encouragement to the flushed-face youngster. "Stick in your toenails, boy," Kirby shouted, "and you will make it!"

Recalling the episode to Kirby three decades later, by which time his former employer was now working for him building Liberty boats, Ford added, "Well, I have been sticking in my toenails ever since." The apprentice-turned-carmaker so appreciated his old boss's gesture of support that in the 1920s he had the letters K I R B Y carved into the frieze of the Ford Engineering Laboratory, his name alongside those of more celebrated—but to Henry, no less influential—figures named Edison, Galileo, Copernicus, and Newton.

∽∘∾

After three years in the city, Henry returned to Dearborn in the summer of 1882. He would live the next nine years there. But to his father's disappointment, he would spend none of them farming. He owned no livestock, no farming implements, and planted no crops. Instead, a few months after his return home, he accepted a job as a Westinghouse agent, traveling throughout the southern Michigan countryside to demonstrate and service the company's portable steam engine—basically, a self-propelled boiler on four wheels. By changing belts and constantly feeding the fire with wood or coal, the steam engine could be used to mechanize such labor-intensive tasks as threshing clover, grinding feed, pressing cider, husking corn, and sawing wood.

Henry had first become acquainted with "the little high-speed, quick-steaming thing" when a neighbor hired him at the rate of three dollars a day to operate the new machine, model number 345, he had just purchased. "I have an idea he was afraid of his machine," said Henry. "To tell the truth, I was frightened myself."

His mastery of the steam engine surprised his doubting father as much as it pleased Henry. "At the end of that first day I was as weary as I had been nervous at its beginning," he said, "but I had run the engine steadily, inducing it to stand up nicely to its work, and I forgot my griminess and weariness in the consciousness I had actually accomplished what I had started out to do. There are few more comforting feelings."*

---

* In 1913, Ford's agents searched long and hard for the Westinghouse steam engine that produced such nostalgia in the auto tycoon. Model number 345 was finally found rusting on a Pennsylvania farm. Its owner surrendered it for ten dollars and a new Model T. Ford had it lovingly restored and later fired it up on his sixtieth birthday, threshing wheat for the cameras. Today model 345 sits inside the Henry Ford Museum in Dearborn, polished, oiled, and looking as it did when Henry Ford first set eyes on it in 1882.

On his twenty-first birthday, July 30, 1884, Henry received a gift of forty acres of land in neighboring Springwells Township from his father, who still had hopes of establishing his oldest son as a farmer. As a bribe, the Moir farm (as the property near present-day Ford and Southfield roads was called) was a failure. Henry spent $250 on a circular sawmill and a portable engine to run it and started clearing the elm, maple, ash, beech, and black oak trees off his property. The cut-up trees were sold as lumber and cordwood. Later that year, anxious to fill in some gaps in his knowledge, he took several courses at a business college in Detroit, gaining a rudimentary knowledge of bookkeeping, mechanical drawing, and general business practices.

Over the next couple years, Henry worked summers setting up and repairing portable farm engines for the Buckeye Harvester Company, then operated his sawmill on the Moir farm the rest of the year. In his free time he read technical magazines and expanded his experimentation into steam and gas engines, struggling to build, among other things, a "farm locomotive" that could be powered by a single-cylinder steam engine. According to Sidney Olson, "The problem that fascinated him most was how to build a machine that ran on the road. He was always working on that: how to increase the power without increasing the weight, how to link up the power with the drive, how to have more than one kind of steering speed (gears), how best to steer, how best to connect the wheels to the frame—and all the things that seem so simple today to motorists who don't even know how to lift the hoods on their cars."

⸎

As Henry entered his twenties, young ladies considered him a good catch. He was handsome, clear-eyed, lithe, and lean, and for all of his long hours at the workbench he had found a balance between labor and leisure. He enjoyed dancing, skating, picnics, hayrides, and taking long walks along the wooded banks of the Rouge, the river that coursed through Dearborn. He had a lifelong appreciation of pranks and practical jokes. He was clearly ambitious and displayed a vigorous self-confidence that was contagious and attracted people to him. This personal magnetism would prove to be a valuable asset when it came time to find investors in his schemes—not to mention the woman who was to become his bride.

On St. Valentine's Day, 1886, twenty-two-year-old Henry sat down and composed a letter to Miss Clara Jane Bryant. He had first met the sweet-faced nineteen-year-old from Greenfield Township at a New Year's dance on the first day of 1885.

Dear Clara

> I again take the pleasure of writing you a few lines. It seems like a year since i seen you. It don't seem mutch like cutter rideing to night does it but i guess we will have more sleighing . . . Clara Dear you did not expect me Friday night and i think as the weather is so bad you will not expect me tonight, but if the weather and roads are good you look for me. Friday or Saterday night for the Opera or Sunday night or Monday night at the party and if your Brother has got some one else let me know when you write but i guess i will see you before then. Clara Dear, you can not imagine what pleasure it gives me to think that i have at last found one so loveing kind and true as you are and i hope we will always have good success. Well i shall have to Close wishing you all the Joys of the year and a kind Good Night.

> May Flowerettes of love around you bee twined
> And the Sunshine of peace Shed its joy's o'er your Minde
> From one that Dearly loves you

H.

Clara, the eldest of ten children, "had quite a few beaux," recalled Henry's sister, Margaret. "She was a popular girl, very sociable." Although initially unimpressed by Henry, Clara was soon won over by this clever young man bubbling over with ideas. He seemed different from the other suitors, showing her a watch with two sets of hands—one for standard railroad time and the other for sun time. "I remember going home and telling how sensible he was, how serious-minded," Clara later said in an interview with the *Ladies' Home Journal*. Two months after receiving this Valentine's Day letter, Clara and Henry became engaged.

Clara was no cream puff, often accompanying—and sometimes assisting—her fiancé as he went about operating his sawmill. She had unshakable faith in Henry and his future, gaining her the sobriquet "The Believer." In private, Henry always called her by his pet name, "Callie." In five years he cut an aggregate one million feet of lumber, selling to shipyards, furniture factories, lumberyards, and individuals. William Ford may have hoped his son was clearing the trees in order to farm the land, but Henry was unequivocal about his intentions: "Cutting the timber gave me a chance to get married."

Henry Ford (*back row, third from right*) with fellow employees of the Detroit Edison Illuminating Company, c. 1892.

And marry he did, on April 11, 1887, Clara's twenty-first birthday. The service was held in the home of Clara's parents. The wedding presents were laid out on a bed, which collapsed when the newlyweds sat on the edge of it. "How we roared," remembered one guest, "as everyone came running to see the bride and groom . . . almost buried in presents!" The couple lived in an old, small house on the Moir farm for a year before moving into a new home built by Henry. Known as the Square House, it was Clara's favorite of all the residences she and her husband would share during sixty years of marriage, possibly because she had laid out the specifications for it herself. There was an organ for her to play in the parlor and finely finished furniture in all of the rooms. The setting was bucolic, peaceful.

Then one day in 1891, Henry consulted with Clara about taking a job with the Edison Illuminating Company, the youngest of the three companies then selling electricity to Detroit's homes and businesses. He explained that in order to pursue his goal of creating a road vehicle, he needed to understand the nascent science of electricity. "It almost broke her heart" to leave the Square House, a relative said, but the Believer lived up to her nickname, uncomplainingly agreeing to make the move to Detroit late that September.

The future Mrs. Ford, Clara
Jane Bryant, in April 1887,
shortly before her wedding.
Henry called her "Callie."

As Henry quickly made a reputation for himself at the Edison station house, Clara quietly put up with a succession of moves, each
rented house or flat representing an incremental improvement over the
previous one. Within a couple of years they were living comfortably
enough in a house at 570 West Forest Avenue, which is where, on
November 6, 1893, Clara gave birth to a bouncing baby boy. "I didn't
run into any difficulty," Dr. David O'Donnell said of the delivery. "Mrs.
Ford didn't give me any trouble at all. She never complained. Mr. Ford
was in the house. He didn't get excited and he didn't bother me. Most
young fathers bother the life out of a doctor." The boy was named
Edsel Bryant Ford. His namesake was Dr. Edsel Ruddiman, Henry's old
schoolyard chum, who had gone on to the success everybody had predicted for him as a university-educated pharmacist.*

---

* There is some anecdotal evidence that suggests that Edsel Ford grew up not entirely
pleased with his name. "I remember [Clara] say once that she wondered sometimes
whether Edsel liked his name," recalled Esther Davis, whose grandmother was William
Ford's sister. "She said she thought it was too bad children couldn't be given a name
the parents liked when they were very small and then when they got to the age of
maybe sixteen or eighteen, if they decided they just didn't like it, they ought to be
allowed to change it. From that I would gather there must have been a little argument
or dissatisfaction with Edsel about his name."

Dr. O'Donnell received ten dollars, while a live-in nurse was paid four dollars for each of the two weeks she spent there assisting mother and child. Henry could afford it. Within days of his son's birth the proud papa had been given a considerable raise, from $50 to $90 a month. On December 1, 1893, he was promoted to chief engineer. Two weeks later, the family moved to 58 Bagley Avenue, near Grand River.

For reasons that can only be guessed at, Clara never bore another child, certainly a disappointment to Henry, who throughout his long life clearly loved children. With Edsel's birth the immediate family unit was complete. It would remain intact for the next half-century as Henry Ford—an unaccomplished thirty-year-old tinkerer destined to become a social engineer on a scale unimaginable to anyone in 1893—took them along on the ride of their lives.

# 2

∽∘∾

# The Horse Is Gone

*There is something uncanny about these newfangled vehicles. They are all unutterably ugly and never a one of them has been provided with a good or even an endurable name. The French, who are usually orthodox in their etymology if in nothing else, have evolved "automobile," which being half Greek and half Latin is so near to indecent that we print it with hesitation; while speakers of English have been fatally attracted by the irrelevant word "horseless." Other nations have been equally unfortunate and it really looks as if the dispossessed or to be dispossessed animals are to get revenge on an ungrateful humanity by stumping us to find a respectable name for our noisy and odorous machine.*

—1899 editorial in the *New York Times*

Henry Ford, following a national craze, bought a bicycle in 1893. Here was a new kind of personal mobility, one that did not involve the mess, cost, and time-consuming responsibilities of hitching up ol' Dobbin.

Henry had never been fond of horses, anyway, not since that day when a spooked colt had dragged the then nine-year-old boy, his foot caught in the stirrup, around the Ford farm. Moreover, like many inhabitants of America's rapidly growing urban centers, Henry was personally affronted by the ubiquitous horse manure and urine. One city dweller complained that streets were "literally carpeted with a warm, brown matting of comminuted horse dropping, smelling to heaven and destined in no inconsiderable part to be scattered in fine dust in all directions, laden with countless millions of disease-breeding germs." It was estimated that in New York City alone, horses and mules dropped up to 1.3 million pounds of manure on streets each day. In Detroit as elsewhere, animal waste was a major health problem only partially alleviated by regular street washings and the army of "white wings" whose job was to sweep up the fetid, fly-blown piles of decaying organic matter.

Although bicycles had been around in one form or another since the 1830s, early models were dangerously unstable and expensive. However, the introduction and mass production of the "safety" bicycle, featuring pneumatic tires and wheels of equal diameter, opened up its use to millions of ordinary men and women. Its ease of operation promised to make the bicycle the "universally accepted steed of the future," gushed one acolyte. Of course, the mud, ruts, and chuckholes that characterized the two million miles of country roads in the United States then weren't the obstacles to horses that they were to cyclists, who were looking to expand their excursions outside the better paved but more congested city streets. Thus the wild popularity of the bicycle in the late 1880s begat a highly organized, public clamor for improved roads, which in turn helped to inspire hundreds of inventors to start serious work on developing a more sophisticated self-propelled vehicle to take advantage of them. "Before this," observed inventor Hiram Percy Maxim, "the bicycle had not yet directed men's minds to the possibilities of independent, long-distance travel over the ordinary highway."

It was the network of paved, publicly maintained highways—a legacy of Napoleonic rule—that helped account for the early French leadership in developing the *automobile*. Names such as Louis Renault, Emile Lavassor, Rene Panhard, and the Peugeot brothers (as well as such words as *garage* and *chauffeur*) regularly appeared in the scientific journals Ford avidly read from cover to cover. At the same time in Germany, Karl Benz and Gottlieb Daimler were creating separate versions of a four-wheel gasoline-powered vehicle. Both were in very limited production by 1889 and are usually pointed to as the forerunners of the modern gas motorcar. The operating principle of the internal combustion engine that powered these vehicles has remained essentially the same since another German, Nikolaus Otto, patented the first commercial four-stroke gasoline engine in 1876. Some years later a trade publication, *Automobile Topics,* described how Daimler's lighter, higher-speed version of Otto's original engine worked.

> The engine is a vertical one, double cylinder, and works on the well known "Otto" cycle, e.g., the downward stroke of the piston sucks in an explosive charge, which at the upstroke is compressed and "fired" by . . . an electric spark. The sudden pressure caused by the firing of the charge forces the piston downward at the next stroke, i.e., the working stroke. At the second upward stroke the exhaust valve is opened by a tappet or cam, and the products of combustion pass out of the cylinder through the exhaust valve. This cycle of operation, known as the "Otto" cycle, is then repeated in the same order.

The now-familiar four-stroke sequence of intake, compression, ignition (power), and exhaust was lost on most inventors, who, nervous about the volatility of gasoline, continued to fit their "horseless carriages" and "power wagons" with steam and electric engines. "You can't get people to sit over an explosion," claimed one builder. Steamers had more power and electrics were easier to start, while both were free of the fumes, sputtering noise, and oil-spitting mess of gas buggies. Also, the steam engine and the electric battery had the virtue of familiarity to inventors, whereas gas engines were something new and strange. There were drawbacks, however. A steamer needed time for pressure to build up in its boiler before the driver could set off to where he was going, and electric cars required regular recharging. Both were extremely heavy, further limiting their range compared with gas buggies.

As builders continued to sort out the relative merits of steamers, electrics, and gasoline cars, the automobile evolved through constant trial and error, with mechanical developments and engineering refinements taking place, usually independently of each other, inside hundreds of scattered barns, basements, stables, and shops. Beyond attempting to perfect the power plant there remained a multitude of other interconnected problems for an inventor to address: engine placement (front, rear, or mid-mount), transmission (transmitting the engine's power to wheels), steering, shifting speeds, and on and on. Converting a wagon or a carriage into a car body and fitting an engine of some type into it was just the start of the battle. Although a few items, such as valves and chains, could be modified for use in creating a motorcar, and others, such as standardized nuts and bolts, could be grabbed off the shelf, every work in progress still needed numerous other parts that had to be individually designed and built from scratch. The necessary tools also had to be created. In short, an entire industry, including everything from terminology to spark plugs, was being built from the ground up. The process was in turn exhausting, exhilarating, and aggravating, with more than enough work to keep busy every interested mechanic, machinist, blacksmith, engineer, scientist, inventor, draftsman, dreamer, and crackpot on both sides of the Atlantic.

American inventors initially lagged behind their European counterparts, but in 1893 Charles and Frank Duryea of Springfield, Massachusetts, designed, built, and drove what is generally recognized as the first gasoline-powered buggy in the United States. Two years later there were some 300 motor-driven vehicles of varying size, shape, and sophistication in the country, enough to warrant staging the first American automobile race, a Thanksgiving Day affair sponsored by the *Chicago Times-Herald*. Charles Duryea covered the 54-mile course in 10 hours, 48 minutes, in a blinding blizzard to capture the top prize. Duryea's average speed of about 5 miles per hour was not nearly as impressive as the fact that his motorcar had been able to make it through treacherous conditions that would have stopped even the stoutest horse. "We had power to spare at all places and had no occasion to get out and push," the winner proclaimed afterward. "Long live the motor wagon!" Such dependability was an aberration among early motorcars, which were prone to breaking down every few miles. Of the hundreds of one-of-a-kind creations then in existence, only a handful of prototypes ultimately went into production. In 1896 the entire U.S. auto "industry" consisted of the Duryea Motor Wagon Company and the Haynes-Apperson Company of Kokomo, Indiana. Their combined output, while meager (the Duryeas hand-built thirteen cars that year to claim the sales lead), marked the first time more than one American automobile had been manufactured from the same design.

Charles Brady King of Detroit never became a nameplate, but late in the evening of March 6, 1896 (a time selected so as not to startle horses on the street), the brilliant young mechanical engineer navigated his rudimentary machine into the local record book. "The first horseless carriage seen in this city was out on the streets last night," reported the next day's *Detroit Free Press*. No early automobile was cruder than King's power wagon: a four-cylinder gas engine fitted into an iron-wheeled wooden cart, steered by a tiller. The contraption weighed 1,300 pounds and trundled over downtown streets at the rate of 6 miles per hour. The *Detroit Journal* quoted King as saying horseless carriages were "much in vogue among the English aristocracy, and will undoubtedly soon be here. . . . I am convinced they will in time supercede the horse."*

Neither newspaper mentioned that the man following King's wagon during its landmark nocturnal run, the derbied fellow dodging snowflakes on his bicycle, was Henry Ford.

∽∘∾

Henry cared nothing about being first in the burgeoning automobile game. A patient and pragmatic man, he was willing to take his time trying to create the most practical car possible. As he soaked in all he could about the machines already out there and the highly publicized endurance races that revealed their best and worst points, he aimed to build what he figured the public would most likely want to buy. The ideal automobile would be lightweight—which meant less fuel consumption and increased range—durable, reliable, and simple to operate and maintain. He didn't set out to build a cheap car for the masses, but after a few detours that is ultimately the road he famously took.

Henry's duties as an operating engineer and machinist at the Edison station on Washington Boulevard—monitoring the steam-pressure gauge, maintaining and repairing the equipment, occasionally shoveling coal—were important but less than onerous, allowing his mind—and feet—to roam. After being promoted to chief engineer he turned the responsibility of being on call twenty-four hours a day to his advantage, moving freely between his workshop at Edison and another he had installed in a brick storage shed in his backyard at 58 Bagley, interspersed with regular side trips to the city's bustling machine shops.

---

* King, five years younger than Ford, was educated at Cornell. He gained a national reputation at the 1893 Columbian Exposition in Chicago, where he won top prize for a pneumatic hammer he invented. He also introduced a steel brake beam for railroad cars at the fair. Among his many other inventions were several that changed the look of the American automobile, including moving the steering column to the left side and the gearshift lever to the interior. King was a man of varied interests and thus lacked the single-minded drive that characterized Ford and other successful auto pioneers. His only manufactured car, the Silent Northern, was a financial flop. He remained lifelong friends with Ford, both surviving long enough to celebrate the golden anniversary of their historic rides in 1946.

"Henry had all kinds of time and he used to come see me," said his old friend, Frederick Strauss, who was now working at the Wain Machine Shop. "He had a little shop of his own back of the Edison Company. . . . Henry used it as a hangout. Other fellows would come sit in there. Henry had a little lathe. He had this idea of making a little gasoline engine out of scrap. We didn't work every night. We would just joke away. Sometimes we would work and sometimes not. It took us about six weeks to get this little engine built.

"Saturday nights we had quite a crowd. Henry had some sort of a magnet. He could draw people to him; that was a funny thing about him."

On Christmas Eve, 1893, while his infant son slept in the next room, Henry clamped his first internal combustion engine to the kitchen sink inside the house on Bagley. He connected a wire from the kitchen light to a homemade spark plug and grounded the engine to a water pipe. Then, while he turned the crankshaft, Clara carefully dribbled some gasoline into the intake valve. The engine coughed, then came alive. Flames shot out of the exhaust. The vibration rattled the dishes and windows. The ungodly noise and noxious fumes finally caused Clara to scoop up little Edsel and carry him upstairs. The incident evidently didn't unsettle the boy. Even before Edsel started kindergarten he was accompanying his father on rides aboard various experimental vehicles.

In the spring of 1896, not long after King's historic trial run, the first of these experimental cars was being painstakingly completed in Ford's backyard shed. Far from being a competitor, King was simply one of the more accomplished members of the fraternity of mechanically minded men in Detroit who over the years pitched in to help Henry build what he called his "quadricycle." In addition to King and Strauss, the group included fellow Edison employees Jim Bishop, Ed "Spider" Huff, and George Cato, and King's assistant, Oliver Barthel. All made some contributions to the very first Ford car. Cato, for example, used his expertise in electricity to devise the ignition system, while Bishop helped fashion the bicycle-like chain drive. Both men worked with Henry to create the two-cylinder, four-cycle engine that was mounted ahead of the rear axle.

Weighing only 500 pounds, Henry's quadricycle—a flimsy wood chassis on four spindly bicycle wheels—was considerably lighter and more streamlined than the vehicles built by King, the Duryea brothers,

Henry Ford poses inside his experimental quadricycle in 1913, seventeen years after his historic 1896 ride through the streets of Detroit.

and most other inventors. As a result it also was faster than most, capable of zipping along at 20 or more miles per hour. The driver sat on a bicycle seat, using a tiller to steer and a large clutch handle to control the two-speed transmission (which had no reverse). There were no brakes.

Clara, as always, lent her support. She pinched pennies to make the household budget stretch to cover the cost of her husband's hardware needs. She shooed away her favorite sister, afraid she'd make fun of Henry's obsession. "Henry is making something," she said mysteriously, "and maybe someday I'll tell you about it."

Sometime in the predawn hours of June 4, 1896, Henry and Jim Bishop readied the quadricycle for its first test drive. First, though, Henry had to apply what mechanics jocularly call "sledgehammer readjustment" to the door frame of the shed. For all of the hundreds of careful measurements made while the car was being assembled inside the workshop, nobody had thought to make sure the finished vehicle could fit through the shed door. A few whacks and crumbled bricks later, the quadricycle was freed and positioned in the alley.

"It was raining," Ford later said of that historic moment. "Mrs. Ford threw a cloak over her shoulders and came outside. Mr. Bishop had his bicycle ready to ride ahead and warn drivers of horse-drawn vehicles—if indeed any were to be met with at such an hour. I set the choke and spun the flywheel. As the motor roared and sputtered to life, I climbed aboard and started off. The car bumped along the cobblestones of the alley, as Mr. Bishop rode ahead on the bicycle to warn any horse-drawn vehicles. We went down Grand River Avenue to Washington Boulevard. Then the car stopped. We discovered that one of the ignitors had failed. When we had repaired it, we started the car again and drove back home. Both Mr. Bishop and I went off to bed for a few winks of sleep. Then Mrs. Ford served us breakfast and off we went to work as usual."

Over the next several days Henry continued to refine his machine. To accommodate passengers, he replaced the bicycle seat with a cushioned bench. Soon he was chugga-chugging into the countryside, Clara and Edsel by his side. Margaret Ford recalled the sight of the quadricycle weaving its way toward the family farm in Dearborn.

"The wheels on one side were high in the center of the road," she said. "Henry had built the car in such a way that the distance between the wheels was less than that of wagons and carriages, so drove in this way on a road which had a rut. Clara and Edsel were on the front seat with him and all of them were sitting on the slanted seat. I remember Edsel was a very small boy in dresses at this time and he was held tightly by his mother on her lap."

William Ford, then in his seventieth year, gave the contraption a good going-over. For years he had regularly journeyed to the city, dropping in at Jim Burns's saloon for a drink or three before continuing on to check up on his oldest son. He expressed interest and support for Henry's experiments, though he occasionally revealed to others his keen disappointment over his son's rejection of farming.

William declined the offer to take a ride in the quadricycle. "He saw no reason why he should risk his life at that time for a brief thrill from being propelled over the road in a carriage without horses," said Margaret. There was something else at play, she suggested. "Father may have resented a bit the success of Henry's machine, which proved that Henry had been right in telling us that horses were not necessary."

Henry's father,
William Ford.

✂∘✄

That August, Henry was invited by Alexander B. Dow, his supervisor at
Edison, to the annual convention of the Association of Edison Illuminating Companies. Henry's inclusion in the select group that traveled
to New York underscored the growing respect peers held for his
demonstrated abilities as an engineer and inventor. His quadricycle,
after all, was one of only a handful of motorcars to be seen on Detroit's
streets. Although he was subjected to the occasional insult or flip comment when his gas buggy conked out—"Get a horse!" was the favorite—
he was far more likely to be surrounded by curious citizens and
quizzed at length wherever he drove. He took to chaining the quadricycle to lamp posts because so many people wanted to take the unat-
tended vehicle for an impromptu spin.

In New York, Dow introduced the star-struck Ford to Thomas Edison during a banquet. If Henry had any reservations about pursuing
gas versus electric as his car's power source, they evaporated when the
world's most famous inventor examined a rough sketch Henry drew on
a menu showing how the vehicle operated. "Young man, you have the
right idea," said the sage of Menlo Park, clapping Henry on the back.

Gone fishing. Edsel, nearly six years old, in September 1899. This photo was taken a month after the organization of the Detroit Automobile Company, his father's first foray into automobile manufacturing.

"Keep right at it." Turning to Dow, Edison explained, "This car has an advantage over the electric car because it supplies its own power."

Edison's words of encouragement were all Henry needed. Upon his return home he sold his quadricycle for $200 to a Detroiter named Charles Ainsley and went immediately to work building an improved version of the original.

"Well," he told Clara, "you won't be seeing much of me for the next year."

∽ою

Irving Bacon, an artist and family friend who later became the Fords' unofficial "court painter," first met Henry in 1898. At the time, Bacon was taking courses in phrenology and physiognomy, and he later recorded a descriptive word portrait of Ford during this pioneering period.

"He was a tall, genteel man, of an athletic build," observed Bacon. "He was crowned with curly brown hair. He was sporting a mustache. His eyes were deeply set. There was a twinkle in his right eye and a keen look in the left. His hands were strong, a clever type, well kept.

I noticed his head was small, well shaped, with a perfect Grecian profile. I noticed his ears too, unusual in form. The lobes joined the
cheeks in a triangle. I heard that this type denoted a genius, or in some
cases, tendencies not too commendable. He was a modest man, devoid
of ego, and his face shone with inspirational enthusiasm."

That enthusiasm enabled Ford, whose salesmanship skills were on
a par with his exceptional mechanical gifts, to line up the right people
to assist him at every step of the way, as he graduated from his first
experimental gas engines to his first attempt at manufacturing a finished vehicle. "I never saw Mr. Ford make anything," insisted David
Bell, the Edison employee who in his spare time created a new steering
mechanism for Henry. "He was always doing the directing."

In later years, Ford, who enjoyed tinkering with his personal history nearly as much as he did with machines, portrayed himself in
interviews and ghosted autobiographies as that typical American hero:
alone, misunderstood, lacking two nickels to rub together, but prevailing against great odds nonetheless. The public readily bought into the
image. But "Crazy Henry" was a myth. As Sidney Olson reminds us,
Ford "was almost never alone or lonely—indeed, he did most of his
inventing in the midst of a crowd of friends handing him tools, money,
valves, ideas, equipment . . . he was not only not scorned but highly
respected . . . he was not only not penniless but in circumstances comfortable enough to afford the theater and vaudeville. . . ."

Taking full advantage of his friends and his freedom to pretty well
do what he pleased at Edison, Ford constructed a first-rate vehicle
whose styling and engineering were comparable to anything else then
on the road, including the respected Duryea. The new model featured
brass lamps, a padded bench seat, and sleek running boards. Among
those impressed was engineer R. W. Hanington, who during an 1898
inspection tour of developing carmakers dropped into the engine room
at Edison. "You were working on an ingenious device for feeding gasoline into the cylinder," Hanington reminded Ford years later, "a sliding
carrier, like the bobbin of a sewing machine, that would pick up the
proper measure of fuel from the tank and transfer it into the cumbus-
tion chamber."

A contemporaneous evaluation of the second Ford motorcar by
Hanington included the following observations:

> The design of the motor is excellent . . . similar to that of the Spring-
> field Duryea's wagon. The sparker is better however. . . .

The cooling tanks show ingenuity and thought. The idea is not original . . . but has not been carried out in such detail. The Duryea wagons have no device for cooling. . . .

The carburetor is good. The measuring device is complete and ingenious. . . . The design of the gearing is compact and well-balanced. I cannot see anything particularly novel or valuable in Ford's arrangement over Duryea's except compactness. . . .

The whole design strikes me as being very complete, and worked out in every detail, and . . . the carriage should equal any that has been built in this country.

The success of a motor-wagon seems to rest on its ability to keep in order and run over all kinds of roads without breakdowns or hitches, and the first wagon to do this will be the successful one. . . .

"Simplicity, strength and common sense seem to be embodied in Mr. Ford's carriage," Hanington concluded.

Among the many Detroiters following Henry's progress was Mayor William Maybury, an old family friend. William Ford had married Mary Litogot in the parlor of the mayor's father's home nearly four decades earlier. Henry dutifully kept a campaign picture of the mayor in his front window.

The mayor's social connections helped Henry raise $15,000 from several prominent citizens to bankroll a commercial venture called the Detroit Automobile Company. The firm was talked about for more than a year, with some backers advancing Henry money to keep his experiments going, before being officially organized on August 5, 1899. In exchange, Henry agreed to share ownership of pending patents to his partners. He was named chief engineer and partner, with no authority over how the business was managed.

Henry's boss at Edison was put out. Alexander Dow understandably was partial to electricity as "the coming thing." He offered to make Henry general superintendent if he promised to abandon his interest in gas-powered cars. Instead, after having spent nine years at Edison, Ford walked away from his $140-a-month job to concentrate on automaking.

The Detroit Automobile Company was installed at a building at 1343 Cass Avenue. It had most recently housed a failed motor manufacturing venture of the mayor's. The new concern didn't fare any better. Instead of building off Ford's prototype, the car that had so impressed key backers, on January 12, 1900, the company introduced a slab-sided delivery truck that was slow, heavy, and fragile as an egg. Orders came in, but they remain unfulfilled as Henry struggled to design the parts needed to complete them. After fifteen months of operation, the city's first auto manufacturing company had nothing to show its investors except a handful of partially assembled trucks and an operating loss of $86,000.

The fault lay with Ford as much as it did with impatient company directors. He had a change of heart about the terms he had agreed to, later describing his backers as exploitative and more interested in turning a quick buck than in building a better car. Displaying the petulance that would come to characterize his behavior in future showdowns, he literally walked away from a difficult situation he had helped create. He held back on sharing his designs, disappearing for hours at a time in the nearby woods. "If they ask for me," he instructed a shop employee as he skipped out on an important directors' meeting, "you tell them that I had to go out of town." Henry would never admit it, but when it came to freezing a design and then figuring out how to manufacture a prototype in quantity, the eternal tinkerer had been in over his head.

The collapse of the Detroit Automobile Company in the fall of 1900 held no long-term consequences for either Henry or the industry. As the world prepared to officially enter the twentieth century, the first U.S. auto show was held at New York's Madison Square Garden. Three hundred motorcars—the majority of them electrics and steamers—were displayed. Fifty thousand people attended the gala exhibition, many of whom left convinced the automobile was a passing fad. Why, remarked some, a few of the so-called horseless carriages came with a socket for a buggy whip! "The horse will continue indispensable for a long time," declared one reporter after visiting the show. Four years later, Charles Platt, the president of the Insurance Company of North America, was still shaking his fist at the future: "I'll never insure a gasoline tank on wheels, the noisy, stinking things!"

Despite the presence of 18 million horses in America in 1900 (compared with just 8,000 automobiles), their demise as the principal mode of personal mobility was at hand. The Detroit Automobile Company was one of seventy-two automobile companies in 1900, and 142 more would start up over the next three years. Most were short-lived enterprises, but the sheer number of entrepreneurs joining in the automobile game signaled the first surge of the socioeconomic tsunami that soon would wash away generations of agrarian thought, culture, and mores. Within twenty short years the census would reveal for the first time more Americans living in the city than on the farm, a population shift greatly accelerated by the advent of the motorcar. There still were twice as many horses as cars in 1920, but by the end of the decade that ratio would be reversed, causing Henry Ford to unsentimentally note in his jot book: "The horse is gone."

# 3

︾

## *Rearview Mirror*

# Ford the "Automobileer" in 1900

*One bitterly cold winter day in 1900, Henry Ford took an intrepid local reporter for a spin in the prototype of a horseless delivery wagon developed by the Detroit Automobile Company. While Ford's first attempt at manufacturing proved to be a bust, the demonstration drive did result in one of the most famous headlines in automotive history. "SWIFTER THAN A RACE-HORSE IT FLEW OVER THE ICY STREETS" blared the headline in the Sunday features section of the Detroit News-Tribune on February 4, 1900. The accompanying three-column narrative told of the "Thrilling Trip on the First Detroit-Made Automobile, When Mercury Hovered About Zero." Within, the "automobileer" and his teeth-chattering companion correctly predicted the demise of the horse while "whizzing" down downtown streets at speeds reaching 25 miles per hour.*

"She's ready," said Ford.

"But you didn't touch a match to something or other."

Ford smiled.

"No necessity. The ignition is by electricity. Didn't you see me touch the switch up there? . . ."

By and by a man opened a factory door and with incomparable swiftness the machine picked up its speed and glided into the snowy, wind-blown street.

Henry inside the Ford delivery wagon in 1900.

"First we'll try her on the rough country road," said Ford, as he veered around an unexpected corner.

The puffing of the machine assumed a higher key. She was flying along about eight miles an hour. The ruts in the road were deep, but the machine certainly went with dream-like smoothness. There was none of the bumping common even to a street car.

"Hold on tight," said Ford. "When we strike the asphalt we will have a run."

"How fast?"

"Twenty-five miles an hour."

"Hold on! I get out."

Bang, bang, went the warning bell underneath the seat. A milk wagon was coming ahead. The horse shivered as though about to run away.

"Ever frighten horses?" I asked Ford.

"Depends on the horse," he replied.

By this time the Boulevard had been reached, and the automobileer, letting a lever fall a trifle, let her out.

Whiz! She picked up speed with infinite rapidity. As she ran on, there was a clattering behind—the new noise of the automobile.

There has always been, at each decisive period of the world's history, some voice, some note, that represented for the time being the prevailing power.

There was a time when the supreme cry of authority was the lion's roar.

After that it was the crackle of fire.

By and by it was the hammering of the stone-ax.

Then it was the slapping of the oars in the Roman galleys.

Next it was the voice of the wind against sails.

It came at last to speak with a loud report, such as announced the reign of gunpowder.

The roar of dynamite was a long time later.

The shriek of the steam whistle for several generations has been the compelling power of civilization.

And now, finally, there was heard in the streets of Detroit the murmur of this newest and most perfect of forces, the automobile, rushing along at the rate of 25 miles an hour.

What kind of a noise is it?

That is difficult to set down on paper. It was not like any other sound ever heard in this world. It is not like the puff, puff of the exhaust of gasoline in a river launch; neither is it like the cry of a working steam engine; but a long, quick, mellow, gurgling sound, not harsh, not unmusical, not distressing, a note that falls with pleasure on the ear. It must be heard to be appreciated. And the sooner you hear its newest chuck, chuck, the sooner will you be in touch with civilization's newest lisp, its newest voice.

Down an asphalted street, Ford rushed her. People came to the windows and looked out with apparent curiosity. Pedestrians stopped to see her pass. She picked up speed as she traveled; and excepting that new noise, the run was smooth as it might have been in a dream.

"Look out," cried Ford.

Before an answer could be given, the danger was past. With a simple twist of the wrist, the big machine turned gracefully to the right just sufficiently to allow a loaded brewery wagon to lumber on its way.

I began to have a creepy feeling and told Ford I wanted to get out.

"Nonsense," he replied. "No danger. All you have to do is to keep a sharp look-out ahead. It's like a bicycle, you see. . . ."

"But that man at the crossing, right ahead."

"Gone," came the broken answer as another block of houses vanished in thin air as the automobile's speed developed. Block after block.

"Now you see how quick we stop her," said Ford. "I'll wager that a race horse going a mile in 1:40 can not be hauled up in less than one-sixteenth of a mile; we'll do it in six feet."

With that, the automobileer pushed something, and with the suddenness of a complete collapse, the auto's speed died instantly away, and the big machine came almost to an immediate standstill.

"Whew!" was all I could say.

Slowly Ford re-applied the power and the big machine picked up speed and flew again up the street, like some frightened ghost.

"How long would it take to learn to run her?" I asked.

"Oh, that depends," replied Ford. "Have you any sense about machinery?"

"Little."

"Well, in a few days, maybe a few hours—there's little to learn. Ride a bicycle? It's the same thing. If you don't look out ahead you may get into trouble. That is the secret of it. When you are running fast, you must keep your eyes open. Then you are perfectly safe. I have a speed-regulator under my foot. If I lift my foot, it stops her instantly. What more could you ask? She simply can not run away."

"But that puffing. Isn't she liable to blow up?"

"Nothing to blow up."

"But we are sitting on three gallons of gasoline."

"That's nothing," said Ford. "It's perfectly safe. There is no fire around here and then, we are in the open air."

Ford pointed to one side of the street and said: "See that harness-maker's shop? His trade is doomed."

By this time, the automobileer had turned into the thick of Woodward Avenue, as far south as Montcalm Street, and was whizzing along through the crowds of vehicles. The speed was about eight miles an hour, but there was not the slightest danger.

"Is there prejudice against the automobile?" I asked.

"Oh, not much," Ford replied. "A number of truckmen have been to see me to have motors attached to their trucks, thinking that it would cheapen their work. But you can't attach the motor to an ordinary wagon. You need special construction."

Downtown Detroit, c. 1900. The traffic mix included bicycles, electric streetcars, and horsedrawn carriages and delivery wagons—but nary an automobile. Note the "white wing" scooping up horse droppings in the lower left.

A loaded truck lumbered slowly into sight. As the auto approached, the irate truckman glared fiercely and then shook his fist. The passengers on the auto saw his lips move, as if he were framing a curse, but not a sound came, for whiz, the auto flew past like a flash of light.

The clanging of street car gongs mingled with the sound of the auto bell, adding a new noise to the alarms of daily life. But she slid over the earth with infinite ease, and careened in and out among trucks, delivery wagons, carriages and bicycles; and everywhere, people had a welcoming smile and an expression of delight. The new chuck, chuck, the newest voice of civilization, sounded like rare music in their ears—a music as yet involved with the delight of absolute novelty.

"The horse is doomed," I said to Ford.

At that moment, the auto whizzed past a poor team attached to a big truck.

"That's the kind," said Ford. "Those horses will be driven from the land. Their troubles soon will be over."

And the chuck, chuck of the new voice sounded for the first time in the strange horses' ears.

Meantime, the auto had slipped like a sunbeam around the corner.

*A piece of sales literature from the period survives. On it a horse is depicted weeping into a towel as a motorcar putters past. The accompanying copy, however, is not nearly as sentimental.*

---

**Comparative Cost.** The cost of an Automobile, and expense of running for five years as compared with a horse and vehicle for the same period:

### Automobile.

| | |
|---|---:|
| Original cost | $1,000.00 |
| Cost of operating, 1/4 cent per mile, 25 miles per day | 114.00 |
| New tires | 100.00 |
| Repairs | 50.00 |
| Painting, four times | 100.00 |
| | $1,364.00 |

### Horse and Vehicle.

| | |
|---|---:|
| Original cost, horse, harness and vehicle | $ 500.00 |
| Cost of keeping horse five years | 1,200.00 |
| Shoeing horse | 180.00 |
| Repairs on vehicle, including rubber tires | 150.00 |
| Repairs on harness, $10.00 per year | 50.00 |
| Painting vehicle four times | 100.00 |
| | $2,180.00 |

Effecting a saving of $816.00 five years, in favor of the Automobile. At the end of five years the motor vehicle should be in good condition, owing to its careful and solid construction, while the value of the horse and carriage would be doubtful. There is always the possibility that the horse may die during the five years, while the Automobile can always be repaired at a nominal cost. Then too, the Automobile will do the work of three horses.

---

# 4

❦

# Who Can't Afford
a Fordmobile?

*We must make the cars simple. I mean we must make them so that they are not too complicated from a mechanical standpoint, so that people can operate them easily, and with the fewer parts the better.*

—Henry Ford, 1903

Auto racing is not something normally associated with Henry Ford. But in the wake of the Detroit Automobile Company debacle it was an activity that not only brought the failed carmaker a measure of fame and respect, it also was directly responsible for attracting backers to his next attempts at manufacturing "the most perfect machine on the market," including his most enduring venture, the current Ford Motor Company.

Automobile races were part spectacle, part product demonstration. Racing champions such as Alexander Winton, William K. Vanderbilt, and Henry Fournier regularly shared space on the front page of sporting sections with pitching sensation Cy Young, prizefighter "Gentleman Jim" Corbett, and other famous athletes of the day. In the case of Winton, his success on the track brought loads of free publicity to the powerful cars built inside his Cleveland factory.

Racing stirred the blood of most men, though it was the deep-pocketed members of the silk-stocking set who were uniquely positioned to take advantage of the motoring bug that races did so much to promote. Detroit, edging toward a population of 300,000 at the dawn of the new century, had its share of bored rich men. To these "sports," an expensive handcrafted automobile with a deep-throated engine and all the trimmings was viewed as the newest expression of success, a novelty that promised far more fun and adventure than the usual symbols of conspicuous consumption.

William Murphy, whose family had made a fortune in lumber and real estate, had been one of the investors in the ill-fated Detroit Automobile Company, but his financial loss did not dampen the middle-aged millionaire's enthusiasm for automobiles or lessen his confidence in Henry's mechanical talents. In the spring of 1901, he began taking an active interest in the racing machine Ford was working on, accompanying him on long test rides through the countryside. It was Murphy who persuaded a handful of other original investors to purchase the assets of the Detroit Automobile Company when it was formally dissolved, then to sit back and patiently wait while Henry continued work on his experimental machine inside the former DAC factory on Cass Avenue.

Henry was ambivalent about racing. For an avowed family man approaching forty, such daredevil driving was considered more than dangerous; it was thought to be downright foolhardy. He was skeptical of the actual benefits of having competing automobiles rip and roar around a dirt track; certainly there were better ways of measuring a motorcar's limits that didn't so blatantly endanger man and machine. But he also understood the enormous public relations value of making a name for himself in that particular arena. Recognition brought financing. "I never thought anything of racing," he said, "but the public refused to consider the automobile in any light other than a fast toy. We had to race."

So Henry poured himself into developing his racer. For a while after the Detroit Automobile Company folded, he shaved expenses by sharing a roof with his aging father, who had moved into a house in downtown Detroit. If the kinship between William Ford and his eldest son continued to have its occasional discordant moments, the triangular relationship involving Henry, Clara, and Edsel remained a close and loving one. Father and mother happily indulged their only child, as the

Father and son,
1902.

following entries from the diary Clara briefly kept during this period
demonstrate:

> January 11, 1901.
> Snowed all day. Edsel got soaking wet. He and Grandpa [William
> Ford] played checkers. Edsel cheated awful and beat every game.
> Went to bed so full of laughs he could not say his prayers.
>
> Sat. January 12.
> Went downtown, got Edsel shoes and leggings. Went into Sheaffers
> store to hear the music. After supper we tried to learn Grandpa to
> play cards.
>
> Sun. January 13.
> Edsel and I went to S[unday] School. . . . Came home, had dinner,
> then Henry fixed Edsel's sleigh to take him coasting, but Edsel would
> not go, said sleigh was no good. He was sent upstairs for punishment
> for his pride. He was sorry.
>
> January 19.
> Henry bought Edsel new coaster.
>
> January 20.
> Henry and Edsel went coasting on the boulevard.

A few months later Henry moved his brood again, this time into a
two-story apartment on Hendrie Avenue. It was the eleventh place he

and Clara had called home since marrying, but in a letter written in the fall of 1901 Clara remained typically upbeat:

> We are keeping house again and very happy to be alone. We have a very nice cozy little house. We did not build on account of Henry building the racer. He could not see anything else. So we will have to put up with rented homes a little longer. We got Edsel a bicycle for his birthday. He rides it to school and thinks it is fine. He and Henry both have raglan overcoats. Edsel thinks he is as big as his father. You would laugh to see him imitate Henry.

Edsel inherited his mother's dark features and his father's wiry frame and long legs. He grew up a gentle, thoughtful, good-natured and obedient lad, one not given to histrionics or fussing. He was a typical boy, falling out of a tree and breaking his arm and later humoring his parents by taking up the violin, a short-lived experiment. During these early years there never was any hint of the strain that would mar the adult relationship between father and son. Once, when Edsel was six, Clara brought him along to visit relatives in Kentucky. Henry, stuck at work, took the time to write him a note on the stationery of the Detroit Automobile Company:

> My Dear Little Son
>
> I am well and hope you are all OK. Say do they carry whiskey jugs and bandwagons in their blouse in Ky. I hope you are having a good time and will be back soon for I am lonesome.
>
> From your loving
>
> Pa Pa

Henry's affection for Edsel was deep and indicative of a lifelong love of children, whose innocence and lack of guile always buoyed his spirits. Helen Gore, an adolescent friend of Edsel's who learned the alphabet with him by picking letters out of bowls of soup, attested to Henry's playfulness. "When I was a tiny child and learning to talk, my mother tried to teach me to say, 'How do you do?' But the nearest I could come to it was 'Ha doodle do?' Mr. Ford used to say, 'Ha doodle do?' to me every time he saw me and I used to say, 'Ha doodle do?' back. As I grew older it didn't make any difference. It was still 'Ha doodle do?' no matter where he saw me."

Henry was not a religious person, but he did believe there was some order and logic to human existence. Nominally an Episcopalian,

as a young man he unsatisfactorily sampled churches of various denom-
inations before finally settling on the theory of reincarnation. He was
greatly influenced by a book written by Orlando J. Smith. In *A Short
View of the Great Questions,* the author laid out his philosophy that the
human soul lived on after death, a person's accumulated knowledge
and experiences carrying over through a succession of lifetimes.

"Until I discovered this theory I was unsettled and dissatisfied—
without a compass, so to speak," Ford explained in a 1928 interview.
"When I discovered reincarnation it was as if I found a universal plan. I
realized that there was a chance to work out any ideas. Time was no
longer a limit. I was no longer a slave to the hands of the clock. There
was time enough to plan and create. I wouldn't give five cents for seeing all the world because I feel there is nothing in the five continents
and on the five seas that I have not somehow seen. Somewhere is a
master mind sending brain wave messages to us. There is a Great
Spirit. I never did anything by my own volition. I was pushed by invis-
ible forces within and without me."

Having been born in the pivotal year of the Civil War, Henry
decided his most recent former life must have been as a soldier, one
whose existence had been prematurely snuffed out on some battlefield.
"We inherit a native knowledge from a previous existence. I do not
know where we come from or go to but we accumulate experience.
Someday it will be possible to measure the soul. We all retain memories from our past lives."

Henry extended his belief in reincarnation to all creatures. Once, a
chicken in the road niftly got out of the way of the car in which he was
riding, causing Ford to observe, "That chicken was hit in the ass in a
previous life."

∾o∾

October 10, 1901, found Henry warily eyeing the dirt oval track in
Grosse Pointe, the lakeside resort community favored by Detroit's elite.
The occasion was a much-ballyhooed day-long series of events sponsored by the Detroit Driving Club and featuring some of the era's top
speed demons, including Alexander Winton, who that autumn day set
a new world record for an exhibition mile with a time of 72.4 seconds.
With a crowd of eight thousand looking on, Winton then brought his
40-horsepower car to the starting line for the main show: a ten-mile

race of gas-powered behemoths. A couple dozen cars were registered for the event, the winner of which would receive $1,000 and a cut-glass punch bowl. To the disappointment of the crowd, only three actually made it onto the track. After one entrant was forced to withdraw because of a leaking cylinder, the field was whittled down to a classic David versus Goliath match: the famous and heavily favored Winton competing against local farm boy Henry Ford.

In the months leading up to the race a first-rate team had helped Ford on his racer, including Charles Brady King, back from naval service in the Spanish-American War; King's former assistant, Oliver Barthel; C. Harold Wills, a young, cocky draftsman who translated Ford's ideas into mechanical drawings; and the indispensable Ed "Spider" Huff, who knew more about the practical applications of electricity to motor-cars than anybody in Detroit. Among Huff's contributions was the special spark coil that, once encased in a porcelain insulating case created by Barthel's dentist, became the first modern spark plug. The engine had opposing cylinders of $7 \times 7$ inches and developed 26 horsepower, allowing Henry on test runs to gobble up a half-mile stretch of downtown boulevard in an impressive 38 seconds. Ford's racer had cost an estimated $5,000 to build, and he was still tinkering with it up to the day of the race.

Despite having much of the crowd behind him, Henry was at a big disadvantage. He was a novice racer, having never taken—much less mastered—the curves of the mile-long track. Henry's inexperience, coupled with Winton's powerful start, left him trailing after the first few laps. Spider Huff, acting as human ballast, crouched low on the running board and hung on for dear life as Ford inexpertly coasted in and out of the corners. Although he lost ground on each wide swing, he began to close the gap on the straightaways. To the grimy, begoggled rivals the packed grandstands were a blur, the collective shouts of the spectators drowned out by the ungodly roar of their machines. Dirt and pebbles flew. Then, on the seventh lap, Winton's car started to lose power, the result of overheated bearings. Smoke poured out of the champion's engine. Henry shot ahead and stayed ahead, proving that—on this day, at least—his car was not only faster but more mechanically reliable than that of America's best known racer-manufacturer.

"Henry had been covering himself with glory and dust," Clara excitedly wrote her brother, Milton. "He rec'd a beautiful cut glass punch bowl for winning his first race. I wish you could have seen him.

Also have heard the cheering when he passed Winton. The people went wild. One man threw his hat up and when it came down he stamped on it, he was so excited. Another man had to hit his wife on the head to keep her from going off the handle. She stood up in her seat & screamed 'I'd bet fifty dollars on Ford if I had it!'"

The winner seemed more relieved than excited. Despite his belief in reincarnation, Henry was in no particular hurry to leave his current existence for a new one. "Boy, I'll never do that again," he said, letting out a deep breath. "That tight board fence was right here in front of my face all the time! I was scared to death."

Ford's upset victory had the intended result. He was treated as a hero when he went to that year's auto show in New York. The most important back-slapping came from Detroit investors. On November 30, 1901, the Henry Ford Company was incorporated, with William Murphy and four other backers kicking in a total of $30,500 cash on a $60,000 capitalization. Henry was given a one-sixth share in the company. Once again, he was named chief engineer. And once again, he had no real say in how the business was run. "Henry has worked very hard to get where he is," Clara wrote Milton. "That race has advertised him far and wide. And the next thing will be to make some money out of it. I am afraid that will be a hard struggle. You know rich men want it all."

What the directors of the Henry Ford Company wanted was to put into production a more conventional version of the racer that Henry had driven to victory at Grosse Pointe. Ford, however, had different ideas, concentrating his efforts on building a larger and faster race car. There was "a barrel of money in this business," Henry confided in a letter to his brother-in-law. "I expect to make $ where I cant make [cents] at manufacturing."

Once again Henry self-destructed by stubbornly defying the wishes of his backers. After Murphy repeatedly warned him to stick to designing a passenger car, a machine-shop legend was brought in to correct the situation. Henry M. Leland, the brilliant and physically imposing head of Leland & Faulconer, was widely respected for his company's ability to tool products to remarkably close tolerances. A rule-of-thumb carmaker like Ford was bound to butt heads with the exacting Leland, a somewhat aloof figure who was unimpressed with Henry's engine.

On March 10, 1902—less than four months into the life of the Henry Ford Company—the firm's namesake resigned, "determined," he said, "never again to put myself under orders." Henry left with a $900 cash settlement, the drawings for his racer-in-progress, and the agreement that the company would reorganize under a new name. As Detroiters had recently celebrated the city's bicentennial, his former partners adopted the familiar name of the city's French founder, Antoine de la Mothe Cadillac. Before long the reorganized firm was manufacturing a Cadillac that was based on Ford's design but which featured a single-cylinder engine of Leland's creation. The reputation for quality that was to become Cadillac's hallmark was evident at the next auto show in New York, when orders for 2,286 of Leland's "one-lunger" were signed. In 1909, Cadillac became part of General Motors.

Resilient and optimistic despite failing in his first two attempts at large-scale manufacturing, Henry went ahead with a full plate of projects. Transferring his operations to a friend's workshop, he continued to revise what was at least the fourth version of his original quadricycle, began designing a four-cylinder car, and started work on a pair of identical giant racers. The yellow race car was dubbed the "999" and the red one was called the "Arrow." These monsters—named after famous express trains of the day—were at the time the biggest, most powerful cars ever built in the United States. Each was nearly 10 feet long and more than 5 feet wide, with 34-inch tires in front and 36-inch tires in back. The engine, relocated from its usual position in a box under the driver's seat to between the front wheels, had four massive cylinders and galloped at 80 horsepower. "The roar of those cylinders alone was enough to half kill a man," Henry said. "There was only one seat. One life to a car was enough. . . . I cannot quite describe the sensation. Going over Niagara Falls would have been but a pastime after a ride in one of them."

This time Henry's financial angel was a handsome, well-to-do young man named Tom Cooper, the world's champion bicycle racer. Cooper had watched Ford whip Alexander Winton at Grosse Pointe, was bitten by the newest speed craze, and approached Henry about forming a partnership. In exchange for his backing, Cooper was to receive ownership of one of the cars. The plan was for the pair to make their money by staging exhibitions and entering challenge races around the country, but their racing circus had one flaw: neither man felt confident enough to drive these hell-roaring beasts in an actual event.

For this they brought in a twenty-four-year-old bulldog named Berna Eli "Barney" Oldfield, an Ohio native who had traveled the

Henry Ford stands beside his famous "999" racer with Barney Oldfield at the tiller. Both men drove the four-cylinder, 80-horsepower racer to world speed records.

bicycle-racing circuit with Cooper. Oldfield was fearless. That he had never driven an automobile before, much less a leviathan like the 999, mattered not. On October 25, 1902, after just a week of lessons, he piloted 999 at the annual day of challenge races at the Grosse Pointe track. This time the field for the main event included five gas-guzzling racers, including Winton in a machine called the "Bullet."

Prior to the race, Ford fretted over the 999's lack of safety features and his driver's inexperience. Oldfield dismissed such concerns. "Well, this chariot may kill me," he said, "but they'll say afterward that I was going like hell when she took me over the bank."

Oldfield then put his bravado on spectacular display, going full-bore the entire way until he covered the five miles in an unprecedented 5 minutes, 28 seconds, lapping the runner-up in the process. Men surged out of the stands, pounded him on the back, shoved cigars into his pockets, and jubilantly carried him around on their shoulders. Barney Oldfield—who the following year would become the first person to travel at the speed of a mile a minute—was on his way to becoming a legend, his name synonymous with daredevil racing. From that day on, Ford and Oldfield formed a sort of mutual admiration society, generously offering that each had "made" the other. "But," Oldfield invariably would add, "I did much the best job of it."

Conversely, Henry's relationship with Cooper, whom Clara Ford later obliquely accused of "sneaky tricks," soured. It would be unfair to wholly blame Cooper for the breakup of their partnership, however, for the day after Oldfield's victory at Grosse Pointe a newspaper reported that Ford's association with "his fast speed freaks" had given way to plans to "put a 'family horse' on the market." While developing racers with Cooper during the summer of 1902, the ever opportunistic Henry had hedged his bets by entering into an agreement with a local businessman to produce a passenger car under the company name of Ford & Malcolmson Ltd. Shortly after Oldfield's record-breaking performance that fall, it was decided the firm should be called the Ford Motor Company. Cooper was left with one of the two racers he'd helped finance and some hard feelings. What he called Henry's newest enterprise is unrecorded. But it can be imagined.

०२००

Alexander Malcolmson was one of Detroit's leading coal merchants, an energetic, self-made Scot with muttonchop whiskers whose wagons bearing the legend "Hotter than Sunshine" were a familiar sight on city streets. Henry had first become acquainted with Malcolmson a few years earlier when, as chief engineer at Edison, he was responsible for buying coal for the electric company's furnaces. Malcolmson, who owned a Winton, was impressed by Ford's 1901 triumph at Grosse Pointe. The losses Malcolmson had experienced in icebox manufacturing and other speculative business ventures did not dampen his enthusiasm for plunging. He agreed to provide $7,000 to build a motorcar based on Henry's designs. That amount quickly proved to be grossly inadequate. Additional capital needed to be raised.

The problem was Malcolmson was already heavily in debt, having recently acquired several competing coalyards. Moreover, with car companies failing left and right, banks were understandably shy about financing automobile start-ups. The only solution was to approach potential stockholders who had not already been burned in previous dealings with Ford. That eliminated nearly every wealthy or influential man in Detroit.

Early investors in the Ford Motor Company. *From left:* John Gray, Alex Malcomson, and James Couzens.

From the autumn of 1902 through the following spring, Malcolmson doggedly approached potential backers, both big and small. Pre-production advertisements were placed touting the "Fordmobile," a sensible, lightweight motorcar "made of few parts and every part does something." At $750, the ads asked, "Who can't afford a Fordmobile?" (The Fordmobile name was soon dropped in favor of the Model A. Subsequent vehicles would bear similarly prosaic letter designations, as over the next several years Ford marched through the alphabet in his quest to build the perfect car.) Eventually, and after much rejection, coaxing, cajoling, and hand-holding, a dozen investors were rounded up. They ranged from Charles Bennett, president of the Daisy Air Rifle Company, to Albert Strelow, a contractor whose involvement was doubly important: he owned the empty two-story building at 696 Mack Avenue that Ford and Malcolmson wanted to use as their factory. The quick-fisted Dodge brothers, Horace and John, whose machine shop was to provide engines, came on board, as did a pair of mild-mannered attorneys, Horace Rackham and John W. Anderson, who did work for Malcolmson. Malcolmson's cousin, Vernon Fry, and his bookkeeper,

Clara, Edsel, and Henry are lined against the porch rail in a 1904 visit to the Square House, the home Henry built to Clara's specifications after they were married. *Below:* Henry and Edsel inside a Model N the following year.

Charles J. Woodall, also were persuaded. At the last minute a doctor wanted in, as well, but the superstitious Ford frowned on it, believing thirteen investors would bring bad luck.

On Tuesday, June 16, 1903, three days after the first stockholders' meeting was held inside Malcolmson's office at the McGraw Building on Griswold Street, incorporation papers for the Ford Motor Company were officially filed in the state capital, Lansing. The automobile industry's newest player was capitalized at $100,000 (1,000 shares at $100 each), with $28,000 cash actually paid in and another $21,000 pledged in notes. The biggest buck Malcolmson bagged was his uncle, John S. Gray, who headed the German-American Bank. Gray's $10,500 investment was by far the largest cash contribution and got him a 10.5 percent stake in the company and the title of president. Between them, Ford and Malcolmson retained a 51 percent controlling interest, each taking 255 shares. Henry was named vice-president and general manager with an annual salary of $3,600.

The treasurer of the Ford Motor Company was Malcolmson's thirty-year-old office manager, James Couzens. Stern, methodical, tenacious, and tireless, the Canadian-born Couzens had kept the coal dealer's books for several years. Couzens had a hair-trigger temper and was so humorless it was later said of him that the ice on the Great Lakes broke when he cracked his annual smile. When he hadn't been all over town buttonholing potential investors, Couzens had managed to scrape together $2,500 to buy twenty-five shares himself. His sister, Rosetta, after much soul-searching and debate, lent him $100—half of her life savings. The frugal schoolteacher received a single share in return. By the time she sold it back to Ford sixteen years later she had netted $355,000.

Even someone as self-confident as Henry could not have imagined such a mind-bending return on investment—certainly not in the summer of 1903, when the Ford Motor Company was down to its last $223.65 and had yet to sell a single car. Then, on July 15, a Chicago dentist named Ernst Pfennig paid $850 for a Model A with tonneau, the detachable leather seating compartment that converted a two-seat runabout into a four-seat touring car. Dr. Pfennig's purchase represented the first sale of the Ford Motor Company. Henry, who turned forty a few days later, was thus able to celebrate a landmark birthday with a historic transaction, the first of tens of millions to come.

# 5

⚞

# Hunka Tin

*It was skyscraper high, hideously ugly, funereally drab, and whether on a city street or in a farmer's barn it looked somehow pathetic, as though, in the hillbilly phrase, it were a widow's pig standing in the cold rain on a Sunday morning. But it was light in weight, simple in construction, easy to repair, and spare parts were soon for sale in the dime stores of the land. Its owners and the public came to regard it with amused affection; it was efficient and put America on the road. Model T became a symbol of economic democracy because it was the car of the people. No automobile for aesthetes or sybarites, it provided a Spartan form of transportation. It got you there and back, and if your bones ached and your ears rang, this was a small price to pay for the novel joys of motoring.*

—David L. Cohn, *Combustion on Wheels*

I t didn't take long for sales of the Model A to take off. James Couzens reported after nine and a half months of operation that the Ford Motor Company had sold 658 of them. This produced a net profit of $98,851—a sparkling 350 percent return on investment. Neither Henry Ford nor Alexander Malcolmson was satisfied, though for different reasons. While Henry continued his quest to build a moderately priced car to rival Ransom Olds's $650 curved-dash Olds, the industry's top seller, his partner looked to put bigger and more powerful models on the market. With both men aware of the value of racing in keeping the company name in the public eye, Ford reluctantly agreed to try to break the world's land speed record for the one-mile straightaway—this time on the cinder-covered frozen surface of

Lake St. Clair. The attempt would come in the rebuilt Arrow (the famous 999's twin), this time featuring an engine nearly identical to the one to be found in the company's new Model B. The first four-cylinder Ford was priced at $2,000, a figure that guaranteed a fat profit on each car while also keeping it out of the reach of the average person. And there, for Henry, was the rub.

On January 12, 1904, as ten-year-old Edsel flapped his arms trying to stay warm and Clara and half a dozen official timers looked on, Henry tore down the ice in the Arrow. Once again his ride-along mechanic was Spider Huff, who stood on the running board feeding gas into the carburetor while Henry, terrified but determined, kept his hands clamped around the steering mechanism.

"The ice seemed smooth enough—so smooth that if I had called off the trial we should have secured an immense amount of the wrong kind of advertising," Henry recalled, "but instead of being smooth, the ice was seamed with fissures which I knew were going to mean trouble the moment I got up to speed. But there was nothing to do but go through with the trial so I let the old 'Arrow' out. At every fissure the car leaped into the air, I was skidding, but somehow I stayed top side up and on the course, making a record that went all over the world." In what the *Detroit Tribune* called "the wildest ride in the history of automobiling," Ford reached a top speed of 91.37 miles per hour (39.4 seconds for one measured mile). Afterward the relieved racer treated Huff and Harold Wills to a muskrat dinner. Two weeks later the mark was broken in Florida by William K. Vanderbilt driving a Mercedes.

In the aftermath of the race, the philosophical differences between Ford and Malcolmson became louder and nastier. Even as sales of the Model B and Models C and F (derivatives of the A) necessitated a move into a larger three-story factory on Piquette Avenue in early 1905, the two majority partners continued to battle over the expanding company's direction. What would it be—large cars or small cars? At Malcolmson's insistence, Ford and Wills designed a massive six-cylinder luxury touring car called the Model K, which was guaranteed to hit 60 miles per hour and sold for $2,500. At the same time, Ford and Couzens did some back-room maneuvering to force the coal dealer out.

Since the company's beginning, the bulk of each Ford car was put together at the Dodge brothers' shop before being shipped by horse-drawn wagons to the Ford factory for final assembly. (This arrangement allowed John and Horace Dodge to profit twice: as shareholders in the

Clara Ford, with the office manager alongside, drives a Model N out of the Piquette Avenue factory. The 300 workers at the "Home of the Celebrated Ford Automobile" were producing twenty-five hand-built cars a day by early 1905.

Ford Motor Company and as the firm's chief supplier.) On November 22, 1905, Ford and Couzens and several other shareholders incorporated the Ford Manufacturing Company. Capitalized at $100,000, the new firm announced its intention to make engines, gears, and other parts for the Ford Motor Company. Because Malcolmson did not have a stake in the start-up, he could not stop the new supplier from charging the Ford Motor Company prices for its parts that would drain all the profits out of the carmaker.

Malcolmson had a strong legal case against this rebellious group of stockholders, but he reacted hastily and foolishly. He announced the creation of the Aerocar Company to manufacture a touring car with an air-cooled engine that would compete with the very company he was a majority shareholder of—a clear conflict of interest. Several months of negotiations followed. Finally, in May 1906, Malcolmson sold his interest in the Ford Motor Company for $175,000. Four other shareholders— Charles Bennett, Vernon Fry, Albert Strelow, and Charles Woodall—also sold out. When the dust settled, Henry had 585 shares, Couzens 110 (including one share held for his sister Rosetta), and John Gray 105. (Gray would die in July, his stock passing on to his family.) Horace Rackham, John Anderson, and John and Horace Dodge each retained

50 shares. With Gray's death, Henry became president of the Ford Motor Company as well its major shareholder. For the first time he was in control of an automobile manufacturing company built around his mechanical genius—a control he would never relinquish.

∾∘∾

Henry now was free to concentrate his energies on what would become his masterpiece, a purely functional automobile that would transform the world and make him a billionaire and an international folk hero in the process. As with the quadricycle and the 999 racer and other vehicles, it was more of a collaborative effort than Henry later cared to admit. But all along the universal car that became the Model T was infused with Ford's unshakable faith in himself and his destiny, and that made all the difference.

"I will build a motor car for the multitude," he had promised. "It shall be large enough for the family, but small enough for the unskilled individual to operate easily and care for, and it shall be light in weight that it may be economical in maintenance. It will be built of honest materials, by the best workmen that memory can hire, after the simplest designs that modern engineering can devise. But it shall be so low in price that the man of moderate means may own one and enjoy with his family the blessings of happy hours spent in God's great open spaces."

The most direct forerunner of the Model T was the Model N, a solid four-cylinder vehicle that could go at the rate of 45 miles per hour. It sold for $600 when it was introduced in 1906. For the first time, that year Ford led all carmakers in production, with some twenty-five cars hand-assembled each day inside the new but already inadequate Piquette plant. Models R and S, priced in the $750 range, were slightly modified versions of the same automobile.

Throughout 1907 and into the following year, Henry and his crew put in long hours working out details of the Model T. While Harold Wills helped Henry perfect the peppy four-cylinder, water-cooled engine, Charlie Sorenson, a gruff Dane who headed Ford's pattern department, earned his nickname "Cast Iron Charlie" by casting the one-piece engine block. Joe Galamb, a Hungarian patternmaker, made wooden molds of parts first drawn up on chalkboards. Spider Huff was largely responsible for the innovative low-tension magneto that, mounted on the revolving flywheel, provided electric current without the need for heavy storage batteries. There were no frills on the T: no gas gauge (owners were instead provided with a ruler to dip into the gas tank), no shock absorbers, no water pump. Gas was drawn into the carburetor by gravity, eliminating the need for a fuel pump. There wasn't even a driver-side door, merely the outline of one embossed in the metal. Agile drivers found it no problem to simply jump into the car; the less nimble entered through the passenger's door and slid over the bench seat until they were tucked in front of the steering column. The car was one of the first with the steering wheel on the left side, giving the driver a better view of oncoming traffic.

The Model T was announced in early October 1908. "No car under $2,000 offers more," advertisements bragged—a claim that proved to be true. Nearly a thousand inquiries came in the mail the day following the first print ads, and thousands more were to follow. Orders had to be paid for in advance, meaning that within a year of its debut the sale of more than 10,000 Model T's had brought in some $9 million cash. Customers had their choice between a gray roadster and a red touring car. Later the color choice was limited to a uniform Brewster green with red trim, which soon gave way to a basic black.

At $850, the 1908 touring car was hardly inexpensive. That amount was equal to a teacher's annual salary and hundreds of dollars more than the Brush "Everyman Car" or the Sears Motor Car offered in the Sears-Roebuck catalog. What separated the Model T from its lower-priced competitors was quality. Its high axles and three-point suspension made it perfect for tackling the ruts that characterized the majority of roads then, while its lightweight vanadium steel construction (common in Europe but unique to Ford among U.S. automakers) made it practically indestructible. (It was later used as armor plating on American battleships.) Anyone handy with a wrench, hammer, pliers, and screwdriver could fix most problems on the T, and parts could usually be found at any hardware store or one of the burgeoning number of Ford dealers aggressively being signed up by the indefatigable Couzens. More than half of the parts that made up the engine could be bought for ten cents or less. Farmers in particular found the Model T an extension of their thrifty, practical selves. The rear end of the car could be jacked up, one of its tires removed, and a device attached to the hub to provide power for sawing wood, pressing cider, or pumping water. "Farmers' dollars are big dollars—because they are hard earned dollars,"

The people's car. An untold number of photo albums had at least one shot of the family posing alongside its proudest possession: a Model T Ford.

read one Model T advertisement in 1912. "It is because the American farmer is ever a careful and painstaking buyer that he is today the happy and proud possessor of more than half the Ford cars in existence."

As production mounted and nonessentials were stripped away, the price of the Model T would drop over the years until it reached a low of $260 in 1926.

Economical, versatile, and built to outlive a horse, the Model T transformed rural America. C. C. Housenick began selling Fords out of his haberdashery in 1906 and thus had a hand in transforming his sleepy little corner of the world, Bloomsburg, Pennsylvania. "Bloomsburg was an unexcitable farm town of 4,000," he recalled nearly half a century later. "In thirty years the only thing that changed was the front page of the paper and that not very much. People raised wheat, corn, and assorted edibles; and the horse was a member of the family."

At the time, more than half of the population lived on the nation's 6 million farms or in towns of less than 2,500 people. And only one in a hundred farm families owned an automobile. "But then came the Model T," said Housenick, "and wonderful things began to happen, but slowly."

From the clothing store we sold a few cars to doctors, mailmen, and schoolteachers. When they began delivering mail through the country with Fords, and they were high enough to clear the ruts, that sort of broke the ice and we were able to do more business. The fact that the farmer loved his horses and didn't want anything to take their place was perhaps the greatest sales resistance that we had. We used the economic argument that the car would use no feed when standing still. We used to go out and drive over plowed fields to show the farmer that he could go any place with his car. It was convincing to many prospects. . . .

Soon a few progressive farmers bought, and along about 1914 life in Bloomsburg began to move with a new sureness and swiftness. People found it was an easy car to drive, so most everyone learned. It was cheap, so many people could buy one. It was built to drive over the bad roads of its day, so horizons spread. Townspeople could go further, faster, and get more things done in a day. Farm families could come to town more often, stay longer. Everywhere people began to congregate more. Social and civic clubs sprung up. Ideas and viewpoints were liberally exchanged.

The economics of the Model T were mildly revolutionary. Columbia County farmers, who formerly needed all day to bring a load of wheat or corn to market by wagon, could make four, five, or six trips with a heavily loaded car, later with a Ford truck. Because they could market more, they raised more and sold more. Their prosperity helped retail stores thrive, furnished incentive for expansion, more building. Businessmen reached more customers with improved transportation. The town grew as more streets were built and more homes clustered around them.

Local products reached more distant markets and brought more money back home to Bloomsburg. The town grew apace and with it the service industries needed to keep it functioning—banks, stores, electric, telephone, and gas companies.

The temperamental Model T deserved its appellation as "the family horse." Essayist E. B. White, who traveled across America in one after his graduation from Cornell, attributed the vehicle's equine characteristics to its unique "planetary" transmission, whose innards became the mechanical foundation for modern automatic transmissions. The three-pedal system required a bit of coordination. The floor pedal on the left allowed the driver to shift the transmission between high and low, while the one in the middle put the car in reverse. The brake pedal

The Tin Lizzie was easy to repair. Most parts could be bought at the local hardware store, and anyone with a rudimentary knowledge of mechanics could work on it.

was on the right. Once mastered it let the driver shift without stripping gears and, when stuck in a mudhole, to rock the car out of trouble. "Because of the peculiar nature of this planetary element," White wrote, "there was always, in Model T, a certain dull rapport between engine and wheels, and even when the car was in a state known as neutral it trembled with a deep imperative and tended to inch forward. There was never a moment when the bands were not faintly egging the machine on. In this respect it was like a horse, rolling the bit on its tongue, and country people brought to it the same technique they used with draft animals."

Starting the engine with the hand crank required a certain finesse, White discovered. It was important not to place one's thumb on the crank handle because, if the engine backfired, a broken arm or wrist often was the result.

"The trick," he said, "was to leave the ignition switch off, proceed to the animal's head, pull the choke (which was a little wire protruding through the radiator) and give the crank two or three nonchalant upward lifts. Then, whistling as though thinking about something else, you would saunter back to the driver's cabin, turn the ignition on, return to the crank, and this time, catching it on the down stroke, give it a quick spin with plenty of That. If this procedure was followed, the engine almost always responded—first with a few scattered explosions, then with a tumultuous gunfire, which you checked by racing around to the driver's seat and retarding the throttle. Often, if the emergency break hadn't been pulled all the way back, the car advanced on you the instant the first explosion occurred and you would hold it back by leaning your weight against it. I can still feel my old Ford nuzzling me at the curb, as though looking for an apple in my pocket."

The owners of Packards, Pierce-Arrows, and other upscale automobiles may have looked down their noses at the Model T, but the masses embraced the cheap, simple, and ungainly "mechanical cockroach" as a kind of national mascot. Many owners affectionately named their car as if it was the family dog or a favorite cow. "Tin Lizzie" became a natural moniker and probably had a thousand progenitors. The origin of another term of endearment, "flivver," also is impossible to pinpoint. One theory is that someone believed the vibration of riding in a Ford was "good for the liver," which was soon phonetically abbreviated to "f'liver," or flivver. That seems a stretch, but in any event lexicographers added the word to Webster's dictionary in 1927, the same year the last of more than 15 million flivvers rolled off the assembly line.

The Tin Lizzie quickly acquired folklore status, its idiosyncratic charm making it the subject of songs, limericks, jokes, riddles, postcards, films, and vaudeville routines. Edsel always cherished the parody of Rudyard Kipling's "Gunga Din":

> Yes, Tin, Tin, Tin,
> You exasperating puzzle Hunka Tin
> I've abused you and I've flayed you
> But by Henry Ford who made you
> You are better than a Packard, Hunka Tin

In 1914, New York songwriters C. R. Foster and Byron Gay had one of the most successful songs of the year with "The Little Ford Rambled Right Along":

> Now Henry Jones and a pretty little queen,
> Took a ride one day in his big limousine.
> The car kicked up and the engine wouldn't crank,
> There wasn't any gas in the gasoline tank.
> About that time along came Nord,
> And he rambled right along in his little old Ford;
> And he stole that queen as his engine sang a song,
> And his little old Ford just rambled right along.

An early Ford dealership.

Ford jokes were a staple of popular culture, the gags helping to popularize the social inferiority of Henry's flivver and the budget-minded folks who proudly drove it. In one joke, a Model T runs over a chicken, who gets up crying, "Cheep, cheep." Another joke asked: "Why is a Ford like a bathtub?" The answer: "Because you hate to be seen in one." Other gags zeroed in on the car's portability, such as the Cadillac owner who always carried a Ford in his tool box in case of an emergency. Then there were the stories that played up the Model T's "tinniness." In one, an Illinois farmer whose barn roof has been blown off in a tornado whimsically ships the mangled tin to the Ford plant in Highland Park. A short time later he receives a reply from the factory, saying his Model T arrived in pretty bad shape but that it would soon be returned to him in perfect running order.

There was much, much more. Humorist Irvin S. Cobb always got a good laugh when he told the story about the lunatic who stole a Model T and then picked up two Chinese laundrymen. The crazy man drove into a train. When people rushed to investigate the accident site, "all they could find was a nut and two washers," said Cobb. Jokes about the Model T were as ubiquitous as the car itself, with publishers cranking out cheap compilations of the latest groaners. These books cost between five and fifteen cents apiece and collectively sold millions of

The Model T was notably versatile, in this case its chassis accommodating a custom-built chapel.

copies. One gag that was always included had someone approaching the "Flivver King" himself and asking, "Have you heard the last Ford joke?" To which Henry wearily replies: "I hope so."

Truth be told, Henry immensely enjoyed the countless Ford jokes that circulated around the country, often repeating them in public. One of his favorites was about the farmer who wanted to be buried with his Model T "because it's gotten me out of every hole so far."

To satisfy the insatiable demand for the Model T, Henry had a new manufacturing plant built on the sixty-acre site of an old racetrack in Highland Park, a few miles north of downtown Detroit. Albert Kahn, the color-blind German Jew responsible for building the first reinforced-concrete auto plant a few years earlier for Packard, designed an airy four-story structure with 50,000 square feet of glass, causing it to be nicknamed "the Crystal Palace." It opened in early 1910. Some 19,000 Model T's were built that first year. Two years later production quadrupled to 78,611—and still demand outstripped supply. In 1913, the first year of the moving assembly line, nearly 183,000 flivvers rolled onto the streets. A decade later, in 1923, Model T production would hit its

Model T's pile up outside Ford's Highland Park plant. In 1912, nearly 80,000 were built—and this was before the introduction of the assembly line. In nineteen years more than 15 million "flivvers" would be produced.

peak: a staggering 2,011,125, a record for one company not to be surpassed for more than thirty years.

There was, of course, a price to be paid for this flood of cars, especially in urban centers, where traffic had the organization of a spilled box of straws. By sheer weight of numbers—by 1921 Ford was building two-thirds of the industry's cars—the Model T was responsible for changing the landscape of America's cities more than any other vehicle. One elderly Detroiter mourned the demise of once stately Woodward Avenue, where gas stations, garages, and parking lots popped up like dandelions to service the new automobile culture. "I am afraid that the old-time charm of Detroit has fled," Charles L. Freer wrote a friend in 1911. "Smoke, dirt, noise and all the unfavorable features of a large manufacturing center are, by degrees, spreading over the entire old residential portion of our city." The traffic mix now included far fewer bicycles and horses and too many novice motorists. New York City, which once had to contend with the removal of forty dead horse carcasses from its streets daily, faced new threats in the form of freewheeling, accident-prone neophytes such as "the East Side butcher who buys a used car and joy rides," complained the *New York Times*. Road regulations everywhere were slow to be adopted and enforcement often was lax, even as accidents and fatalities piled up. It wasn't until 1920, for example, that the first primitive traffic light appeared in the Motor City. The levels of pollution and congestion rose to heights unthinkable to an earlier generation of city dwellers, and would continue unchecked for decades to come. Henry and Edsel would both flee upscale neighborhoods in the city for less crowded spaces outside Detroit.

The Model T was instrumental in American carmakers turning the table on their European counterparts, whose luxury models had been penetrating the U.S. market for years. In 1912, German, French, and British auto manufacturers all petitioned their governments for tariff protection, the result of the flivver's universal popularity. Henry, who had created a Canadian subsidiary in 1904, opened his first overseas manufacturing plant in Manchester, England, in 1911. By 1930, plants in two dozen countries, including Chile, Malaya, Australia, and South Africa, would be building Ford cars, trucks, and tractors.

William Ford died in 1905, a dozen years before his son opened an assembly plant in Cork County, Ireland—the very place the Fords had left in 1847. Many years later, when the Flivver King was himself a very old man, he expressed a single regret: "I wish my father could have lived to see what happened."

# 6

∽o∾

# The Five-Dollar Day

*We believe in making 20,000 men prosperous and contented rather than follow the plan of making a few slave drivers in our establishment multi-millionaires.*

—Henry Ford, January 5, 1914

H enry Ford was on his way to becoming a wealthy man even before the runaway success of the Model T made him fabulously rich. In 1907 he was paid $36,000 as company president—a substantial figure, given that baseball's most sensational young player, Ty Cobb, earned $2,400 that year while leading the Detroit Tigers into their first World Series. But Henry's salary was peanuts compared with the hundreds of thousands of dollars in dividends he initially raked in as majority shareholder, a figure that quickly climbed into the millions.

Money was never Ford's primary motivation. He lived comfortably, but not nearly as ostentatiously as a man of his means could have. After years of residing in rental properties, he and Clara moved into a custom-built $300,000 house at 61 Edison Street. The brick and stone residence sat on a double lot, allowing Clara to indulge her passion for gardening. Wisteria, roses, lilacs, forsythia, and rhododendron blossomed under her care. Meanwhile, Edsel lost a fingertip to a lathe inside the fully equipped workshop Henry had built over the garage. The accident didn't discourage the mechanically inclined boy, who had been driving cars since he was ten years old. (Henry's only concession to his son's tender age was to require that a butler crank the starter.)

At fourteen, Edsel drove a Model N to Detroit University School, the exclusive prep school he attended once the money started rolling into the household, and then drove customized "speedsters" thereafter.

Edsel often worked after class at his father's auto plant, helping with the mail or hanging around the experimental lab. As a teenager he attached numbered brass tags to Model T's as they were built inside the noisy, cavernous confines of the Crystal Palace. "If that kid can only continue the way he is going," Henry happily told an associate, "I've got a boy I can be proud of."

An excellent student, Edsel ended his formal education with his graduation from high school in the spring of 1912. "I think Edsel rather regretted that he didn't continue his school work further and go on to college," observed one of his teachers, Frederick Searle. "Edsel had a reasoning mind and liked to sit down and talk things over." Instead, he went straight to work for his father, who had garnered industrywide praise and admiration with his recent triumph over the Selden cartel—a victory that at the time was much bigger news than the success of the Model T.

The Selden controversy had hung like a black cloud over the Ford Motor Company since it was founded in 1903, when Henry refused to be signatory to an agreement that paid royalties from each car sold to the Association of Licensed Automobile Manufacturers. The ALAM administered the licensing of the patent granted to George B. Selden, the dubious inventor of the gasoline-powered automobile.

Selden, a patent attorney in Rochester, New York, never built a car in his life, but he did know how to manipulate the system to his advantage. In 1895 he received U.S. patent no. 549,160 for a two-cycle internal combustion engine that he had first developed on paper in 1879. During those sixteen years he had calculatingly filed more than a hundred amendments to his original patent application, each one drawing on the technical refinements of other inventors. Soon all American manufacturers of gas-powered cars were sent notices that they must secure a license from Selden and pay a royalty on each vehicle built.

Selden lacked the financial resources to enforce his claim, so in 1899 he sold patent rights to the Electric Vehicle Company, which aggressively went after the money it felt it was owed. Carmakers ultimately decided it was cheaper to simply pay the royalties than slug it out in court. In 1903 a group of nearly thirty auto companies, including major manufacturers such as Winton, Oldsmobile, Packard, and

Cadillac, reached a compromise with the Electric Vehicle Company. They would form a syndicate, the ALAM, to function as a collection agency and watchdog group. In addition to collecting royalties of 1.25 percent on each gasoline car made (three-fifths going to Electric Vehicle, the balance to the ALAM), the syndicate would be the sole authority in determining what future companies would be licensed under the patent. It also could dictate a company's production.

Paying royalties for a doubtful patent was one thing, but Ford and other emerging carmakers also saw the Selden group as potentially using their regulating power to intimidate them and squash competition. Nonetheless, Henry initially sought ALAM's sanction to build cars. But after the syndicate refused to license the company on the ground that it was an assembler and not a manufacturer, Ford began production in open defiance of what he and James Couzens brilliantly labeled "The Trust" in print advertisements. This characterization put the ALAM in the same odious category of other monopolies then under attack by that "trust buster" in the White House, Theodore Roosevelt. When the syndicate sued Ford and threatened legal action against his dealers and customers, Henry guaranteed them protection "against any prosecution for alleged infringements of patents."

It took six years and 5 million words of testimony for a verdict to be reached. All along, public sentiment was with Ford, who shrewdly played up his underdog role in advertisements, interviews, and court testimony. But he was to be seriously disappointed. On September 15, 1909, the New York District Court handed down its decision: the Selden patent was legal. Henry was distraught over the prospect of once again having "outsiders" telling him how to run his company, as he felt had happened during his two previous attempts at manufacturing. That October, he and Couzens held secret negotiations to sell the company to Billy Durant's newly formed General Motors Corporation. Couzens reported Durant's offer of $8 million to Henry while he was lying in pain on the floor of his New York hotel room.

"Tell him he can have it if the money's all cash!" said Henry, who offered to throw in his lumbago. The deal fell through a few days later in Detroit when Durant could not raise the money.

While Durant and other unlicensed automakers fell into line, agreeing to pay the ALAM past due and future royalties, Ford decided to fight on alone. He appealed the court's ruling. As lawyers on both sides spent the next year generating the necessary written briefs and arguments, the ALAM and Ford Motor Company continued its war of words in ads and notices that appeared in national publications. "Don't buy a lawsuit with your car," the cartel warned potential car buyers. Ford responded by pledging the entire assets of his company, $12 million, as a bond to protect his customers against legal action. The financial stakes were huge for Ford, who by now was the largest automaker in the world. In 1910 alone, he had sold more than 32,000 Model T's, which represented one-fifth of all U.S. sales.

On January 9, 1911, the Court of Appeals of New York unanimously overturned the lower court's ruling. The three-judge panel decided that not all internal combustion engines were alike. The one used by Ford and nearly all other auto manufacturers was the Otto four-cycle type, not the two-cycle version described in Selden's patent application. As the patent was due to soon expire, the ALAM decided against appealing the decision.

Henry and Edsel were in Detroit, preparing to leave for the auto show in New York, when word of the court's decision reached them. Three days later, father and son joined Couzens as invited guests at the annual ALAM banquet, where Henry took a few puffs from the ceremonial peace pipe passed around by his former adversaries. The reconciliation was genuine, a "love feast," reported the New York press. As seventeen-year-old Edsel listened with a mixture of awe and pride, the banquet hall rocked with cries of "Ford! Ford! Ford!"

∽o∽

One afternoon in 1911, Henry invited a reporter from one of the local dailies into his office. With the Selden case settled and off his mind, he mused over several other topics, particularly the relationship between wages and profits. It was a subject about which the homespun capitalist was spending more time thinking as Model T sales and corporate profits continued to soar.

It wouldn't be too long, he predicted, before "automobiles will be going two abreast, in two directions on Woodward Avenue, and at the same time. And just as sure as that day is coming, so is coming a shorter workday, and so is a daily wage. It will be a daily wage of five dollars, perhaps as much as ten dollars, and maybe more. We are just beginning to get moving in the automobile industry, and the men who build the cars are entitled to better wages and better hours."

Back at his office, the reporter chewed over Ford's extravagant and unformed ideas with his city editor, who asked, "Do you believe it?"

"No," admitted the reporter, who could not imagine unskilled factory hands ever making more than a couple of dollars a day.

"Neither do I," agreed the editor. "So let's do Ford a favor, and not print it. He's probably getting enough crank mail as it is without us adding to it."

Less than three years later, on January 5, 1914, the same reporter was among those summoned to the Model T plant for a momentous announcement. Seated inside his office, Couzens read a statement:

> The Ford Motor Company, the greatest and most successful automobile manufacturing company in the world, will, on January 12, inaugurate the greatest revolution in the matter of rewards for its workers ever known to the industrial world.
>
> At one stroke it will reduce the hours of labor from nine to eight, and add to every man's pay a share of the profits of the house. The smallest amount to be received by any man 22 years old and upward will be $5 per day. The minimum wage is now $2.34 per day of nine hours.
>
> All but 10 percent of the employees will at once share in the profits. Only 10 percent of the men now employed are under 22 and even every one of those under 22 will have a chance of showing himself entitled to $5 per day.
>
> Instead of waiting until the end of the year to make a distribution of profits among their employees in one lump sum bonus sum, Mr. Ford and Mr. Couzens have estimated the year's prospective business and have decided upon what they feel will be a safe amount to award the workers. This will be spread over the whole year and paid on the regular semi-monthly days.
>
> The factory is now working two shifts of nine hours each. This will be changed to three shifts of eight hours each. The number employed is now about 15,000 and this will be increased by 4,000 or 5,000. The men who now earn $2.34 per day of nine hours will get at least $5 per day of eight hours.
>
> This will apply to every man of 22 years of age or upward without regard to the nature of his employment. In order that the young men from 18 to 22 years of age may be entitled to a share in the profits, he must show himself sober, saving, steady, industrious, and must satisfy the superintendent and staff that his money will not be wasted in riotous living.

Young men who are supporting families, widowed mothers, younger brothers and sisters will be treated like those over 22.

It is estimated that over $10 million will be thus distributed over and above the regular wages of the men.

"The commonest laborer who sweeps the floor shall receive his $5 per day," Ford declared.*

As the press conference wound down, Henry looked out the window, where hundreds of men—some heading for work, others seeking it—lined the sidewalks below. He motioned to reporters. "There's the principal reason for the eight-hour day," he said. "With the eight-hour day and three shifts working we can put on 4,000 more of those men who are anxious to be at work."

While Henry had long pondered the relationship between labor and capital, the immediate genesis of the Five-Dollar Day was the bitterly cold evening James Couzens had spent flipping through the pages of a socialist magazine. It was just a few days before Christmas in 1913, and while Couzens was able to stay toasty inside his elegant home on Longfellow, outside of it hungry, haggard-looking men hunched their shoulders against the cold. Couzens was struck by the disparity between the almost obscenely rich stockholders in the Ford Motor Company— he and Henry Ford foremost among them—and the ordinary working stiffs who, toiling away for $2.50 a day, had made those profits possible. Too often these men were tossed into the street by Detroit's industrial employers, left to scrounge for food, coal, and self-respect.

The next day, Couzens spoke to Henry about a wage increase. Henry was receptive, especially in the light of a recent incident. While walking through the plant with Edsel, Henry had noticed a worker staring hard and long at them while menacingly gripping a mallet—a violent gesture that, to Henry, suggested an ordinary working man's frustration

---

* But not women, stressed Couzens. "They are not the same economic factors as the men are," he explained. "They do not control the standard of living. There are 200 or 300 women employed in the electrical department. The rest that are here do office work. The average woman employee cannot be regarded as a fixture in a business as a man can be. A woman will leave at almost any time, for almost any reason, and when she stays long enough to be a dependable worker, she is apt to get married and have someone else support her. It is the man we aim to benefit." However, within a couple of years women were raised to the same pay level as men.

James Couzens and Henry Ford, c. 1910.

with the lack of opportunity in his life. "He was saying, 'Look at Henry Ford's boy! What has mine beside him?'" Henry told Couzens.

Over the next few days the two men went back and forth over the size of the raise. Should it be three dollars? Three and a half? Four? Couzens, knowing Henry's views on philanthropy, couched his argument in terms he could understand. "A straight five-dollar raise will be the greatest advertising any automobile concern ever had," he said. Ford agreed, though he reserved the right to call the raise "profit sharing" in case he needed to rescind it down the road.

News of Ford's profit-sharing plan exploded like a thunderclap inside kitchens, saloons, editorial offices, and boardrooms everywhere. In an editorial typical of the general press reaction, the following day's *Detroit News* congratulated Ford on the "striking" use of the phrase "social justice": "It is this element which makes the whole affair more than one man's munificence, more than a real distribution of material benefits, and gives it the quality of an attempt at constructive social and economic readjustment." The *New York Sun* assessed Ford as a "wholesale Santa Claus" while ministers sermonized that the Five-Dollar Day heralded a new era of cooperation between workingmen and employers. Ford workers were understandably ecstatic. Woljeck Manijklisjiski told a reporter, "My boy don't sell no more papers. My girl don't work in the house of another and see her mother but once in the week no more. Again we are a family." Ford was seen as an "inspired millionaire" looking out for the common good.

Some took a dim view, however, considering Ford a traitor to his class. The *Wall Street Journal* was among the harshest critics, arguing that "to inject ten millions into a company's factory, and to double the minimum wage, without regard to length of service, is to apply Biblical or spiritual principles into a field where they do not belong. . . . he has in his social endeavor committed economic blunders, if not crimes. They may return to plague him and the industry he represents, as well as organized society." The antiunion Employers Association of Detroit, along with its many automaker members, thought Ford's action would destroy the capitalist system. The *New York Times* opined, "The theory of management at Ford Motor Company is distinctly Utopian and runs dead against all experience."

Nonetheless, Ford's generosity produced its own dividends. Prior to the Five-Dollar Day, turnover at Highland Park was incredibly high: 963 workers had to be hired for every 100 that stayed on the payroll. It cost $100 to train each new worker, meaning turnover cost the company $3 million annually. After the introduction of profit sharing, however, the number of people hired to maintain a steady work force of 14,000 employees dropped to just one-eighth of what it had been. The abysmally high rate of absenteeism, the bane of every foreman and shop supervisor, also was corrected. A more stable work force resulted in greater productivity. "I felt that Mr. Ford was doing something to help me and I wanted to show my appreciation by doing better than ever," was how one worker expressed it. More and more, men could be found proudly wearing their company badges to dances on Saturday night and to church on Sunday morning.

The introduction of a living wage also created a new class of consumers: workers able to purchase the very product they built. "Fordism," a term coined to describe the "mad socialist's" penchant for human engineering, would soon lose its original 1914 luster, but not before revolutionizing industry by demonstrating how an employer could successfully boost wages, productivity, and sales all at the same time.

The Five-Dollar Day came with a heavy dose of paternalism. Henry had always practiced and espoused the virtues of sobriety and industry. Now, with wage increases tied to such factors as an employee's demonstrated thrift, cleanliness, or morality, Ford had a carrot to dangle in front of his workers. Couzens spoke to the "sociological side" of profit sharing, "one of great importance and one to which we have given some consideration already, but will give a great deal more from now on. We have a Sociological Department to look after our employees' welfare, and this will be greatly extended. Young men who have plenty of money may spend it wastefully or in riotous living. . . . We want to see that our employees do not lose their efficiency because of prosperity and will have our Sociological Department work along that line."

Henry believed men down on their luck should be given the opportunity to remake themselves—given a leg up, not a handout. He could be downright evangelistical, often picking up hitchhikers and transients and giving them jobs inside his factory. He was particularly drawn to the plight of ex-convicts and African Americans, hiring far more of each than any other automaker. He once refused to fire a young man for stealing. "Give him a better job," Henry instructed, "and see if that will make him a better man."

The Sociological Department implemented Ford's ideas about self-help. Between 1913 and 1921, as many as eighty investigators at a time fanned out to visit workers' homes, interview neighbors, and examine personal documents, all in an effort to determine wage increases and discharges. "Employees who cannot remain sober and industrious will be dismissed," explained Couzens, "but no one will be let out without being given every possible chance to make good. No one will be discharged until we find that he is of no use to us in any way whatever."

Ford, like all automakers, actively recruited immigrants for his factory. In 1915, there were 18,028 workers representing forty-nine different nationalities at Highland Park. Signs had to be posted in several languages, but there was no guarantee that a recent arrival from Poland or Italy could read in *any* language. Foreign-born employees were enrolled in an Americanization program that stressed instruction in reading, writing, and speaking English, and were given lessons in civics and personal hygiene as well. Upon the successful completion of the seventy-two-session program, graduates participated in an elaborate commencement ceremony that culminated with their symbolic passing from the model of an immigrant ship into a giant melting pot. As teachers stirred the pot with oversized ladles, "out came the men dressed in their best American clothes and waving American flags," said one social worker present at the 1916 ceremony.

Although intrusive, the company's sociological program generally was viewed favorably, particularly by immigrants, many of whom were patiently taught how to use a toothbrush, change a diaper, or clean a sink. In addition, thousands of boys were given a practical education at the Henry Ford Trade School, another rehabilitative effort administered by the Sociological Department.

∾∾

What enabled Henry to maximize production and profits while lowering prices and raising wages was the assembly line, which he was no more responsible for inventing than the automobile. He was, however, the first to apply mass-production techniques to the building of cars, an innovation that, when coupled with the publicity generated by the Selden case, the Model T, and the Five-Dollar Day, made him into a towering and world-famous figure.

The first quarter-million or so Model T's were built in the fashion of all automobiles then. Skilled mechanics and craftsmen did the actual assembling. Unskilled workers literally ran all over the plant, fetching parts from bins and bringing them back to each car in progress as it moved from a stationary workbench (where an engine was built) to a central assembly area (where a chassis was fitted with engine, axles, and wheels) to the upholstery department (where seats were installed), and so on until the vehicle was finished. Most automakers recognized the waste of this leisurely system, particularly as Frederick "Speedy" Taylor, the acknowledged guru of time-and-motion techniques, went around Detroit with clipboard and stopwatch preaching better ways of increasing production. At the same time, an efficient method of delivery and assembly had yet to be figured out. Cyrus McCormick (who made reapers), Samuel Colt (firearms), and Isaac Singer (sewing machines) had already demonstrated the cost-effectiveness of assembly lines in manufacturing. But those were simple products when compared with the thousands of parts that went into the building of an automobile.

Charlie Sorenson, now Ford's plant superintendent, first experimented with a crude version of an assembly line in July 1908 at the Piquette plant. As Ford and Harold Wills looked on, a rope was used to pull a frame on skids along the length of the floor. Parts and materials

The first moving assembly line in action inside the magneto department at
Highland Park.

had been strategically arranged in a long row, and every few feet the
chassis stopped and components were added: wheels, radiator, dash-
board, steering wheel, and spark coil, most of which had been put together on subassembly lines. Gradually the vehicle took shape. Henry
was intrigued by the demonstration run, but nothing could be done on
a grand scale owing to the small size of the factory and the upcoming
unveiling of the Model T.

It became a different story by 1913, when the spacious Crystal
Palace and a four-month backlog of orders created the right environment for a radical change. Assisting Sorenson in making that change
was Clarence Avery, Edsel's former manual arts teacher, who had been
hired after expressing an interest in entering the automobile business.
In August 1913, after nearly two years of studying and estimating the
time and cost savings involved in building axles, radiators, and other
components on a moving conveyor, Avery and Sorenson launched the
new concept in the magneto shop.

"We began with a minor sub-assembly; the flywheel magneto,"
recalled Wills. "It had been customary for one man to do the entire job
of assembling a magneto. It had taken him 20 minutes. Splitting the

work into 29 operations, and pushing the magneto on a conveyor, the assembly time was cut to four minutes." Through trial and error, similar techniques were worked out for building a complete car. Within months, entire Model T's were being assembled on three lines, with each flowing river of steel being fed by scores of subassemblies. Overhead conveyors helped move parts between work stations.

"It must not be imagined that all this worked out as quickly as it sounds," Ford later wrote. "The speed of the moving work had to be carefully tried out; in the fly-wheel magneto we first had a speed of 60 inches per minute. That was too fast. Then we tried 18 inches per minutes. That was too slow. Finally we settled on 44 inches per minute. The idea is that a man must not be hurried in his work—he must have every second necessary but not a single unnecessary moment. We have speeds for every assembly. . . . Some men do only one or two small operations, others do more. The man who places a part does not fasten it—the part may not be fully in place until after several operations later. The man who puts in a bolt does not put on the nut; the man who puts on the nut does not tighten it. On operation 34 the budding motor gets its gasoline; it has previously received lubrication; on operation number 44 the radiator is filled with water, and on operation 45 the car drives onto John R Street."

Within two years the time to build a Model T dropped as dramatically as a dinner plate off a tabletop, from 12 hours and 28 minutes to a mere 93 minutes. Skilled craftsmen were replaced wholesale, in most cases by a poorly educated, unskilled worker willing to perform the same task over and over and at a pace dictated by the boss. "You wouldn't tell them to go faster," said one production manager, recalling the twice-the-work-for-twice-the-pay mindset that accompanied the implementation of the Five-Dollar Day. "You would just turn up the speed of the conveyor to go faster, that's all, until they kicked it was going too fast and they couldn't do it. Then we would drop it back a notch." The speed of the assembly line and general working conditions would remain constant issues—in 1916 alone, workers at Highland Park lost 192 fingers and suffered 68,000 lacerations—but getting paid the industry's highest wages helped take some of the sting out of the repetitive nature of the work. Each year more and more Model T's rolled off the assembly line, output reaching nearly 803,000 in 1917—a tenfold increase in just five years. To further streamline production, beginning in 1914 the color of the Model T—previously available in

The body drop at Highland Park, 1913.

black, green, red, blue, and two shades of gray—was limited to black, which was the fastest drying enamel paint. It would remain the only available color for a dozen years. Although Ford coined the phrase, "The customer can have any color he wants as long as it's black," nearly all automakers adhered to the same dark-hued policy until General Motors chemists introduced Duco pryoxylin lacquer, a new fast-drying finish available in several colors, in 1924.

The nearly simultaneous introduction of the Five-Dollar Day and the assembly line profited Ford, his workers, and the public. Car buyers saw the cost of the Model T steadily fall by $50 to $100 each year. In 1915 new Model T customers even received a $50 rebate from Ford, an unprecedented public relations gimmick that cost the automaker $15,410,650. Profits continued to grow, from $24 million in 1915 to $60 million the following year.

Ford's largesse naturally extended to his only child. One November day in 1914, Henry strode into a local bank, Edsel in tow.

"Bill," he announced to the banker, "I have a million dollars in gold here. This is Edsel's twenty-first birthday, and I want him to have it."

Two Ford workers inside their Detroit boardinghouse in 1914. All workers were subject to being visited by inspectors from the Sociological Department.

Visibly astonished, Edsel would have been forgiven for taking the rest of the day off to celebrate—or recuperate. Instead, displaying his customary diligence, he went back to his office and spent the rest of his birthday at his desk. He did admit later, however, that he'd never made as many mistakes as he did that day.

7

～o～

*Rearview Mirror*

# The Crystal Palace in 1914

*In East Pittsburgh, Pennsylvania, fifteen-year-old Frank Marquart and his father were just two of countless laborers astonished and inspired by Ford's momentous announcement of the Five-Dollar Day. They immediately joined the throngs from all over the United States and Canada headed for Highland Park.*

My father hated his job as a common laborer in the chain mill and he hated me for not finding a steady job, and life became a living hell for me. Then came that memorable day in January 1914 when my father came home from work excitedly waving the *Pittsburgh Press* and shouting at us: "Look, in Detroit Henry Ford is paying five dollars a day to all his workers. I'm going to quit my job tomorrow and Frank and me will go to Detroit. We'll both get jobs at Ford's—why, we'll be making 10 dollars a day, think of it, 10 dollars a day!" Then he read aloud excerpts from the front-page story about the Flivver King philanthropist, who was revolutionizing wage scales in America. The more my father talked the more enthusiastic he became.

My mother, however, did not share the enthusiasm. "But how do you know you'll get work in Detroit?" she ventured. I don't recall all that was said but I do remember that her misgivings threw my old man into a rage. He accused her of not cooperating, of not lending moral support; he said she wanted to hold him back. "How to hell can we ever get ahead if you always pull back like that," he demanded, half in

German and half in English. While he berated my mother, I picked up the *Press* and read the story for myself. I immediately sided with my father. With the thought of getting away from the hell-hole that was Braddock, of escaping the abuse of my father because I could not find work, of going to a big city—especially a city like Detroit where automobiles were made—I was all for pulling up stakes and heading for the Motor City as soon as possible. . . .

It was agreed that my father and I would go to Detroit, find work at five dollars a day, and send for the rest of the family later. Never, as long as I live, will I forget those days in Detroit in early January 1914! I can't recall how we found the boarding house run by Mrs. Hartlieb . . . but I do recall how we rose early on the following morning, gulped down breakfast, and walked to Jefferson Avenue to take the Jefferson car to Woodward and then transfer to the car that was to take us to the Ford plant in Highland Park.

Nor will I ever forget the sight that greeted our eyes when we walked toward the Ford employment office. There were thousands of job seekers jam-packed in front of the gates. It was a bitterly cold morning and I had no overcoat, only a red sweater under a thin jacket. I don't know how long we stood in that crowd, but I became numb from cold. The crowd kept getting larger and larger and there were angry cries of "for Christ's sake, stop shoving" from men who were near the gates. Some of those men had been waiting there for hours; they were cold, ill-tempered, and in a snarling mood. Several times the company guards ordered the men to stand back and not push against the gates. But those near the gates were pushed by those behind them, who in turn were pushed by those behind them. Suddenly a shout went up—a shout that soon became a roaring chant: "Open the employment office, open the employment office!"

Whether the employment office was ever opened that morning I do not know; whether anyone was hired, I do not know either. But I do know that a man shouted over a megaphone, "We are not hiring any more today; there's no use sticking around; we're not hiring today." An angry roar went up from the crowd: "You sonsabitches, keeping us here all this time and then telling us you ain't hiring, you bastards!" The crowd did not break up; it kept pushing toward the gates. With chattering teeth I suggested to my father that we ought to leave. He cursed me and shouted at me in German that he didn't bring me to Detroit so I could loaf like a bum.

The Five-Dollar Day made Ford famous. When it was announced in January 1914, thousands of job seekers from across the country mobbed the Model T plant in Highland Park.

Again the man came with the megaphone: "We ARE NOT hiring today. Go away; no use standing out there in the cold for nothing." And then the ominous warning: "If you don't stop pushing against these gates we're gonna use the firehoses."

I guess everybody thought that was an empty threat made to scare people away. It scared no one. The crowd showed no signs of being intimidated. In fact, it became more unruly. Someone yelled, "Let's crash the goddamn gates!" I can remember how the mood of the crowd suddenly changed; it became ugly, threatening. I heard a roar of approval as someone yelled: "We oughta take down the goddamn place brick by brick." There was shouting and cursing and confusion. Then from near the gates a cry was raised: "For God's sake the bastards are gonna turn the hoses on us!" Someone near me shouted: "Aw, that's bullshit, they wouldn't dare do a thing like that." He had hardly finished the sentence when the water came, the icy water that froze almost as soon as it landed on our clothing.

The hoses were turned at an angle and moved from side to side so that the spray hit all sections of the crowd. There was a wild scramble to get away; some people were pushed down and trampled. Several fist fights broke out when some workers shoved those ahead of us. My father cursed, in the way he always cursed when infuriated, his curses beginning in English and rising to a crescendo in German. But he was lucky; the water did not soak through his overcoat as it soaked through my jacket and sweater. By the time we were able to board a Woodward streetcar I was shivering from head to foot.

My father said it was a "Jew plot." A rabid anti-Semite long before Hitler arose to horrify the world, my father said Ford was a Jew and what we suffered that morning was the result of a "dirty Jew trick." When I suggested that "Ford" was not a Jewish name, he told me not to be stupid: "Don't you know Jews change their names for business reasons!"

∽◦∾

*Not long after the Marquarts were chased off with hoses in Highland Park, a writer for Collier's was given an ear-bruising guided tour of the plant's inner workings. Julian Street returned to his magazine's offices to type out a colorful and impressionistic account of the factory that was transforming the world.*

Of course there was order in that place; of course there was system—relentless system—terrible "efficiency"—but to my mind, unaccustomed to such things, the whole room, with its interminable aisles, its whirling shafts and wheels, its forest of roof-supporting posts and flapping, flying, leather belting, its endless rows of writhing machinery, its shrieking, hammering, and clatter, its smell of oil, its autumn haze of smoke, its savage-looking foreign population—to my mind it expressed but one thing, and that thing was delirium.

Fancy a jungle of wheels and belts and weird iron forms—of men, machinery and movement—add to it every kind of sound you can imagine: the sound of a million squirrels chirking, a million monkeys quarreling, a million lions roaring, a million pigs dying, a million elephants smashing through a forest of sheet iron, a million boys whistling on their fingers, a million others coughing with the whooping cough, a million sinners groaning as they are dragged to hell—imagine all of this happening at the very edge of Niagara Falls, with the everlasting roar of the cataract as a perpetual background, and you may acquire a vague conception of that place.

Fancy all this riot going on at once: then imagine the effect of its suddenly ceasing. For that is what it did. The wheels slowed down and became still. The belts stopped flapping. The machines lay dead. The noise faded to a murmur: then to utter silence. Our ears rang with the quiet. The aisles all at once were full of men in overalls, each with a paper package or a box. Some of them walked swiftly toward the exits. Others settled down on piles of automobile parts, or the bases of machines to eat, like grimy soldiers on a battlefield. It was the lull of noon.

I was glad to leave the machine shop. It dazed me. I should have liked to leave it some time before I actually did, but the agreeable young enthusiast who was conducting us delighted in explaining things—shouting the explanations in our ears. Half of them I could not hear; the other half I could not comprehend. Here and there I recognized familiar automobile parts—great heaps of them—cylinder castings, crank cases, axles. Then as things began to get a little bit coherent, along would come a train of cars hanging insanely from a single over-head rail, the man in the cab tooting his shrill whistle; whereupon I would promptly retire into mental fog once more, losing all sense of what things meant, feeling that I was not in any factory, but in a Gar-gantuan lunatic asylum where fifteen thousand raving, tearing maniacs had been given full authority to go ahead and do their damnedest.

# 8

⌘

# War on Several Fronts

*Events were moving swiftly for Henry. Involved in lawsuits, politics and national affairs as well as auto production, he was like a juggler with several balls in the air at once. Another man might have felt overpowered, but he thrived on the pressure and activity. Later he looked back on this period and said simply, "It was the time of my life."*

—Collier and Horowitz, *The Fords: An American Epic*

The Five-Dollar Day made Henry Ford a national figure overnight, with the *New York Times* alone publishing thirty-five articles about him in the three months following its announcement. Meanwhile, several large-circulation magazines published profiles of the automaker in 1914. A feature in the *New York Sun* reflected the generally adulatory tone of the press coverage. "Forty years ago he was doing chores on his father's farm at Dearborn, Michigan, six miles from Detroit. Twenty-five years ago he was drawing a mechanic's wages. Today he is giving away millions of dollars. . . . In the first place, be it said, Henry Ford seems to have been endowed with a mechanical genius as distinctly as great painters, great musicians, great poets are specially endowed for their respective careers in the world."

Henry was a poor public speaker and disliked personal publicity; consequently, the company had lacked an identity since its inception. That was before 1914, when the world rushed in. Thanks to the massive media attention given his profit-sharing plan, Ford was introduced to the public as a self-made, self-effacing, and selfless man, a simple genius in touch with his—and, by extension, America's—pastoral roots. Before the Five-Dollar Day, his shyness had made it easy for him to share the credit for the company's success with men such as James Couzens and C. Harold Wills. But now, having had fame unexpectedly thrust on him at a late age—he was in his early fifties—he reacted in the manner that the world today automatically expects from "specially endowed" actors and first-round draft picks. He started believing his press clippings, and in short order his head got too big for his bowler.

Ardent admirers and the simply curious joined reporters and photographers in making Henry's everyday comings and goings more difficult. The crush of attention caused him to briefly experiment with wearing a fake beard around the Highland Park plant and ultimately forced him to move from his Edison Street home to a more secluded residence he built along the shore of the Rouge River in Dearborn.

Despite some occasional grousing over the inconveniences of his newfound celebrity, Henry easily slipped into the homespun robes of the new industrial messiah, laconically issuing statements that enjoyed instant and widespread circulation. "I do not consider the machines which bear my name simply as machines," was typical of the pronouncements that helped make him the unofficial representative of the common man. "If that was all there was to it I would simply do something else. I take them as concrete evidence of the working out of a theory of business which I hope is more than a theory of business—a theory towards making this world a better place to live." Reporters treated this grass-roots capitalist almost as an oracle, asking his opinion about everything under the sun: foreign trade, railroads, the gold standard, the war in Europe. Of the latter, Henry was more expansive than on other subjects. The clash of nations had resulted in the unprecedented slaughter of millions of combatants and civilians at places such as Gallipoli and Ypres (where poison gas was used for the first time), and no end was in sight. Americans were engaged in an internal debate over U.S. neutrality, one that heated up with the torpedoing of the British liner *Lusitania* on May 7, 1915, by a German U-boat. Of the 1,198 men, women, and children lost, 128 were Americans. The sinking accelerated anti-German feeling and had President Woodrow Wilson preaching preparedness. In August 1915, the one-year anniversary of the outbreak of hostilities, Ford promised his "life and fortune" to the cause of peace, a pledge that led to one of the most quixotic adventures in his life.

Ford abhorred war. Among the 650,000 Americans who died during the Civil War was his mother's brother, who had accepted $1,000 from a local businessman to serve as his substitute. That tiny piece of family history underscored his belief that war was a rich man's game, fought by ordinary citizens for the sake of Wall Street "parasites." "New York wants war," he declared, "but not the United States." He followed up that observation with another: "If one-tenth of what has been spent on preparedness for war had been spent on the prevention of war the world would always have been at peace."

Ford's vigorously stated sentiments impressed Rosika Schwimmer, a stout thirty-eight-year-old suffragist, and young peace activist Louis Lochner. Both pacifists separately contacted the celebrity industrialist, and the three met for lunch at Ford's Estate, Fair Lane, one November day in 1915. There they discussed Schwimmer's grandiose plan for ending the war—the formulation of an independent peace commission that would mediate continuously with world leaders. Typically impulsive, Ford decided to immediately arrange a trip to New York and Washington, his new friends in tow, to stir up press coverage for the cause and to visit Wilson in the White House.

A few days later, Ford was able to have a face-to-face chat with Wilson. He even got the stone-faced president to smile over a favorite Model T joke. But Wilson was noncommittal when asked to support the activists' plan—conceived the previous evening during a dinner with fabled social reformer Jane Addams—of chartering a ship to take a special peace delegation to Europe. Wilson, who had previously met with Madame Schwimmer and rejected her as strident and impractical, now dismissed the carmaker as a castle builder. Ford was similarly unimpressed. "He's a small man," Henry said to Lochner after the meeting.

Moving with a haste that startled and upset many of the activists, on November 24, Ford informed the press he had already chartered a Scandinavian American liner, the *Oscar II*, for his mission. It was scheduled to leave New York in eleven days. He hoped to have aboard some of the country's biggest names and most influential citizens, including President Wilson. Exactly what this blue-ribbon delegation would do once the so-called Peace Ship steamed out to sea was still up in the air, reporters discovered.

"We're going to stop the war," Henry said.

"Going to stop the war?" asked a reporter.

"Yes, we're going to get the boys out of the trenches by Christmas."

"But how are you going to do it?"

"Oh, you'll see," said Ford.

"Where are you going?"

"I don't know."

"But what makes you think you can put it over?"

"Oh," said Ford, "we have had assurances."

Ford's well-intentioned but unformed scheme found little support among politicians and the media. "Mr. Ford's visit abroad will not be mischievous only because it is ridiculous," said ex-president Theodore Roosevelt. To the *Louisville Courier Journal*, it was "worse than ineffable folly for pestiferous busybodies in this country like Henry Ford and Jane Addams to nag the president to make an ass of himself by mediating in behalf of a peace which is impossible."

The delegation faced a potentially hazardous voyage. Although the German ambassador announced in September that liners would no longer be targeted by U-boats, mariners had good reason to doubt such promises. In the days leading up to the Peace Ship's scheduled departure, several ships were attacked. The prospect of a premature grave in the icy North Atlantic, coupled to the ridicule that the Peace Ship was getting in the press, accounted for the woeful response to the flurry of invitations sent to prominent citizens. Telegrams had gone out to ex-president William Howard Taft, Thomas Edison, William Jennings Bryan, Helen Keller, and every state governor but only magazine publisher S. S. McClure and North Dakota governor Louis Hanna agreed to come along. Of the 202 first- and second-class passengers on board the *Oscar II* on December 4, less than half were delegates; the rest were "technical staff" and journalists. Ford was paying everybody's expenses. (Another 450 passengers, mostly Scandinavians returning home for Christmas, were booked in third class.)

The day-long drizzle on the day the Peace Ship sailed added to Clara Ford's sense of foreboding. She was so sure her husband was doomed that she wept and tried in vain to convince him to abort the mission. Edsel, nattily attired in a derby and chesterfield topcoat, was more stoic in his send-off. When Henry invited Clara to accompany him, saying he had drawn up a will that left everything to their only child, Clara declined because both might be lost, leaving their bachelor son without a parent. Two bands, one aboard ship and the other on the Hoboken pier, played such songs as "I Didn't Raise My Boy to Be a Soldier" and "Onward Christian Soldiers." Finally, at dusk, what one

Michigan editor termed the "loon ship" pulled in its gangplank and steamed out of the harbor. Splashing after the boat was a character who called himself "Mr. Zero." His mission, he explained after being yanked out of the water, was to deflect German torpedoes.

It took about a week into the fifteen-day crossing for Henry to lose his enthusiasm for the project. Bickering broke out among the delegates while reporters peppered Ford with questions that exposed just how ignorant he was about the half-baked mission he had embarked on. Henry was happiest when he was below decks, among the machinery he understood so well. One day he was almost washed overboard and caught a cold, causing him to stay in his cabin for the rest of the trip. There he was counseled by Samuel Marquis, an Episcopalian minister that Clara had assigned to be her husband's spiritual crutch during the trip. Marquis helped turn Henry against the autocratic Schwimmer, who, much to Ford's relief, had taken over control of the delegation. When the *Oscar II* reached Oslo, Norway, Ford was worn out, homesick, and disillusioned. Two days before Christmas, he sneaked out of his hotel room and caught the next ship back to the United States, having told the thoroughly shocked Lochner, "Guess I had better go back to Mother. You've got this thing started and can get along without me." The demoralized delegation regrouped and pressed on. Over the next year they met with a succession of junior government officials in Scandinavia and Europe before coming back home having accomplished little more than burning through another half-million or so of their benefactor's dollars.

Meanwhile, Henry returned to New York, insisting the adverse press was no big deal. "I was bothered only because my wife didn't like some of the criticism," he said. "My son Edsel didn't mind and I am really strong for it"—that is, the ridicule was good medicine for the fractious peace movement.

Ford's ego was bruised by the criticism he received from the more intellectual segments of society, but ordinary folks saw something noble in his attempt to end the fighting. At least he had tried to do something, harebrained as it was. Most people sat on the sidelines, unwilling to enter the game. Irving Caesar was one of the idealistic people for whom Henry Ford's populist reputation was enhanced. The nineteen-year-old college student in New York had read about the peace mission, sent Ford a telegram, and was brought on board as a stenographer. "I don't consider the Ford Peace Ship a lost mission," he reflected nearly forty years later. "The cause of peace was well served. Millions and millions of people throughout the world were exposed to a brief moment of hope. And who shall say that even a brief moment of hope isn't worth the millions of dollars it cost Ford."

◆◆◆

A few weeks prior to getting involved with Madame Schwimmer, Ford's budding megalomania resulted in the departure of his most dependable partner. Henry may have been an exalted national figure, but James Couzens knew him as the circa-1903 Henry Ford and treated him accordingly. Couzens wore several hats at once: purchasing agent, advertising manager, sales manager, and office manager, as well as serving as secretary and treasurer. Henry would have had a hard time managing a sandwich shop by himself, so from the very beginning he happily let Couzens assume all the nitty-gritty details of sales, finance, and personnel. Couzens swiftly built a network of 7,000 Ford agencies, roughly half of the entire industry total. The worldwide sales organization left competing automakers in the dust. A fiercely independent man, Couzens was fiscally conservative but socially liberal. It was he, not Ford, who was primarily responsible for such humanitarian initiatives as the Five-Dollar Day and the Sociological Department. These created an untold amount of free and positive publicity for Ford—the company *and* the man. A lot of industry observers, then and now, felt the Ford Motor Company would not have survived, much less prospered, without James Couzens. It was a sign of Henry's distrust of similarly strong-willed men that he felt he had to get rid of him.

Any excuse would do. He assigned someone to tail Couzens, then complained to an editor at the *Detroit News* that the executive had been at the plant only 184 days in the past year. Ford, stirring the pot, stated he disliked "absentee control." Much of Couzens's time out of Highland Park had been spent in California, where he had gone to recuperate after his son died out there in an accident, his new Model T plunging off a narrow mountain road. "I've had enough of his goddam persecution," Couzens said after learning of Ford's espionage.

Ford's antiwar and antipreparedness sentiments were enough to ignite the final confrontation. One October evening in 1915, Couzens came across an article being prepared for publication in the *Ford Times,* the company's magazine. "You cannot publish this," said Couzens, not-

ing the pacifist theme of the piece. When the advertising manager protested, he barked, "These are Mr. Ford's personal views, not the views
of the company."

"You cannot stop anything here," Henry told Couzens the next
morning.

"Well, then," said Couzens, "I will quit." And he did, though the
forty-three-year-old multimillionaire kept his stock and stayed on the
board of directors for another four years. Most of his duties, but none
of his clout, were assumed by Henry's loyal and docile personal secretary, Frank Klingensmith, who was named treasurer of the company
and made a director.

At the same time Ford was parting ways with Couzens, an ongoing
imbroglio with two other shareholders also was reaching its climactic
stage. John and Horace Dodge had grown rich supplying parts to, and
drawing dividends from, the Ford Motor Company. They'd also grown
impatient to build their own car. On July 17, 1913, after Ford finally
rejected overtures of buying the Dodge Brothers and operating it as a
subsidiary, the Dodges formally ended their relationship with the Ford
Motor Company. In June 1914, the new Dodge Brothers Motor Car
Company was incorporated. Later that year the first Dodge automobile
rolled out the door: a sturdy, peppy four-cylinder model that was the
first mass-produced car to feature an all-steel body. John Dodge was
so sure of its quality he personally drove several into a brick wall at
20 miles per hour. "I might as well," he explained, "because someone
else is going to do it when these cars get on the road." The Dodge sold
for $785, which put it in the middle range of new car prices. (The
Model T sold for $450.) The public and the press gave the new Dodge
a warm welcome. In 1915, Dodge Brothers built 45,000 cars; only
Ford and Willys-Overland produced more.

The Dodges invested heavily in their start-up, spending a couple
million dollars on expanding and retooling the factory they had originally built in neighboring Hamtramck to accommodate turning out
parts for the Model T. Now that they were no longer getting $10 mil-
lion a year in Ford business, they were more dependent than ever on
the millions in regular and special dividends they were accustomed to
receiving each year as Ford stockholders.

Henry, looking to expand his own operations while also recogniz-
ing the rise of a formidable competitor, decided to turn off the spigot
of cash. In early 1916, not long after returning from his Peace Ship

adventure, he stopped by the Dodge plant for a friendly talk with the brothers. He wanted to discuss his plans for mass-producing tractors, which he correctly thought would revolutionize farming in the same fashion as the Model T.

"There had been considerable talk about the forming of the tractor plant," John Dodge said later, "and there had been some objection on the part of some of the stockholders of the Ford Motor Co. My understanding was that it was his purpose to use the engine of the Model T and the facilities and resources of the Ford Motor Company to produce this tractor and still own the tractor plant himself."

What Henry had in mind as a site for his tractor factory was a 2,000-acre tract along the Rouge River in southeast Dearborn. The tractor plant was just a part of his grand dream. He had visions of developing the area into an industrial complex of unprecedented magnitude, bringing in rubber, wood, coal, and other raw materials to be processed into the components he was currently dependent on outside suppliers to provide. Ford wanted to be wholly self-sufficient as an industrialist, and that philosophy extended to his refusal to go to the banks to help pay for it. The Rouge complex would be completely self-financed.

This is where Ford shocked the Dodges. "He said he did not propose to pay any dividends except the nominal dividend," recalled John Dodge, "that the stockholders had already received a good deal more than they had put into the company, and he did not propose to pay any more. He was going to put the earnings of the company back into the business to expand it. He was going to double the size of his plant and double the number of cars produced and sell them at half price."

Ford intended to restrict dividends to just $1.2 million a year. Every dollar beyond that would be plowed back into expanding operations. The Dodges were up in arms. If Ford wanted to run the company for his own pleasure instead of for profit, he should buy them and other shareholders out. Henry didn't need to, of course. He was the majority stockholder and could do what he wanted. His imperious decisions to lower the price of the Model T and to withhold dividends had the effect of undercutting the Dodge brothers just as they were trying to gain a foothold in the market.

This was where the situation stood on November 1, 1916, when Edsel Ford married Eleanor Clay inside the Boston Boulevard mansion of her uncle, Joseph L. Hudson, the city's leading retailer. Eleanor, three years younger than the groom, had recently graduated from the exclusive Liggett School. A lively, self-confident brunette with an appetite

Eleanor Clay in her
wedding dress,
November 1916.

for skating, dancing, basketball, and good works (she was a volunteer
at various local charities), she had first met Edsel at Miss Annie Ward-
Foster's dance class, held in a room over the downtown Women's
Exchange. Edsel, partial to jazz, also had a romantic side, as evidenced
by the title of one of his favorite ballads, "Let's Make Love Among the
Roses." For a proper couple such as Edsel and Eleanor, heeding that
song would have to wait until marriage, of course. The ceremony was
elegant but understated, with one society reporter later sniffing over
the absence of any jewelry worth more than $1,000. After honeymoon-
ing in Hawaii and western Canada, the newlyweds moved into a grand
home on Iroquois Street in Indian Village, a new neighborhood of opu-
lent homes that was all the rage for fashionable and privileged young
couples like themselves.

Henry and Clara had not expected their son to marry as young as
he did (he was a few days shy of turning twenty-three), and had hoped
to keep their little family unit together as long as possible. Aside from
that, they were pleased with his development and his choice of bride.
Edsel had grown into a dapper man already widely admired for a level
of maturity and sense of responsibility and consideration not often
found among other children of the nouveau riche. At the wedding, John
Dodge came up to Ford and said, "Henry, I don't envy you a damn
thing except that boy of yours." The father of the groom didn't have
long to drink in the compliment. The next day newspaper headlines
screamed that the Dodge brothers had filed suit against Ford, charging
him with illegally withholding dividends.

The Dodge brothers: Horace (*left*) and John.

Ford fought back in the papers, piously arguing that the company should be run for the benefit of its customers ahead of its stockholders, whose initial risk had already been rewarded well beyond their wildest imaginations. Moreover, rebates like the $15 million returned to car buyers in 1915 and regular price reductions were smart business moves. "Did you ever before in your life hear of any concern being complained of as violating state, federal and common laws because the goods were sold at too low a price, as the Dodge Brothers allege we are doing? They say my course is likely to injure them. They own 10% of the stock and I own 58%. I can't injure them $10 without at the same time injuring myself $58, and I don't think they can reasonably accuse me of pursuing such a course."

The case didn't come to trial until the following year. In the intervening months, America formally entered the war on April 6, 1917, transforming the spiritual commander of the Peace Ship into a "fighting pacifist." Henry, morally conflicted by his about-face, pledged he would "work harder than ever before" on behalf of the allies while promising not to take "one cent profit" out of his defense work. Always aware of the public relations impact of a grand gesture, Henry at various times talked of building a thousand one-man submarines a day, of cranking out two-man "flivver" tanks at the same pace, of blackening enemy skies with 150,000 aircraft. Ordinary people, familiar with Ford's reputation, thought him perfectly capable of pulling off such miracles of mass production. He didn't come anywhere close, which is not to say that Ford's industrial output on behalf of the allies wasn't impressive.*

Ford's first significant contribution to the war effort was decidedly nonmilitary. On July 27, 1917, he formed a separate company, Henry Ford & Son, to manufacture tractors, hurrying into production his "kerosene burning donkey" for delivery to the British. The $750 "Fordson" tractors were sold at cost. By war's end some 7,000 of the hand-cranked tractors, which featured cleated tires and a twelve-inch double-bottomed plow, were helping English farmers combat a desperate food shortage throughout the British Isles. Another 27,167 were sold domestically.

Tractors were only the beginning. The company built 39,000 military cars, trucks, and ambulances, more than a million steel helmets, nearly 4,000 Liberty airplane engines, and more than 415,000 cylinders, as well as caissons, submarine detectors, and armor plating for tanks. It also designed a robot airplane bomb that foreshadowed Germany's V-1 terror weapon of World War II.

The company's most dramatic project was building "Eagle" submarine chasers. With no shipyard in the country capable of manufacturing the 615-ton vessels in quantity, the government agreed to spend $3.5 million in plant and waterway improvements on Ford's River Rouge property. A massive steel shipbuilding plant—1,700 feet long, 350 feet wide, and 100 feet high—went up. Building "B" (still in use today for auto production) housed three assembly lines, each of which could handle seven boats in progress. Nearly 4,000 welders, erectors, riveters, pipe fitters, caulkers, electricians, and painters worked on the boats, which crept from station to station on 200-foot-long flatcars. To

---

* According to historians Allan Nevins and Frank Ernest Hill, the Ford Motor Company made nearly $8.2 million in profits from defense work, an amount that shrank to almost $4.4 million after taxes. Henry Ford's 58.5 percent share of the balance was $2,549,129, of which $1,622,348 was paid in taxes. Henry's $926,780 in profits were never returned to the U.S. Treasury, as he had pledged.

Henry Ford and the "Peace
Ship" set sail from Hoboken,
New Jersey, in December 1915.

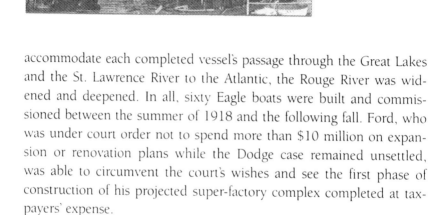

accommodate each completed vessel's passage through the Great Lakes
and the St. Lawrence River to the Atlantic, the Rouge River was wid-
ened and deepened. In all, sixty Eagle boats were built and commissioned between the summer of 1918 and the following fall. Ford, who
was under court order not to spend more than $10 million on expan-
sion or renovation plans while the Dodge case remained unsettled,
was able to circumvent the court's wishes and see the first phase of
construction of his projected super-factory complex completed at taxpayers' expense.

As Americans rallied 'round the flag, the Dodge lawsuit finally moved into the courtroom. In preliminary testimony, Henry cagily sparred with the Dodges' attorney, Elliott G. Stevenson, who questioned his motives for lowering the cost of the Model T. "Your conscience would not let you sell cars at a price that you did last year and make such awful profits?" Stevenson asked. "That is what you said, isn't it?"

"I don't know that my conscience has got anything to do with the case," Ford responded.

"Why did you say that it wasn't right to get such 'awful' profits, if it wasn't your conscience?"

"It isn't good business," said Henry, who stayed unflappable as Stevenson bored in. "You say you do not think it is right to make such profits?" the attorney asked. "What is this business being continued for, and why is it being enlarged?"

"To do as much good as possible for everybody concerned."

Stevenson wanted to know what Ford meant by that.

"To make money and use it, give employment, and send out the car where people can use it . . . and incidentally to make money."

"Incidentally?"

"That's right," said Henry. "Business is a service, not a bonanza."

"Your controlling feature, then, is to employ a great army of men at high wages, to reduce the selling price of your car so that a lot of people can buy it at a cheap price, and give everybody a car that wants one?"

"If you can give all that," replied Ford, "the money will fall into your hands; you can't get out of it."

It was a good performance by Ford, but it wasn't enough to prevent the court's ruling that his withholding of dividends was both arbitrary and illegal. On October 31, 1917, the Michigan State Circuit Court ordered him to make immediate payment of $19,275,385. The decision was appealed to the Michigan Supreme Court, which fifteen months later upheld the lower court's ruling. The skeptical judge chastised Ford: "Where a corporation with an unsatisfied demand for its cars and the output of 500,000 per annum deliberately makes a cut of $80 in the price of the car, and enters upon a duplication of its present enormous plant, not to speak of other large expenditures, suspicion will arise that its motives are not wholly philanthropic; domination quite as much as philanthropy comes to mind." Interest brought the total due to about $21 million.

✎⌀✎

Henry was never truly comfortable with his about-face from peace activist to munitions maker, rationalizing his decision by convincing himself that "the war to end all wars" would truly do just that. "After the war you can throw that uniform away," he regularly told officers who visited his factories on government business. "We won't be having armies and navies then." On the day the Armistice was announced, he immediately put a halt to all ongoing defense work. "You call Washington and get permission to stop," he ordered his executives. Told that his decision would cost the company a million dollars in lost government orders, he replied, "Peace will be worth it." It took Ford just three weeks to switch back to making Model T's, the quickest changeover by any automaker.

It took him much longer to get over the mud-slinging of the 1918 U.S. senatorial race, the only time Henry ever officially ran for a political office. Woodrow Wilson, aware of the magical pull of the Ford name, prevailed upon him to run. At stake was control of the Senate, which was hostile to Wilson's plans for a "League of Nations" and other initiatives that, once the war was over, would ideally allow the world to maintain its hard-fought peace. "Mr. Ford, we are living in very difficult times," the president wrote Henry in June 1918, "times when men must sacrifice themselves for their country. I would give anything on earth if I could lay down this job that I am trying to do, but I must carry on. . . . You are the only man in Michigan who can be elected and help bring about the peace you so desire. I wish you therefore to overcome your personal feelings and interests and make the race."

Henry admitted to voting only half a dozen times in his life, and then only when dragged to the polls by Clara. He was as reluctant a candidate as can be imagined, stating, "While I am willing to give whatever time, thought and expense is necessary to do the work well, I am not willing to spend a single cent to get the place." Ford wouldn't even declare a party affiliation. He ran in both primaries, winning the Democratic nomination by a four-to-one margin and finishing second to Truman H. Newberry in the Republican election. The results meant Wilson's unenthusiastic candidate would square off against Newberry in the November election.

Much of the national press was critical of Ford, and many Democratic supporters were dissuaded from voting for him because of his nonpartisanship. However, all of the Detroit newspapers endorsed him, as did the American Federation of Labor.

Ford's opponent was a member of one of the wealthiest and most prominent families in Detroit. The Newberry fortune had been made in the mining and lumber industries, and the candidate himself was a major investor in the Packard car company, which set up the inevitable "gas-guzzling rich versus tin lizzie" comparisons by cartoonists and editorial writers. It was one thing to have the backing of the powerful Republican State Committee while your opponent did no campaigning. But Newberry, secretary of the navy in Theodore Roosevelt's cabinet, also had the advantage of running as a war veteran against a man whose son had been granted a deferment from the draft.

It's not entirely clear who initiated Edsel Ford's request for an exemption in 1917, but the best evidence points to his father. Edsel, who was twenty-three years old and healthy when America entered the war, may have wanted to serve in uniform, but he also had legitimate grounds for an exemption. He was married; his first child, Henry II, was born on September 4, 1917, making him the supporter of two dependents; and he was integral to his company's operation. The request filed by Edsel's lawyers was initially refused in October 1917. But a subsequent change in the selective service laws allowed him to be reclassified as 2-A (having dependents) and 3-L (being indispensable to a war industry).

Most Americans had little patience with "slackers" such as heavyweight contender Jack Dempsey, who was photographed in the overalls of a shipyard welder—the well-tailored suit he wore underneath clearly visible—in an attempt to deflect criticism of the prizefighter's questionable draft deferment. And they ostracized conscientious objectors such as Harold Studley Gray, a member of one of Detroit's wealthiest families, for boldly stating that he was "unalterably opposed to the principle of conscription and believe[d] it to be un-American as well as the very backbone of militarism." Dempsey was dogged for his refusal to enlist for years afterward. Gray, convicted of insubordination by a military tribunal, began serving his twenty-five-year sentence at Fort Leavenworth four days after the armistice of November 11, 1918, ended the fighting. The widely publicized case of Gray was of particular interest to the Fords because the Harvard-educated young man was the grandson of John S. Gray, the first president of the Ford Motor Company. (Gray ultimately served less than a year of his sentence before

**NOTHING LIKE THIS IN
HENRY FORD'S WINDOW**

The controversy over Edsel's military deferment cost his father crucial votes in the 1918 Michigan senatorial race. This cartoon, which appeared in *Detroit Saturday Night,* didn't help.

being released, his dishonorable discharge bearing the notation, "Character, Bad.")

Edsel's character was unimpeachable, but for those who wanted to hurt his father his deferment was a convenient target. "Young Ford should take his medicine just like the rest of the boys," declared *Detroit Saturday Night,* a publication that Newberry had a small stake in. "He has developed no inventive ingenuity that we have ever heard of that would entitle him to exemption from military duty. We do not wish to be understood as making this criticism in a spirit of enmity nor even unkindness, but only because we like to see fair play. Many thousands of fathers have sons whose services they need in shops, stores, plants, and on farms, yet these boys are at the front, fighting for their country."

Friends wondered why Edsel didn't simply allow himself to be drafted, then assigned to the Ford Motor Company. "I want no stay-at-home appointment," he said privately. "I will accept none. I don't want to don a uniform with the assurance that I will be expected to do nothing but sit in a swivel chair. There is one job in this war I do not want and will not take, and that is the job of a rich man's son." According to one newspaperman gauging the reaction to Edsel's deferment, "it took more courage for Edsel Ford not to put on a uniform than it would have taken to put one on."

Just days before the election, Theodore Roosevelt weighed in with a lengthy letter to Newberry that was published in the *Detroit Saturday Night*. "The failure of Mr. Ford's son to go into the army at this time, and the approval by the father of the son's refusal, represent exactly what might be expected from the moral disintegration inevitably produced by such pacifist propaganda," wrote Roosevelt, whose four sons had all seen action, including the youngest, Quentin, an aviator killed in a dogfight with seven German planes.

> Mr. Ford's son is the son of a man of enormous wealth. If he went to war he would leave his wife and child immeasurably distant from all chances of even the slightest financial strain or trouble, and in his absence would not in the smallest degree affect the efficiency of the business with which he is connected. But the son stays at home, protesting and appealing when he is drafted, and now escaping service. Your two sons have eagerly gone to the front. They stand ready to pay with their lives for the honor and the interest of the American people, and while they thus serve America with fine indifference to all personal cost, the son of wealthy Mr. Ford sits at home in ignoble safety, and his father defends and advises such conduct. It would be a grave misfortune to the country to have Mr. Ford in the Senate when our question of continuing the war or discussing terms of peace may arise, and it would be equally grave misfortune to have him in any way deal with the problem of reconstruction in this country.

"Michigan is facing a test," Roosevelt warned, "clear-cut and without shadow of a chance for misunderstanding, between patriotism and Americanism on one side and on the other pacifism." Roosevelt's son-in-law, Ohio congressman Nicholas Longworth, declared there were seven men certain to get through the war unscathed: Kaiser Wilhelm's six sons and Edsel Ford. Pressing the attack, Newberry's camp reworked one of Henry's Peace Ship promises into the campaign slogan: "He kept his boy out of the trenches by Christmas."

Ford didn't respond to these and other personal attacks on Edsel. However, when a paid advertisement entitled "Henry Ford and His Huns" appeared in the *Detroit Free Press*, unjustly charging a company draftsman named Carl Emde with being a German alien and sympathizer and challenging Ford to fire the man, he angrily decided to shoot back. "We would not allow injustice to be done to an old trusted and valued employee, even though he was born in Germany," he said in a forceful and convincing rebuttal published throughout the state on November 5, election day. However, it appeared too late to make that morning's statewide edition of the *Free Press*, thus failing to influence tens of thousands of voters. Despite spending almost no time or money on the campaign, and refusing to effectively respond to most of the criticism and allegations thrown his way, Ford just narrowly lost the election, 217,088 votes to 212,751. A swing of just 2,169 votes would have sent the Flivver King to Washington. Instead he stayed—and stewed—in Dearborn.

Like a dog chewing his favorite old slipper, Henry sunk his teeth into Newberry and didn't let go. Over the next several years he made the senator's life miserable, sending a team of private investigators to pry into allegations of excessive spending. When this failed to turn up anything, Ford convinced the Department of Justice to empanel a grand jury, which wound up indicting Newberry and 134 others under the Federal Corrupt Practices Act. Newberry was convicted and sentenced to two years in prison and a $10,000 fine, but on appeal the U.S. Supreme Court narrowly overruled the conviction and Newberry was able to keep his seat. At the same time Henry turned his wrath on those who had been in his adversary's camp, bankrolling the campaigns of anti-Newberry candidates in various elections. Senator Charles Townshend's 1922 defeat to ex-governor Woodbridge Ferris marked the first time Michigan sent a Democrat to the upper house since before the Civil War. More significantly, Ferris's election gave the Democrats control of the Senate. When it was announced that Newberry's case would be reopened, Newberry resigned rather than face the likelihood of being removed in disgrace. In an ironic twist, the man appointed to serve out the departing senator's term was James Couzens, who Detroiters had elected mayor on the same day his former boss lost to Newberry.

～⌒～

The war years were a crowded period for Henry, with some of the heaviest salvos in the ongoing Ford saga not fired until after the Armistice. In May 1919, after two years of legal wrangling, a lawsuit he had filed against the *Chicago Tribune* finally came before a jury in Mount Clemens, Michigan, north of Detroit. The small resort community, famous for the restorative powers of its mineral baths, was chosen when the court decided a fair trial was not possible in either Detroit or Chicago.

The issue was whether Henry Ford had been slandered by an editorial that appeared in the *Tribune* on June 23, 1916. The powerful newspaper was responding to a comment made by a Ford spokesman that employees who bore arms as National Guardsmen in the current crisis on the Texas-Mexico border (where Pancho Villa was raising havoc) would not be guaranteed their jobs when they returned. "If Ford allows the rule of his shops to stand," the *Tribune* stated, "he will reveal himself not as merely an ignorant idealist but as an anarchist enemy of the nation which protects him in his wealth. A man so ignorant as Henry Ford may not understand the fundamentals of the government under which he lives." Ford sued, asking for $1 million in damages. Henry, aware of the reach and influence of the *Tribune*, installed a company news bureau in Mount Clemens to put his own spin on the proceedings. The staff of writers daily cranked out tens of thousands of words in bulletins and features, which were then fed to nearly 2,800 daily and weekly newspapers all over the country.

The defense team was headed by Elliott G. Stevenson, whose ability in the Dodge trial had impressed *Tribune* publisher Colonel Robert R. McCormick. The archconservative McCormick had been hammering Ford about his lack of patriotism since the Peace Ship, but the prosecution was able to establish early in the trial that the company had not released any workers called to National Guard duty during the Pancho Villa expedition. In fact, the families of Guard volunteers had been taken care of by the Sociological Department. For all intents and purposes, that should have been the end of the trial then and there, but the judge ruled that the defense could broaden the scope of its questioning, thus bringing into play the sad state of the Flivver King's intellect.

Alfred Lucking, Ford's chief counsel, attempted to tutor his client on current events and American history prior to his taking the witness stand. Henry played the class clown during these sessions, gazing out the window and drawing Lucking's attention to a passing plane or a chirping bird. Ford's lack of preparation would soon jump up and bite him in what one Indiana newspaper inhospitably characterized as his "pale, green ass."

Stevenson first jousted with Ford over the "educational" advertisements he had published before the United States entered the war.

"You call yourself an educator?" the lawyer asked. "Now I shall inquire whether you were a well-informed man, competent to educate people."

Stevenson then brought up a comment that the industrialist had made during an interview with *Tribune* reporter Charles Wheeler in the spring of 1916. "History is more or less bunk," Ford said at the time. "It's tradition. We want to live in the present and the only history that is worth a tinker's damn is the history we make today. That's the trouble with the world. We're living in books and history and tradition. We want to get away from that and take care of today. We've done too much looking back. What we want to do, and do it quick, is to make just history right now. The men who are responsible for the present war in Europe knew all about history. Yet they brought on the worst war in the world's history."

Stevenson read Ford's remarks back to him, then asked, "Did you say that?"

"I did not say it was bunk," he answered. "It was bunk to me. . . . I did not need it very bad."

Stevenson set out to prove the newspaper's contention that the plaintiff really did "not understand the fundamentals of the government under which he lives."

    S:   What are the fundamental principles of the United States government?

    F:   I don't know what you mean by fundamental principles.

    S:   You don't know what the fundamental principles of the government mean?

    F:   Do you mean the Constitution?

    S:   What do you consider the fundamental principles of government?

    F:   Justice, I think.

    S:   Justice? Is that all?

    F:   That will do.

    S:   Is that the only idea that you have of the fundamental principles of government?

    F:   Well, it's quite a long subject, you know.

Stevenson, anxious to make the witness look ridiculous, began to badger him with more specific questions.

    S:   Have there been any revolutions in this country?

    F:   There was, I understand.

    S:   When?

F: In 1812.

S: In 1812, the Revolution?

F: Yes.

S: Any other times?

F: I don't know.

S: You don't know of any other?

F: No.

S: Don't you know there wasn't any revolution in 1812?

F: I don't know that. I didn't pay much attention to it.

S: Don't you know that this country was born out of a revolution in 1776? Did you forget that?

F: I guess I did.

S: Now, can you tell us anything about what the revolution was about in 1812?

F: About aggression, I guess.

S: About aggression; don't you know there wasn't any revolution in 1812?

F: I didn't know that.

S: You don't know that?

F: No.

S: Don't you know there was a war in 1812? Don't you know what the cause of the war is?

F: I don't know much about it.

S: Do you know anything about it?

F: Not very much.

S: Do you know whether we had an army in 1812?

F: I understand we did.

S: Don't you know our Capitol was burned down in 1812?

F: I heard so.

And so it went. Over the next several days Ford defined Benedict Arnold as "a writer, I think" and chili con carne as "a large mobile army." Almost as appalling as Ford's ignorance was Stevenson's rude, mocking manner of inquiry. At times it was good theater, the fifty-five-year-old capitalist leaning back on the rear legs of his chair like a schoolboy cornered by his teacher, and exasperating the pompous Stevenson with some innocent response. When the lawyer asked him to explain "what the United States was originally," Ford hesitated for effect before answering, "Land, I guess." To John Reed, the famous socialist journalist, Ford was a "slight boyish figure with thin, long sure hands unceasingly moving . . . the fine skin of his thin facewbrowned by the sun; the mouth and nose of a simpleminded saint."

Although the army didn't draft Edsel, Ford admirers weren't shy about drafting Henry for office.

Simpleminded proved to be the operative word of the three-month-long trial. "I admit I am ignorant about most things," Henry said as his testimony wound down. In the end, the jury ruled Ford had indeed been libeled—and awarded him six cents in damages. Both sides declared victory.

The verdict handed down in the early evening hours of August 14, 1919, was a humiliating end to what had been a humbling and painful experience for Ford, and it left him a profoundly changed man. Prior to the *Tribune* trial, he never knew what he never knew. Afterward, though, detractors would happily remind him of his ignorance. As Stevenson remarked in his summation to the jury, "They forced us to open the mind of Henry Ford and expose it to you bare." Metropolitan publications, as interested in defending the free-speech rights of one of its own as in examining the industrialist's persona, jumped in on the *Tribune's* side. The *Nation's* response was typical: "Now the mystery is finally dispelled. Henry Ford is a Yankee mechanic, pure and simple; quite uneducated. . . . He has achieved wealth but not greatness; he cannot rise above the defects of education, at least as to public matters.

So the unveiling of Mr. Ford has much of the pitiful about it, if not of the tragic. We would rather have had the curtain drawn, the popular ideal unshattered."

Many educated Americans who had been enamored of Ford's success and convinced of his homespun genius were disillusioned by the *Tribune* trial. By and large, though, "plain folks" living on farms and in small towns saw things differently. In their view it simply was an intellectual flogging of an ordinary, poorly educated citizen by a battery of big-city lawyers, just one more example of the growing cultural rift between rural and urban America. But for the grace of God it could have been Louie, the immigrant barber in Peoria, or Maggie, the Iowa farmwife, on the stand, revealing their shortcomings to the whole world. Their affection for, and trust in, the folk-hero tinkerer not only remained undiminished, in many cases it grew. One Ohio newspaper spoke for this grass-roots faction when, after acknowledging the carmaker's regretful ignorance, it added, "We sort of like old Henry Ford, anyway."

# 9

༄ஃ༄

# Joy Ride

*After the name of Henry Ford became a household word, men in the Ford Motor Company who might temporarily get more publicity than he did aroused his jealousy, and one by one they were purged.*

—Charlie Sorenson

In the fall of 1918, as Henry Ford was involved in lawsuits, war production, and a Senate race, he managed to upstage all these ongoing news events with the surprising announcement that he was resigning the presidency of the Ford Motor Company, effective December 30, 1918, in order to pursue other ventures. He explained he wished "to devote my time to building up other organizations with which I am connected." On January 1, 1919, Edsel, who had just turned twenty-five, officially succeeded his father as president.

What other ventures did the Flivver King have in mind? Tractor manufacturing was sure to be one. A hometown newspaper he had recently purchased, the *Dearborn Independent,* was another. Then, in early March 1919, just weeks after he lost his appeal in the Dodge suit, he told the press while vacationing in California that he planned to build a new car that would be superior to the Model T and would cost half as much, to boot. "We shall have a plant on this coast and all over the country," Henry said. "In fact, we propose to dot the whole world with our factories."

"But what about the Ford Motor Company?" Henry was asked.

"Why," he said innocently, "I don't know exactly what will become of that."

The Dodges logically complained that the majority shareholder of the Ford Motor Company should not be permitted to come out with a competing product. But Ford's private secretary, Ernest Liebold, responded for his boss: "The Ford Motor Company has no mortgage upon Mr. Ford's body, soul, or brains. He is a free agent."

Most of the minority stockholders correctly suspected that Ford's intention to head a "huge new company" was a ruse to drive down the value of their holdings and force them to sell out cheaply. While Edsel calmly told agitated dealers that it would probably take at least two or three years for his father to actually put a new model into production, brokerage agents were quietly approaching shareholders with buyout offers. One by one, they signed agreements. The offers started at $7,500 a share before the going price of $12,500 was finally established. James Couzens, having been through this charade before with the squeezing-out of Alex Malcolmson, held out until he got $13,000. This still was a bargain for Henry. Before he spoke of building a new super-car, S. K. Rothschild had offered the Dodge brothers $18,000 a share for their Ford stock.

Regardless, it was a buy-out bonanza rarely seen before or since. John Dodge, Horace Dodge, Horace Rackham, and John Anderson each received $12.5 million for their original $5,000 investments. John Gray's 1903 stake of $10,500 brought his heirs $26,250,000. The biggest winner was Couzens, who was paid $29,308,858 for his original $10,900 investment. His sister's single share, purchased for $100, sold for $262,036.

The last of the shareholders capitulated in July 1919, just as the *Tribune* trial was winding down. When informed of the news, Henry was so ecstatic over finally achieving complete control of his company, he danced a jig around the room. "Of course," Edsel told the press, "there will be no need of a new company now." Henry redistributed the family shareholding, retaining 55 percent while giving Edsel 42 percent and Clara 3 percent.

Much of Ford's cash was tied up in expansion of the Rouge, whose steelmaking capabilities began May 17, 1920, with the ceremonial blowing in of the world's largest blast furnace by Edsel's three-year-old son, Henry II. The little boy, snuggled into his grandfather's arms, at first had a little trouble lighting the little pile of coke and wood, but then the furnace came to life—a dynastic moment that had three generations of Fords smiling and clapping their hands.

To finance the $105 million he needed to buy out the minority stockholders and to pay the court-ordered $19 million in back dividends, Henry had been forced to borrow $60 million from a consortium of three banks. Final payment on the eighteen-month note was due in April 1921, a deadline that, because of the pent-up demand for cars in postwar America, he was confident he'd have no trouble meeting.

He and other automakers didn't take into account a disastrous series of labor strikes in the coal, steel, and railroad industries, which crippled manufacturing, and a dramatic interest rate increase by the Federal Reserve Board, which put a damper on car loans. In September 1920, Ford reacted to this double whammy by slashing Model T prices by an average $148—an unprecedented 25 to 30-percent across-the-board reduction that failed to move inventory. The country remained mired in a deep economic slump. For the first time in the seventeen-year history of the Ford Motor Company, Henry was forced to shut down production. Seventy thousand workers were idled just before Christmas. The media, which had gushed over the price cuts in a way it hadn't when Ford announced a six-dollar daily wage in 1919, now openly fretted that the company might be taken over by bankers or acquired by General Motors. "Henry Ford has reached his limit. It is beyond the powers of any one man to raise money and carry forward single-handed the manifold enterprises in which he has started," one major investment service warned its clients.

Rolling up his sleeves, Ford initiated a "waste elimination" program that looked into every corner and crevice of the company for ways of saving a dime. Surplus materials were recycled or sold. Hundreds of telephones were disconnected; every pencil sharpener in sight was taken away and clerks ordered to bring in their own pocketknives. Everything deemed nonessential, from filing cabinets and wrenches to entire departments, was sold or eliminated. The belt-tightening resulted in a savings of about $7 million.

It still wasn't enough to meet his obligations, so in February 1921 Henry started up the assembly line again, this time with 20,000 fewer workers. The Highland Park plant built 90,000 cars in six weeks. Playing hardball, Ford then demanded that dealers, who were obligated to pay cash on delivery, accept the unconsigned Model T's being shipped their way or risk forfeiting their franchise. This forced thousands of dealers to go to their local banks for a loan. The flow of cash back to Dearborn, coupled with company-wide cost-cutting measures, allowed

The Fordson tractor.

Henry to meet his April deadline. Newspapers from coast to coast ran stories and editorials praising Ford's remarkable "victory" over Wall Street bankers. Getting rid of longtime employees and force-feeding unwanted cars to financially strapped dealers hardly fit Ford's public persona. But as one contemporary noted, most Americans "do not mind if he frequently turns a trick for which they would denounce any well-known Wall Street operator." And such ruthlessness was part of the game. As Ford had come to admit, "A great business is really too big to be human."

The Rouge complex, a mile wide and a mile and a half long, was too gargantuan to be anything but impersonal. Beginning with the making of submarine chasers during the war, switching to the production of tractors and then automobiles, the Rouge was the fulfillment of Ford's dream of continuous, integrated manufacturing. "It would go beyond simply being a place where the car was built," wrote Neil Baldwin. "All the constituent materials contributing to the creation of the automobile from the ground up would converge there: iron and timber and rubber from Ford-owned rail lines and sailing in on Ford-owned freighters by sea, via Great Lakes ports and the St. Lawrence River, enacting the captain of industry's obsession with self-sufficiency." Raw materials moved along ninety-three miles of railroad track and twenty-seven miles of conveyor belts. At its height in the 1920s, nearly 80,000 men (including an army of 5,000 janitors) worked at the twenty-three major buildings that comprised the Rouge, including steel and glass mills, a cement plant, a by-products plant, two foundries, a pressed-steel stamping plant, assembly plants for motors and automobiles, and a massive powerhouse with eight towering smokestacks. Nowhere in the world was there such a concentration of men and machinery. One time in 1923, "just to flex its industrial muscles, the company performed a remarkable feat," recalled a Ford executive. "On a Monday a certain load of ore was delivered at the River Rouge docks; it was cast, machined, assembled as a unit, shipped to a branch three hundred miles distant to be assembled into a finished car, sold to a dealer, and sold by him to a customer—by Thursday night." After auto production was shifted entirely from Highland Park to the Rouge with the introduction of the Model A in 1927, it took a mere thirty-three hours to turn raw materials into a finished car.

∽o∾

Although the average person didn't see it, the optimism and cheerful adaptability that characterized Henry's early years had been spanked out of him by the Peace Ship fiasco, Senate-race mud match, and *Tribune* humiliation. They were replaced by inflexibility and a cynicism of the common man that flew in the face of the egalitarian populism he was widely thought to exemplify. "We have to recognize the unevenness in human mental equipment," he said. "The vast majority of men want to stay put. They want to be led. They want to have everything done for them and have no responsibility." In Ford's opinion, the average worker "wants a job in which he does not have to put forth much physical exertion—above all he wants a job in which he does not have to think."

It followed axiomatically that the thinking was best left to a "friendly autocrat" such as Ford, who alone would determine what was fair in the way of prices, wages, and profits. With no stockholders, no bankers, no unions, no outsiders, nor parasites of any type to answer to, Henry was in an unprecedented position for an industrialist of his size. He, along with his wife and son, owned everything free and clear and enjoyed absolute control of the company. Even John D. Rockefeller in his heyday never owned more than 27 percent of Standard Oil.

Henry on the banks of the Rouge, c. 1913.

Henry would never be satisfied until he rid the company of all but the most acquiescent and low-profile executives. The purge had actually started years earlier with the squeezing out of Alex Malcolmsom, continued through the buy outs of James Couzens, the Dodge brothers, and the last of the stockholders, and then reached its apex with the postwar housecleaning of 1919–21. Among those shown the door were Frank Klingensmith, C. Harold Wills (whose many contributions included designing the distinctive Ford script logo in 1903), and Bill Knudsen, who had supervised the construction of fourteen branch assembly plants. "This is my business," said Ford in explaining Knudsen's ouster. "I built it, and as long as I live, I propose to run it the way I want it run. . . . I let him go, not because he wasn't good, but because he was too good—for me."

Much was irretrievably lost in this exodus. With the departure of many key managers and the slashing of the office staff from 1,074 to 528 employees, the administrative infrastructure of the world's largest automaker was gutted. The company would become as disorganized as its founder, filled with waste, corruption, and competing cliques. "To my mind," Henry explained afterward, "there is no bent of mind more dangerous than that which is sometimes described as 'genius for organization.' It is not necessary for any one department to know what any other department is doing." The various Ford factories and enterprises, he pointed out, "have no organization, no specific duties attaching to any position, no line of succession or of authority, very few titles, and no conferences. We have only the clerical help that is absolutely required; we have no elaborate records of any kind, and consequently no red tape."*

Gone, too, was the institutional sense of benevolence. "The old group of executives, who at times set justice and humanity above profits and production, were gone," observed Sociological Department head Samuel Marquis, whose position and program were eliminated. "With them, so it seemed to me, had gone an era of cooperation and good will in the company. There came to the front men whose theory was that men are more profitable to an industry when driven than led, that fear is a greater incentive to work than loyalty." By 1928 Henry Ford was being called "an industrialist fascist—the Mussolini of Detroit" by the *New York Times.*

Ford was openly disdainful of college graduates and experts of any type. In fact, his favorite story, one he never tired of reciting as a sort of precautionary tale, revolved around a dinner he had once attended where the guests began by mentioning their alma maters. "I knew they were all after me," said Ford. "It went all around the table, and Yale, Harvard and many other colleges were mentioned. They were all college men but me. When it came to my turn, I said, 'Well, gentlemen, it was a damned good thing that some of us didn't go to college to keep you fellows employed that did." To Henry, out-slicking the city slickers required a certain native intelligence, not a sheepskin. Managers and engineers who did have degrees and professional credentials were wise to keep them a secret from the company patriarch.

What Ford wanted was men such as Charlie Sorenson, who had moved over from Highland Park to join him in developing the Rouge. Sorenson was totally devoted to Ford, a take-charge guy with no ambitions beyond making sure Ford plants continued spitting out as many

---

* Henry hated office routine, recalled Ernest Liebold. "You couldn't sit down with a stack of letters and go through and ask Mr. Ford about each one. When you got to the second one, he'd get up and walk out. He just didn't want to be bothered about that. If he saw I had any number of letters in the drawer or anything I was going to talk to him about, he'd get up and walk out. He'd say, 'I'll be back in a few minutes,' or 'I'll be back later on.' That's the last I'd see of him. He didn't have a set routine. I never knew when he was coming."

cars as humanly possible. On a single day in 1925, a total of 9,575
Model T's poured off the line, a figure roughly equivalent to the total
number of automobiles in the entire country a quarter-century earlier.
"Part of Sorenson's great value to the company was that he could
always visualize the finished product when something was under dis-
cussion," said Harry Bennett, another hard-boiled loyalist who profited
from the purge. "He was capable of giving quick, positive decisions.
But above all, Sorenson really got things done in the plant. He was a
driving, efficient executive who thought of nothing but the car.

"Sometimes men had nervous breakdowns, trying to keep pace
with him. When some fault in a car was in the process of being corrected, Sorenson went at the job at a brutal clip. If a man was made
of tough stuff and stuck it out, he was all right. But if he broke down
and had to go away for a rest, Sorenson simply dealt with the fellow
who took over his work and was rugged enough to stick it out. When
the first man came back, he found out he wasn't exactly fired, but
he didn't have a job." As Ford's axe man, Sorenson supervised the
purge of executives as the Ford center of gravity moved from Highland
Park to Dearborn. "I wonder what that fellow is doing here," Henry
would casually mention to Sorenson. The next day "that fellow" was
gone.

Although the Ford Motor Company, like all competitive work envi-
ronments, had always had a certain amount of internal jockeying, an
era of dog-eat-dog was ushered in. Henry often did the prodding—
then stood back and enjoyed watching the results. "He openly tried to
foster hostility between us," Bennett said of Ford's attempt to drive a
wedge between him and Sorenson. "Once he said to me, 'You be careful, Harry, Sorenson is no friend of yours.'" Henry also told Bennett the
same thing about Edsel, helping to draw early battle lines between the
two men.

Emil Zoerlein spoke of Ford's Darwinian approach. "Even among
the smallest people, he was always interested in setting up one man
against the other," the engineer said. "Sometimes it wasn't handled
quite right, so to speak, in banging two men's heads together and making them sore at each other, but the idea behind it was, I believe, to
build up competition between these two, and something good would
come out of it." Ford never felt the need to expand on this theory,
added Zoerlein. "He just said, 'Competition must be existent to achieve
something.' He felt it was inherent in human beings."

〜∽◌〜

The Ford Motor Company came out of the war firmly established as an international institution, its products as ubiquitous in fields as on roads. The Fordson tractor was becoming the agricultural counterpart of the Model T, revolutionizing a postwar Europe bereft of manpower and horses and aiding in Stalin's ambitious collectivization of Russian peasant society. The distinctive blue tractor was the result of millions of dollars of research and scores of different experimental models. Despite the Fordson's early tendency to tip over backward and pin the driver, a characteristic that according to one study killed or maimed 136 people before various safety devices were introduced, the company led all U.S. tractor manufacturers in production through most of the 1920s. Growing competition from International Harvester and foreign manufacturers (whose "implements of agriculture" were allowed to enter the U.S. market duty-free) caused Ford to shift all production from the Rouge to its plant in Cork, Ireland, in 1928. By then the movement known as Fordizatzia was helping to transform Soviet Union, where 24,600 tractors were shipped between 1920 and 1926. In the eyes of ordinary Russians, the great emancipator from Dearborn would be responsible for freeing them from generations of back-breaking labor and poverty. A writer for *Outlook* magazine returned from a 1927 visit to report that "more people have heard of him than Stalin. . . . Next to Lenin, Trotsky, and Kalinin, Ford is probably the most widely known personage in Russia." Babies and communes were named Fordson, and Henry's name and picture regularly appeared in print and on banners in socialist parades. To fascinated Russians, to "Fordize" something was the same as to "Americanize" it. In 1929 the Soviets paid millions for the tools, dies, jigs, and fixtures needed to manufacture Ford cars at Gorky, a factory complex modeled after the Rouge. Among the skilled workers who went to work at the Russian *avtozavod* (auto factory) was Walter Reuther, a budding Socialist who had spent five and a half years working as a tool-and-die man at the Rouge, and his older brother, Victor. "Soviet power plus American technique will build Socialism" was the front-page motto of the *Moscow Daily News*.

In Russian villages and throughout the American heartland, the Ford name was revered among rural folks. His values of thrift, sobriety, hard work, and self-reliance were those traditionally admired in villages and farm communities. A fundamentalist Dunkard sect, for example, banned its members from driving Buicks but not Model T's; the Ford car, they judged, was not "haughty and sinful." The universal car was of a piece with its commonsensical creator, and millions of Model T owners were grateful for both. A farm wife wrote Ford in 1918: "You know, Henry, your car lifted us out of the mud. It brought joy into our lives. We loved every rattle in its bones." When Henry was being pilloried by the press during the *Tribune* trial, tens of thousands of ordinary Americans followed a newspaper columnist's suggestion to sign and mail a preprinted note of support that read: "Dear Ford: I am glad to have you for a fellow citizen and I wish we had more of your brand of anarchism, if that is what it is. Yours truly. . . ." And when the company was having severe financial problems over the winter of 1920–21, countless citizens sent him unsolicited cash donations and offers of help. Thomas Edison declared that if Henry Ford publicly asked for assistance, sympathetic admirers would send him $100 million.

Ford's popularity was such that his name was constantly floated for the presidency. Write-in campaigns always flattered him, as did the results of a 1923 *Collier's* poll that showed him easily beating the likes of Warren G. Harding, Herbert Hoover, and other professional politicians. But after his bitter loss to Truman Newberry, even a run for the White House was unappetizing to Ford, as well as to those who knew him intimately. "How can a man over sixty years old who has done nothing but make motors, who has no training, no experience, aspire to such an office," asked James Couzens in the fall of 1923, by which time Ford for President clubs had sprung up all over the country. "It is most ridiculous."

Perhaps, but Americans turned off by the corruption in Harding's administration openly wondered whether the straight-shooting industrialist would run and, if he did, whether it would be as a Republican, Democrat, or third-party candidate (the "Auto-cratic Party," some mused). Without answering any of these questions, even in a ghost-written *Collier's* article entitled "If I Were President," Henry was able to turn the groundswell of popular support to his advantage. What Ford had his eye on was not the White House, but a white elephant known as Muscle Shoals.

During the war, with nitrate shipments from Chile cut off by the threat of German U-boats, the federal government had authorized the construction of two plants in Muscle Shoals to manufacture the nitrate needed for use in producing explosives. Muscle Shoals was a waterpower site on the Tennessee River, in northern Alabama. However, the war ended before the plants became operational, leaving the government in a dilemma. Should the project, which included the unfinished mile-long Wilson Dam, be completed? If so, should the nitrates be used to produce artificial fertilizer for farmers? Should Muscle Shoals remain a public project or be sold to a private company? As these questions were debated in Washington, the secretary of war announced the opening of bids on leasing Muscle Shoals. The only condition was that the lessee provide the government with some kind of a return on its original $85 million investment.

In July 1921, Ford submitted a proposal to lease Muscle Shoals for a period of 100 years. He would buy the nitrate plants, quarries, equipment, and land for $5 million. In addition, he would assume an annual obligation of $1.5 million that would include the gradual payback of the estimated $40 million the government would spend to complete the dam. These were fire-sale prices, but Henry pledged to limit profits to 8 percent. His intention was to manufacture nitrates—used for fertilizer—at a cheaper price than American farmers were used to paying, as well as steel and aluminum. Thinking large, as usual, he laid out his vision of a new wonder city seventy-five miles long and fifteen miles wide, a metropolis bigger and grander than even Detroit, with the power of the Tennessee River delivering electricity to farms, businesses, and factories. Many prominent Southerners supported Ford's plan to inject life into the historically impoverished and underdeveloped region of four million people. Said one Alabama banker: "We hope Ford will get Muscle Shoals because if he comes down here he will undo what Sherman did. Ford will make it possible for us to help ourselves."

Before Ford could make the South forget General Sherman's march to the sea a couple of generations earlier, he needed congressional approval, and that was held up for more than a year by political wrangling and the submission of additional bids. To speed things along, Henry took part in the kind of back-room deal making that he professed to detest. A few days before Christmas in 1923, he publicly declared his support of Calvin Coolidge, who had assumed the presidency on Harding's death in office a few months earlier. The surprising announcement ended Ford's own ad hoc presidential bid and had critics of his Muscle Shoals proposal, as well as disappointed political supporters, pointing to a December 3 meeting at the White House. There, it was alleged, Coolidge had guaranteed to deliver Muscle Shoals to

Ford in return for his endorsement. Indeed, on March 10, 1924, Congress approved Ford's bid. But when a telegram interpreted as proof of the secret pact came to light, the Senate launched an investigation. Henry, already under attack for trying to profit at taxpayers' expense, withdrew his bid in October, more than three years after he had originally submitted it. Once again, Henry and his admirers painted the issue as the little guy versus "the nefarious financiers of Wall Street." The disappointed residents of the region would have to wait until the establishment of the Tennessee Valley Authority in 1933 for a new promise of prosperity.

As for Henry's presidential bid in 1924 or any other year, Clara, as she often did, had the final word. "Mr. Ford has enough and more than enough to do to attend to his business in Detroit," she declared at the national convention of the Daughters of the American Revolution. "The day he runs for President of the United States, I will be on the next boat to England."

∞∞

Beginning with the first rush of cash brought in by the Model T, Henry started buying up land along the north branch of the Rouge River in Dearborn. He originally intended to create a wildlife sanctuary, but the public adulation that followed in the wake of the Five-Dollar Day caused him to reconsider using the property for a private estate. The result was Fair Lane, which he and Clara moved to in 1915. "Hereafter," said Henry, "I am going to see to it that no man comes to know me so intimately." The fifty-six-room mansion, a hybrid of Late English Gothic and Prairie-style architecture and made of rough-hewn limestone quarried in Ohio, was built on a bluff overlooking the twisting river. The $2 million house was elegant, but more intimate and welcoming than the cavernous and lavishly appointed mansions of fellow auto tycoons in Grosse Pointe. One of its main features was an ornate stairwell carved from a single piece of oak. Etched into the mantelpiece at Fair Lane were the words of Henry David Thoreau: "Chop your own wood and it will warm you two times." Henry took Thoreau's aphorism to heart, regularly hiking into the countryside, ax in hand, to harvest kindling and firewood. A small staff kept the place running smoothly enough, with Henry's window-rattling snoring upstairs and Clara's cheek-to-jowl storage of dust-collecting household goods in the basement (neither she nor Henry ever threw anything out) giving the hired help something to gossip about.

Henry may have become a towering figure in American cultural life, but with the building of the Rouge complex and Fair Lane he had set up shop and home in the comfortable bosom of his hometown. "He has lived all his life practically in the same spot and even today he seldom leaves the vicinity for any length of time," wrote Sarah T. Bushnell, author of one of several largely favorable Ford biographies to hit bookstores during the 1920s. In fact, Fair Lane was only a couple of miles from the house Henry was born in. "We have lived here always," Clara told Bushnell, "and here we love to stay."*

Henry's lifelong interest in ornithology made Fair Lane into practically a bird preserve. At Highland Park he had kept a telescope handy inside his president's office, but the meager sightings on noisy and smoky Woodward Avenue were nothing compared with the thousands of robins, blue jays, cardinals, wrens, swallows, doves, sparrows, finches, kingfishers, starlings, meadowlarks, and other birds enjoying luxury accommodations on the heavily wooded Ford estate. There were hundreds of birdhouses scattered around the property, including an elaborate "bird hotel" with seventy-six compartments and equipped with an electric heater and brooder. A man was employed full-time to do nothing but keep up the feed and water. At Christmas, a special tree hung with suet and seeds provided Henry's feathered friends with a holiday feast. To Henry, birds were "the best of companions." He always

---

* Clara's side of the family, the Bryants, were regular visitors to Fair Lane, and Henry suffered them well enough. The same couldn't be said of Henry's brothers and sisters, whom for the most part he ignored. Of his five siblings who survived childbirth, two didn't live to see the phenomenon of the Model T. Robert died in 1877 when he was four years old, and Jane passed away in 1906 at the age of thirty-seven. Henry remained fairly close to Margaret, who had married James Ruddiman, the brother of his childhood friend, Edsel Ruddiman. But he had contentious relationships with William and John. William managed to go bankrupt selling Ford tractors, while John continued working the family farm. John, who died at the age of sixty-two in 1927, once turned down his famous brother's peace offering of a Model T, ordering the man who delivered it, "Take that danged thing back and tell him to keep it, because I don't want it." William died in 1959 when he was eighty-eight. Margaret passed away the following year, at ninety-three.

Henry and Clara's Fair Lane estate.

announced his arrival home with a long, happy warble; Clara would respond with one of her own.

Ford was influenced by fellow bird lover John Burroughs. The famous poet-naturalist with the flowing cotton-candy beard had been critical of the motorcar until he accepted Henry's gift of a new Model T in 1912 and found the contraption actually put him in closer contact with the natural wonders of the countryside. In June 1913, the seventy-five-year-old Burroughs left his farm in the Catskills to visit Fair Lane, where Henry unveiled an elaborate bird fountain he'd built in his honor.

Outside of regularly scouring the pages of the Bible for inspiration and solace, Henry was not a big reader, but he did wear out several copies of the collected essays of Ralph Waldo Emerson, the rustic philosopher in whose footsteps Burroughs, a former pupil, had followed. Henry took away a lot from Emerson's essays, particularly the notion that reason and rationalization can take a man only so far in the world. One of Ford's favorite passages was, "Only in our easy, simple, spontaneous action are we strong." He identified with that sentiment and, to the growing detriment of his business, remained a hunch player to the end. Henry, who had a strong persecution complex, undoubtedly also saw himself in the oft-quoted line from Emerson's essay on self-reliance: "To be great is to be misunderstood."

In keeping with the teachings of Emerson, Thoreau, and others, Ford lived about as austere a lifestyle as a man of his stature and wealth ever has. "He was not of the profligate type who sought to get joy out of life by carousing, gambling, smoking, and licentious habits," Irving Bacon observed approvingly. "His pleasures were simple ones: old-style dancing, skating, hiking, social gatherings, baseball games, and collecting antiques of every description. His disregard for money was notorious. Two hundred dollars was always concealed under his desk blotter in case it was needed, but very seldom was any of the filthy lucre around in his pockets. Once he was handed a check for a very large sum of money and shoved it in his pocket. Months after it was discovered not to have been cashed, and a frantic search began to try and find it."

Clara, in complete control of all household matters, remained practical and frugal. Henry bought her many fine and expensive gifts over the years, including a $322,000 emerald and diamond necklace and a $135,000 string of pearls. Nonetheless, she continued to darn her husband's socks. Henry, not wanting to offend, sometimes had his driver take him to a store where he could buy a new pair that he would then change into in the car. For his part, Henry also recognized a good bargain, buying his reading glasses over the counter at one of S. S. Kresge's department stores.

The Ford Motor Company was considered by 1926 to be the greatest industrial empire in the world, a manufacturing colossus that had in its first twenty-three years *averaged* $39,166,913 in annual profits. Total profits for this period were an estimated $900,839,000. How much was Ford—the man, the company, which were one and the same—worth? In the mid-1920s the *New York Times* estimated his assets to be in the range of $1.2 billion, making the Ford fortune the greatest in the world. (That figure would be roughly equivalent to $13 billion today.) Henry personally drew an average of about $4.5 million in dividends each year during the decade (about $50 million in today's dollars). "I'm in a peculiar position," he admitted. "No one can give me anything. There is nothing I want that I cannot have. But I do not want the things that money can buy. I want to live a life, to make the world a little better for having lived in it."

A noble sentiment, and one that accounted for his continual dabbling in social engineering. By 1923 he employed thousands of so-called substandard men—deaf-mutes, epileptics, amputees—and half of the African Americans working in the entire automobile industry. From such ambitious and far-reaching undertakings as the Five-Dollar Day, the Peace Ship, and the Sociological Department, the scope of his tinkering often narrowed to just an individual creature whose destiny he could, with godlike power and satisfaction, determine. He would go out of his way to rescue a bird fallen out of its nest or fish found floundering on the banks of the Rouge. His soft spot for children was legendary. Whenever he came across news of an afflicted child, remembered Bacon, "it was necessary to move the child's entire family to Detroit and give the father a job, also a place to live, while the child was given special treatment." Ford once instructed the artist to visit a boy at the children's clinic. One side of the young patient's face was disfigured by a terrible cancer. "Make a picture of the good side of his face and give it to him so he can see how he would look if he were a normal boy," he said.

Henry was not without his vanities. He refused to be photographed wearing his glasses. He was always immaculately dressed in a suit and tie. Trim and in fine physical shape, he enjoyed showing off his vigor, often challenging someone to an impromptu foot race. "He liked to jump over things," recalled Clarence Davis, a grade-school classmate of Clara's and a regular visitor to the Ford home. "He used to jump over this big davenport in their living room. He would just start from one end of the room and jump right over the back of it. He thought that was quite a little stunt. He loved that."

He also was comically superstitious. If in the morning he put on a sock inside out, he refused to change it the rest of the day. On a Friday the thirteenth you couldn't budge him out of the house. He tried to rationalize his fears by saying, "If a black cat crosses the road and you're superstitious, then you'll drive more carefully, and that's a good thing." Moreover, anyone foolish enough to walk under a ladder "deserves to get a paint pot on his head."

☙

On April 9, 1923, two days before Henry and Clara celebrated their thirty-sixth wedding anniversary, Evangeline Dahlinger gave birth to a seven-pound, eleven-ounce baby boy at Henry Ford Hospital. As the infant, named John, grew up, people remarked on his startling resemblance to Edsel Ford. The likeness was understandable, because circumstantial evidence heavily suggests he was Henry Ford's illegitimate son.

Evangeline Cote was a petite, vivacious brunette of French-Canadian descent who started working at the Highland Park plant as a stenographer in 1909, when she was sixteen. Her dark good looks ran in the family: a first cousin was screen idol Tyrone Power. Ford was as attracted to her energy as to her beauty. He nicknamed her "Billie." During her lifetime Evangeline excelled in a variety of athletic pursuits. She was an accomplished equestrian, at one time being crowned the women's harness-racing champion of Michigan; an expert pilot (she was the first woman to be issued a pilot's license in the state and owned a seaplane); and a capable speedboat driver, docking her powerful thirty-six-foot Hacker, the *Evangeline*, at the Rouge plant. All of these activities required money, of course, and finances were never a problem after young John came along.

Evangeline was twenty-nine when she gave birth to her only child. If she *was* Henry's lover, the exact start of their affair remains unknown. She was married to Ray Dahlinger, a capable and calculating high school dropout who served Ford in a variety of ways over the years. He was a handyman, personal driver, and ultimately the general manager of Ford's many farmlands. Dahlinger was tough enough to serve as Ford's armed bodyguard and "bag man" aboard the Peace Ship, making sure no harm came to either the tycoon or the large sums of cash he'd brought along. In 1927 Dahlinger drove a new Model A from coast to coast, a publicity stunt that put 8,328 miles on the odometer. A couple of years later, he supervised the landscaping of Greenfield Village. Henry had actively encouraged the Dahlingers' 1917 marriage and presented them with a farmhouse near Fair Lane as a wedding present.

That was just the beginning of Ford's remarkable largesse. After John was born, he installed the family in a magnificent 150-acre estate that featured a gatehouse, several garages, a boathouse, a blacksmith shop, an artificial lake with skating rink, a show barn, and a half-mile racetrack. A Tudor mansion—Ray Dahlinger called it the "goddamn castle"—had eight bathrooms, nine fireplaces, and a secret staircase leading up to Evangeline's bedroom suite. Ray and Evangeline slept in separate bedrooms on opposite sides of the house. The staircase evidently was to accommodate clandestine visits by Ford, who would take Clara's electric boat about a mile up the Rouge River to the Dahlinger estate. More substantial gifts to the couple followed, including a 300-

Evangeline and baby John.

acre farm near Romeo, Michigan, and vacation property on Lake Huron, near a Ford home.

Evangeline's duties were social in nature. She taught classes in social etiquette and horsemanship at Greenfield Village, where she also helped in the ongoing selection and furnishing of historic buildings.

Clara could not ignore the gossip surrounding her husband's lavish attention on the ex-typist and her child. At some point she made peace with the arrangement, which—because of the thirty-year difference in age between Henry and Evangeline—eventually evolved from a sexual to strictly fraternal relationship. There was a certain tension whenever little John was brought over to Fair Lane to play with Henry's grandchildren, with Edsel's older boys often picking on their smaller playmate. John thought Henry II and Benson were "two fatties" and contented himself with the occasional tramps through the woods with the man he knew as "Mr. Ford." There they would sit on logs and play mouth harps. Once Henry watched as Ray tried unsuccessfully to fix one of the boy's model trains. Ford took over the task and solved the problem in a flash. "Gee, Mr. Ford," exclaimed the boy, "you're a genius!" Henry laughed so hard he cried. When John enlisted in the army during World War II, he asked Henry for the pocketknife he had once given the old man as a gift. John carried it on him throughout the war as a good luck charm and came home unscathed.

The Dahlingers would remain a part of the Fords' daily lives and on the payroll until Clara's death in 1950. Ray died in 1969. Ten years later, Evangeline passed away in a nursing home in Port Huron, Michigan, at age eighty-six. To the very end, she refused to discuss John's paternity, brushing off her son's queries with a brusque "I don't want to talk about it." If she had been sleeping with Ray Dahlinger and Ford at the same time, it's very possible she wasn't sure herself who the father was. John, a smart-alecky sort who enjoyed introducing himself as "Henry Ford's illegitimate son," obviously had no doubts, writing a book, *The Secret Life of Henry Ford,* before his death in 1984. While most members of the Ford family have privately dismissed Dahlinger's claims (as adults, Edsel's boys were known to refer to their former playmate as "that creep"), Clara's opinion can be perhaps gleaned from one significant act. The night Henry died at Fair Lane, the first person she summoned to his bedside was Evangeline Dahlinger.

# 10

♋

# Farewell, Lizzie

*When she's coming down the street*
*All the boys say "Ain't she sweet?"*
*Henry's made a lady out of Lizzie.*
*No more bruises, no more aches,*
*Now she's got those four-wheel brakes,*
*Henry's made a lady out of Lizzie.*
*There's ev'rything inside her now*
*Except a kitchen sink,*
*A mirror and a powder puff,*
*A shower bath, I think.*

— "Henry's Made a Lady Out of Lizzie" (1928)

America roared in the 1920s, economically and otherwise, and thanks to the president of the Ford Motor Company the men on the assembly line got more time off to enjoy the fruits of their six-dollar-a-day labor. In the early spring of 1922, the company became the first carmaker to install a forty-hour work week, running three shifts around the clock on weekdays and shutting off the conveyor belts on Saturdays and Sundays. Three years later most other auto plants would still be averaging a fifty-hour week: nine hours Monday through Friday and a half-day on Saturday, the traditional payday.

"The Ford company has always tried to promote an ideal home life for its employees," Edsel explained. "We feel that every man needs more than one day a week for rest and recreation. We believe that he should have more time for his family, his home, his garden and his reading."*

Although he had almost nothing in common with the largely immigrant work force that kept the Highland Park plant humming, the young executive understood the importance of a stable domestic life. He'd had one growing up and he now enjoyed one with Eleanor, who in 1919 had given them a second son. Initially, the baby was named after his father, but after a day or so Edsel had a change of heart and renamed him Benson.

Henry, proud of the Model T's populist image, always liked to say that "a Ford will take you anywhere except into society," but that was hardly the case with his son. With Edsel drawing an average of about $3 million each year in dividends—an amount roughly equal to the combined annual incomes of 3,000 auto workers—the Edsel Fords could well afford to live a Gatsby-esque lifestyle, though one with more dignity and taste than many of their Jazz Age contemporaries. They took four-day shopping trips with friends to New York for the spring and fall fashions; wintered in a house they bought in exclusive Hobe Sound, Florida, north of Palm Beach; and spent summer vacations in the fog-shrouded splendor of Seal Harbor, Maine, where their hilltop retreat (today owned by homestyle guru Martha Stewart) overlooked the Atlantic Ocean. Weekends were spent closer to home, at a sprawling 2,400-acre country estate north of Detroit known as Haven Hill. Edsel called it his "nerve retreat." It was a world of fabulous privilege, of tennis, golf, sailing, and horses, of engraved invitations and monogrammed cuffs, but Edsel kept a level head throughout. "I have never been able to see that the ability to earn money should be a curse or a burden," he said, "unless one chooses it to be so."

As the money continued to flow in, the fashionable couple moved from the house on Iroquois Avenue, on which Edsel had spent $60,000 redecorating in Art Deco style, to a grand mansion on the Detroit riverfront, where they hosted a lavish dinner for the Prince of Wales during his 1924 visit to "the colonies." (The United Auto Workers' international headquarters, Solidarity House, occupies the site today.) Two more children were born there: Josephine in 1923, followed by William Clay a couple of years later. In 1926 they commissioned Albert Kahn

---

* Federal employees had enjoyed the eight-hour day since 1912. It wasn't until 1938 that Congress extended the right to include all nonagricultural workers, and the normal American work week became five eight-hour days.

to design their dream home at Gaukler Pointe, a prime piece of lake-front property that Henry had originally bought as a potential building site for his own estate. Once it became clear that Henry's son and daughter-in-law were not going to move onto the land he had reserved for them adjacent to Fair Lane, Henry sold Edsel the fifty-five-acre parcel. Situated on Lake St. Clair in Grosse Pointe Shores, it was fifteen miles from downtown Detroit and about as far from Papa as Edsel could get without being out in the country.

Edsel and Eleanor wanted a mansion, but not a palace. Kahn criss-crossed the Atlantic and came back with plans for a rambling estate patterned after the stone houses in England's Cotswold district. Centuries-old fireplaces and staircases were torn down, shipped across the ocean, and reassembled inside the sprawling 30,000-square-foot house. The site included 3,000 feet of Lake St. Clair shoreline, along with an artificial lagoon, which provided mooring for an armada of vessels. Edsel was an avid sailor, owning several sloops and an eighty-eight-foot schooner. On nice summer days, he often piloted his speedboat up the Detroit and Rouge rivers to work. More than fifty servants and maintenance people were required to keep the estate running smoothly, though Edsel, true to his sense of noblesse oblige, "never had a valet in the sense that some Grosse Pointers may have," recalled his secretary of twenty-five years, A. J. Lepine. "He was a little more democratic than that. He didn't have a man around laying out his clothes daily. . . . I have heard that he packed his own trunk and suitcase. Apparently he knew where he wanted things put and he did that himself."

Edsel and Eleanor and their four children moved into the three-story, sixty-room house in 1929. The couple primarily wanted a home to service a comfortable family life and a hectic social calendar. But for all its imposing size and lavish appointments, there was an undeniable warmth and intimacy. On any given day, a noted artist, athlete, architect, or aviator might be found inside Edsel's study, reflecting his wide circle of friends and interests. Just as likely would be the sight of young William or Josephine pedaling their tricycles pell-mell down a hallway, narrowly avoiding a collision with some priceless piece of furniture.

One of Edsel's most enjoyable hobbies was photography. He took many of the photographs displayed inside his various residences and kept a darkroom in his study. "A feature of his travels was that he carried, on a great many occasions, a fine camera," said Lepine. "He was an expert with the camera. Keeping busy with that resulted in his having a lot of mementos in the way of pictures representing his activities

The main hall of Edsel and Eleanor Ford's mansion in Grosse Pointe Shores. Although the house was designed to be more human in scale than those erected by other auto barons, there never was any danger of mistaking the fabulous wealth of its occupants. At far left is a rare thirteenth-century white marble sculpture of the Virgin and Child; hanging on the wall at right is a 1525 oil on canvas by Titian.

outside. He would get the films developed by the company's Photographic Department. He knew cameras, he did fine work and he had the patience to do it. No matter what kind of crowd was out, he undoubtedly was the one doing the work with a camera, and then he'd give everyone prints of the pictures. That was just another sidelight of his character—that good-fellow disposition." It was that kind of disposition that, during a 1928 trip to a spa in Warm Springs, Georgia, caused him to impulsively write a check for $25,000 to New York banker and politician Franklin Delano Roosevelt, who had been crippled by polio. The unsolicited donation launched the Infantile Paralysis Fund, which subsequently became known as the "March of Dimes." About this time Edsel and Eleanor helped found the Roscoe B. Jackson Cancer Research Foundation in Bar Harbor, Maine, a cause to which they contributed $200,000.

"Good fellows" and "flappers" were all out to have a swell time in the twenties. The uproarious decade was characterized by speakeasies, marathon dancers, flagpole sitters, talking movies, and ticker-tape parades. The sense of national buoyancy was helped along by a booming consumer industry, with savvy entrepreneurs such as Powell Crosley— the "Henry Ford of radios"—applying the famous tycoon's principles of mass production to put once pricey luxury items into the hands of the growing middle class. Novelist F. Scott Fitzgerald called the era of easy credit, fast living, and overconsumption "the greatest, gaudiest spree in history." Young women scandalized their parents by shucking their corsets, hiking their skirts, rolling down their stockings, bobbing their hair, sipping from flasks, squeezing cigarettes between painted lips, and exploring the link between cars and courtship. In 1920 they also got the right to vote, though it can be argued that the invention of the self-starter several years earlier—which eliminated the dangerous task of hand-cranking and opened up a whole new segment of car buyers— was an act of greater liberation. The Diana, manufactured in St. Louis during the decade, featured lighter steering and balloon tires and was an obvious attempt to appeal to female drivers.

For all of the freedom modern women were now tasting, it was still indisputably a man's world—no more so than in the upper echelons of the auto industry, where prostitutes, mistresses, and discreetly arranged adoptions and abortions were all part of the lifestyle that didn't make it into Detroit's society pages. Despite all the temptations available to someone with Edsel's looks, power, and wealth, by all accounts he and Eleanor maintained a close, monogamous relationship throughout their twenty-seven years of marriage. Edsel always called his wife "Ellie," while Eleanor's pet name for her husband was "Ned."*

---

* As a group, Ford executives were perhaps no lustier than their counterparts in other auto companies, but individual appetites varied. Harold Wills was known as a dapper and somewhat vain fellow whose conquests, some thought, had helped lead to his ouster from the company. "Women!" Henry Ford responded when a young engineer, Harold Hicks, speculated about Wills's departure. "Why Hicks, women won't do you any harm. You can screw any woman on earth excepting for one thing—never let your wife find out!" It was Wills who introduced Evangeline Dahlinger to Ford, whose dalliance with the pretty secretary may not have been his only extramarital affair. Harry Bennett, another top Ford executive, was married three times, regularly sampled the favors of party girls, and collected pornographic films such as *The Casting Director* and *A Stiff Game* (some of which he viewed with Henry). In his autobiography Bennett tells the story of how Henry once instructed him to quickly and quietly relocate two maids—one to California, the other back to her native Finland—because of a possible misunderstanding. One of the girls had caught Ford stroking the hand of the other in the garden at Fair Lane and he was afraid the eavesdropper would tell Clara. It's entirely possible Ford's bizarre behavior in this particular matter was purely innocent. "But," as biographer Robert Lacey would point out, "since the drift of Henry Ford's later life displayed a conspicuous tendency to gratify his own appetites and to exploit the power that wealth gave him over other men, there is no reason to believe that he did not also seek, on occasions, to extend his power over women."

If Ellie or Ned ever displayed a roving eye, it was to calmly map out an exit route whenever one of the older Fords approached with a lecture forming on their lips. They endured Henry and Clara's regular scoldings about the dangers of alcohol and tobacco and "high living"—then climbed into formal wear and enjoyed a fun but perfectly sane outing anyway with other "smart" couples such as the Books, Calkins, Macauleys, Newberrys, and Potters. Henry, distrustful of Grosse Pointe's "old money" types and jealous about the influences they might have on his son, sometimes resorted to paying household staff to spy on their activities. The Edsel Fords' disregard for the prohibition laws, in effect in Michigan from 1918 to 1933, particularly frustrated the old tee-totaler. On one occasion, he had an aide drive him to 1100 Lakeshore Drive while they were gone, then went inside and smashed their liquor supply. On another, having heard rumors that Edsel had nearly died from drinking some bootleg booze at a New York party, he seriously considered having someone slip him a Mickey Finn in hopes the reaction would make him swear off drinking.

∽o∾

In Henry's mind, one of the most corrupting influences on Edsel was a man he had hired himself. Ernest Kanzler was Edsel's brother-in-law, having married Eleanor's older sister, Josephine. Kanzler, a Harvard graduate, was a regular guest at Fair Lane during his and Edsel's court-ship days with the Clay sisters. At the time Kanzler was employed at a law firm doing work on the Dodge versus Ford lawsuit. Henry freely discussed the case in front of Kanzler, who asked him to stop.

"You ought to be on my side," Henry retorted. "Why do you want to be a lawyer, anyway? They're parasites. Come to Highland Park, and I'll give you a job." Offered a salary of $5,000 a year, Kanzler quickly accepted and eventually wound up with the office next to Edsel's. He had a demonstrated talent with numbers and organization, setting up a "just-in-time" parts delivery system that saved the tractor firm millions of dollars. He drew up production and inventory timetables for the Model T and injected a much-needed sense of organization into the company. As Edsel's brother-in-law, close friend, and right-hand man, it was Kanzler, not Charlie Sorenson, who seemed to have the brains and connections to emerge as the overall head of production at the company.

Unfortunately, Kanzler also had a big mouth, which he unzipped around the plant and at social gatherings. "God damn it, we are way behind the times," he'd say. "Why are we manufacturing an out-of-date car?"

His loud and constant criticisms irritated Sorenson but somehow never got back to Henry. Kanzler took care of that himself with a six-page memo he brashly sent Ford. In it he spelled out all the short-comings of the Model T. It was dated January 26, 1926. Henry never responded to it. Exactly five months later Kanzler was fired. Edsel learned of it while he and Eleanor were en route to Europe to collect antiques for the house being built at Gaukler Pointe. On their return, Eleanor cried and begged Henry to change his mind, to no avail. Henry wanted no separate power structures forming around Edsel. Meanwhile, it was up to Sorenson to break in the heir apparent.

"Sorenson's job in the Ford Motor Company is to train Edsel for the big job when he can take it over," Ray Dahlinger explained one day to an inquisitive co-worker. "Edsel just isn't tough enough."

∽∘∾

By the early 1920s nearly three-quarters of all new cars were being bought on credit, but Henry continued to disapprove of installment payments. He well remembered the lessons of his youth, when thrift was a virtue and being in debt was considered an evil second only to intemperance. However, although Ford built more than two million cars and trucks in 1923—half the industry total—the growing strength of the competition during the decade forced him to grudgingly make concessions. He allowed Edsel to subtly restyle the '23 Model T, giving it a lower profile with a sloped windshield. Further signs of Henry's concern over shrinking market share was the decision to resume adver-tising after a six-year hiatus and to offer a weekly purchase plan, whereby the customer could take delivery of a new Ford only after the full purchase price was paid for in five-dollar installments. More than 300,000 Model T's were sold in this fashion in two years. It wasn't until 1928, with the creation of Universal Credit Corporation, that Ford dealers were finally able to offer their customers traditional bank loans.

Long before then, Ford dealers in America and Europe were clam-oring for a new product to stave off competition from low-cost alterna-tives such as Chevrolet and Dodge. Especially worrisome was Chevy,

Edsel, Eleanor, and Henry II sailing with Josephine Kanzler, c. 1927.

where Bill Knudsen was wreaking revenge on his old boss and gobbling up market share by coming out with stylish products that featured balloon tires, hydraulic brakes, and smart-looking extras such as disc wheels, step plates, and bumpers. Now that just about everybody who wanted a car had one, a crowded field of automakers faced the challenge of convincing car owners to make this major purchase more than once or twice in their lifetime. General Motors's strategy of "artificial obsolescence" revolved around annual styling changes and an array of sprightly paint finishes. Chevrolet ads proclaimed their products to be "in vogue," something nobody ever said about the dowdy Model T.

When Henry went abroad for two weeks in 1924, Edsel and some engineers used the opportunity to perform a major cosmetic overhaul of the Model T, crafting a mock-up that was less boxier and painted bright red. The night before they had a chance to properly prepare Henry for the sight of this sacrilegious prototype, however, Ford unexpectedly walked into the garage where it was parked at Highland Park. His unannounced arrival startled George Brown, the purchasing agent who had helped procure parts for it.

"What's over there?" Ford asked, his suspicions aroused.

Brown gulped. "Well, Mr. Ford, that's the new car."

"Ford car?"

"Yes, sir."

Edsel and Henry size up the quadricycle and the 10 millionth Model T in June 1923.

Oh, no, it wasn't. As Brown looked on in slack-jawed amazement, the sixty-one-year-old Ford singlehandedly dismantled Edsel's creation. "He walked around the car three or four times, looking at it very closely. Finally, he got to the left side of the car, and he gets hold of the door, and BANG! One jerk, and he had it off the hinges! He ripped the door right off! God, how the man done it, I don't know! He jumped in, and BANG! goes the other door! BANG! goes the windshield! He jumped over the back seat and started pounding on the top. He wrecked the car as much as he could."

Brown ran shouting up to the second floor to warn some of the engineers who had been in on the project. "Look out, boys! Mr. Ford's kicking the car all to pieces downstairs!"

If only Ford were doing that to the competition. In 1926 Henry slashed the price of the runabout to an all-time low of $260, but despite the discount and some attractive design changes by Edsel, production fell by more than a quarter-million. Meanwhile, Chevy sales passed the 600,000 mark. Edsel, whose cufflinks bore the legend *Omnium Rerum Vicissitude* ("All Things Change"), had watched in agony as Ford's once dominant share of the market fell from 67 percent in 1921 to 46 percent five years later. The cult of the Tin Lizzie was being swept away by the reality of a fickle and more sophisticated car-buying public. For years it was price—not comfort, styling, or mechanical innovations—that had kept flivver sales going. Now customers demanded more style and conveniences than the Model T, with its 1908 technology, offered. And with installment payments, "pay as you ride" car buyers didn't mind shelling out a few more dollars each month for the extras.

After several years' worth of contentious meetings and diminishing market share, Henry finally gave in. He would retire Lizzie, replace the old gal with a fresh face, and arrest the free fall. The momentous decision had taken longer than Edsel and others had liked, but, according to Warren I. Susman, "Ford had perhaps belatedly learned a fundamental fact about the new and affluent mass society he had done so much to shape, if not create: price and efficiency alone would not dictate consumer choice." Henry "had not perceived that the common man did not want to feel common; mechanical perfection, although often desirable, was not enough." Ford, of course, would go to his grave convinced that he had built the perfect car, that its demise was the result of superficialities and not because of any basic internal flaws. "The only thing wrong with that car," he would insist, "was that people stopped buying it."

On May 25, 1927, Ford announced the pending end to Model T production and the introduction of an all-new vehicle to be called the Model A. No details of the latter were released, principally because there were none to give out. At this point the car was almost as big a mystery to Ford as it was to the public. The next day, with Edsel at the wheel and Henry in the back seat, father and son drove the 15 millionth flivver off the line at Highland Park and through the drizzle to the Engineering Laboratory in Dearborn. There several hundred people watched them pose alongside two other historic vehicles, the 1896 quadricycle and 1908 Model T prototype.

The public treated the end of the Model T as a death in the family. In all, a total of 15,007,033 of them had rolled onto America's roads since Henry's universal car debuted in the fall of 1908. The country had undergone great changes during those nineteen years, even if the car had not. Songwriters Jack Meskill and Abner Silver caught the prevailing nostalgic mood with their likable lament, "Poor Lizzie":

> Poor Lizzie, what'll become of you,
> Now that your sister is here?
> Poor Lizzie, tho' we've made fun of you,

We're mighty sorry, old dear.
Right now your big sister's
The talk of the town.
You were a good wagon
Until you broke down.
Oh, Poor Lizzie, since Henry's done with you,
What'll become of you now?

Poor Lizzie, what'll become of you
Now that you're old and passé?
Poor Lizzie, they're making fun of you,
Now we can't give you away.
Now we'll take two flivvers,
Make sure that they're mates;
Tie one to each shoe
And just use them for skates.
Oh, Poor Lizzie, since Henry's done with you
What'll become of you now?

Five years earlier, on February 4, 1922, Ford had bought the Lincoln Motor Company, which had fallen into receivership. Henry Leland, who had started the firm in 1917 with his son Wilfred, found himself in the uncomfortable position of working for the man he had displaced two decades earlier at the Henry Ford Company. The Lelands assumed they would continue running the show. But Ford's reasons for spending $8 million on the company were twofold: to provide an outlet for Edsel's creative urges and to exact a little revenge on Leland, not necessarily in that order. After the Lelands' predictably quick and bitter departure from the scene, Edsel was made president of a second car company, which he hoped to make Ford's luxury arm. "Father made the most popular car in the world," he declared. "I would like to make the best car in the world." Taking charge of design, he revamped the Lelands' mechanically sound but stodgy sedan. He used custom coach builders in the United States and Europe to create what was soon recognized as one of the most fashionable luxury lines in the country—no small feat, given the large number of high-end carmakers then in operation.

Edsel's admired makeover of the Lincoln and successful tweakings of the Model T gave Henry confidence that his son could do the same with the new Ford. "We've got a pretty good man in my son," he admitted. "He knows style—how a car ought to look. And he has mechanical horse sense too." As work began in earnest on the Model A, Henry

The *New York World* waved a fond farewell to the Model T with
this cartoon in November 1927.

supervised the engineering aspects of the new vehicle while Edsel was
given free reign with the design, inside and out. The way in which each
approached his respective task says everything about what was right—
and wrong—about the company at this critical juncture in its history.

Henry had $250 million cash in various banks and was in no dis-
cernible hurry to bring out the new Ford, even as his idled work force
of 50,000 went without paychecks and competing carmakers took
advantage of the industry leader's unprecedented shutdown to snatch
big bites out of the sales pie. The pace of discovery might have picked
up had there been some sort of formal system in place to adequately
test the car in progress. Instead, Henry relied on the terse summations
of Ray Dahlinger, whose real job was managing Ford Farms when he
wasn't driving test vehicles—on public roads, no less. No engineer and
not much for conversation in any case, Dahlinger could only offer two
opinions at the end of a run. "It's no damn good," he'd say. Or "It's goddamn good." Dahlinger's verdicts left engineers begging for more, but
Henry seemed satisfied and would make adjustments accordingly.

Some copywriters from the Philadelphia agency hired to do advertising for the Model A could not believe how slowly and haphazardly the
product they were preparing to ballyhoo—any time now—was evolv-

ing. "There stands the car in the middle of the floor, nearly finished so far as we can make out," one of the writers reported to his boss on his return from Dearborn.

> Every morning the engineers gather around it, just looking at it, waiting for Ford to appear. When he comes he reaches inside, rattles something, shakes his head and says, "That won't do. You've got to think of something better than that." One of them says, "Can you think of anything, Mr. Ford?" He rattles the thing again, walks off a little and comes back, makes some pencil marks on a piece of paper, hands it to them and says, "Try something like that." The next morning they gather round the car again, and when Ford comes in he asks, "Got it on?" They say, "Yes, Mr. Ford." He reaches in, rattles the thing again, whatever it is, makes a gesture of disgust and says, "That's worse." With that he walks off, leaving them there gazing at the car. It's like that day after day, with the whole country screaming for the new Ford car. We don't understand it.

The months of trial and error dragged on, through the summer and into the fall. The delay added to the suspense that was keeping hundreds of thousands of potential customers from settling on a new car until they had seen what ol' Henry Ford was up to. The unveiling of the first new Ford car in almost two decades promised to join Charles Lindbergh's solo flight across the Atlantic as one of the top news stories of 1927. What would it look like? A poem entitled "The New Ford," which appeared in papers across the country, tried to satisfy the speculation:

> The new Ford car, Dame Rumor says,
> Will have a Turkish bath attached;
> A radio that sweetly plays the moment that the door's unlatched;
> An ice machine, a baby grand, a year's supply of pepsin gum,
> An earth-inductor compass and a sun-porch, or solarium.
> (P. S.—I have to mention, tho, that Edsel says it isn't so.)

The Model A wasn't quite that elaborate when it finally debuted on December 2, 1927, but most of the estimated 10 million people who stampeded showrooms to see it within thirty-six hours of its arrival thought it was a mighty fine automobile. The design mastery of Edsel and his only engineering assistant, Joe Galamb, carefully if crudely carried out on blackboards, was evident in the final product. Inspired by work previously done on the Lincoln, the Model A's cupped fenders

A Model A moves down the assembly line. Ford's
changeover to the new car cost $50 million and threw
men out of work for six months.

and graceful radiator shell had the look of more expensive cars. In fact,
the new Ford was dubbed the "baby Lincoln." However, the cost was a
very competitive $550 for the coupe. Buyers had their pick of several
colors, including Niagara Blue, Arabian Sand, Cobra Drab, Andalusite
Blue, and Dawn Gray. These were a salve for Sorenson's tired eyes,
which over the last dozen years had watched an unremitting river of
black metal flow out of the Model T plant. "I was sick of looking at
them," he admitted.

Mechanically, Henry and his crew had also done their jobs. A sliding gear transmission replaced the old planetary transmission. The
presence of a more powerful four-cylinder engine, hydraulic shock absorbers, four-wheel brakes, and a safety glass windshield (unheard of in
a low-priced car) made a ride in the technologically modern Model A
a smooth, safe, and quiet one. The Cartier brothers wrote Edsel: "Perhaps you could let us mount a few Model A's up as broaches and
bracelets." That first day some 50,000 orders were placed in New York
alone. By mid-December more than 400,000 people had added a new
Ford to their Christmas shopping list. Edsel's friends in Washington
and Hollywood, unwilling to wait for the months-long backlog of orders

to be fulfilled, got preferential treatment. Thus Douglas Fairbanks Jr. and Franklin Delano Roosevelt wound up tooling around in their new Fords before most of the rest of the world.

The process of overhauling the manufacturing equipment in the Rouge and forty-seven other plants—thirty-five in the United States and Canada and a dozen overseas—to accommodate the 5,580 individual parts in the Model A proved incredibly complicated, expensive, and time-consuming. Chevrolet sold more than one million cars in 1927 to shoot past its incapacitated rival, and continuing production difficulties at Ford kept Chevy in the lead in 1928 as well. Finally, with the wrinkles ironed out by the end of 1928, Ford reclaimed the top spot in 1929 with more than 1.8 million produced—a third of the industry total. It was a remarkable comeback, but it didn't last.

Within five years the Model A was totally obsolete. Not only did Chevrolet and other competitors storm back with their annual new offerings, but their superior organizational methods—the kind Edsel and Kanzler were itching to introduce—allowed them to make changeovers without costly breaks in production. On top of that, Ford now had to contend with another low-cost challenger, Plymouth. Henry and Edsel knew they needed to update the Ford line in order to keep up.

Henry had one last engineering marvel left in him. He closed his plants in the summer of 1931 and didn't reopen them until five months and $50 million later. In early 1932 the new Ford V-8 was unveiled, featuring eight cylinders galloping for the first time inside a single-casting block. Finding the exact alloy mix to ensure the blocks would not crack under the strain was a triumph of metallurgy. The most spectacular of the new manufacturing processes Ford installed at the Rouge to handle the production of the V-8 was a giant pouring furnace, a two-ton pitcher that dipped to fill engine molds with molten metal as they moved down the line. Most of the styling work took place at Briggs Manufacturing, where Edsel set up a small, out-of-the-way design studio much in the manner of Harley Earl's revolutionary Art and Colour Section at GM. Several body types were offered, with sticker prices ranging between $460 and $650.

Producing 65 horsepower, the V-8 was the most powerful car ever offered to mainstream America. Bank robbers Clyde Barrow and John Dillinger were boosters, writing letters to the company praising the

The Ford V-8, introduced in 1932, gets a going-over at Navin Field by the entire squad of the Detroit Tigers.

new Ford. "I have drove Fords exclusively," Barrow wrote, "when I could get away with one." Despite such testimonials, Chevrolet still outdistanced its rival in sales. Outside of an odd year here and there, it would hold onto its number-one position throughout much of the next half-century.

## 11

ᏧᏍᏋ

# Chronicle of the Neglected Truth

*I was sad and I was blue*
*But now I'm just as good as you*
*Since Hen-ry Ford a-pol-o-gized to me*
*I've thrown a-way my lit-tle Che-vro-let*
*And bought my-self a Ford Cou-pe*
*I told the Sup-'rin-ten-dent that*
*the Dearborn In-de-pen-dent*
*Does-n't have to hang up where it used to be*
*I'm glad he changed his point of view*
*And I even like Edsel too,*
*Since Hen-ry Ford a-pol-o-gized to me*

—"Since Henry Ford Apologized to Me" (1927)

The *Chicago Tribune* trial may have revealed America's greatest industrial genius to be a self-confessed ignoramus about most matters not directly involving automobiles or manufacturing. But on the subject of "the international Jewish conspiracy," Henry Ford considered himself an expert. Rosika Schwimmer got an unsettling introduction to Ford's anti-Semitism at a luncheon meeting prior to their sailing on the Peace Ship.

"I know who started the war—the German Jewish bankers," he had exclaimed, slapping a pocket containing one of his notebooks. "I have the evidence here. Facts. The German Jewish bankers caused the war. I can't give out the facts now, because I haven't got them all yet. But I'll have them soon."

The "facts" did not get widespread play until a few years after the Peace Ship fiasco, when Henry purchased a little-read hometown newspaper. Ford's intention when he launched the revamped *Dearborn Independent* in 1919 was to have a vehicle for his opinions, which he felt were being ignored by the mainstream press. He hired an experienced staff headed by former *Detroit News* editor Edwin G. Pipp, a respected journalist with a worldly view. The paper was published out of the empty Ford tractor factory on Michigan Avenue. The sixteen-page "organ of unbiased opinion" (which would ultimately grow to forty-eight pages) "comes to put its shoulder to the car of social justice and human progress," claimed Pipp, who shared Henry's vision of turning the *Dearborn Independent* into the equal of the *New York Times* and *Wall Street Journal*. Early issues did offer "straight" news and commentary about a variety of social issues, with the auto magnate's pedagogy confined to a single-paged editorial called "Mr. Ford's Own Page." By the time the *Independent* ceased publication eight turbulent years later, however, the original premise and editor were both long gone and Henry Ford's weekly was being ridiculed as "the best periodical ever turned out by a tractor plant" and roundly denounced for its "stupid slander against the Jews." And Pipp, just one more person uplifted and then disillusioned by his association with Ford, had become one of its harshest critics.

❧

Given his rural upbringing and the Populist tenor of the times, Henry's anti-Semitism was hardly surprising. Even the McGuffey's anthologies he'd enjoyed as a boy featured such stereotypical figures as the Shakespearean moneylender, Shylock. In Henry's unsophisticated mind, "Jew" was synonymous with the traditional enemies of the bedrock Gentile life he had known: bankers, hucksters, warmongers. Over time, the word became more of an all-purpose pejorative than a direct reference to a particular race or religion. He was known to call Gentiles he disliked or distrusted "Jews." Ford also expressed a wariness of Catholics, whom he vaguely understood took orders from the Pope.

"Mr. Ford was prejudiced against Jews and Catholics," said Harry Bennett, Ford's security chief. "But he liked many individual Jews and

Catholics. When he liked a Jew—as he did the Tigers' Hank Greenberg and Michigan's quarterback, Harry Newman—he'd say to me, 'He's mixed, he's not all Jewish.' When he liked a Catholic, and he liked a lot of them, he'd say, 'He isn't a good Catholic.' Then when one of these people would do something wrong, he'd say, 'What could you expect of them?'"

Henry occasionally had Bennett dig up a man's background to see whether there was any Jewish blood. Ford engineers already knew not to incorporate brass in their designs—in their boss's mind, brass was "a Jew metal."

The opening salvo of Ford's assault on Jewry came with the May 22, 1920, issue of the *Independent*. The cover story, which carried no byline, was headlined "The International Jew: The World's Problem":

> There is a race, a part of humanity which has never yet been received as a welcome part, and which has succeeded in raising itself to a power that the proudest Gentile race has never claimed—not even Rome in the days of her proudest power.

And so it began. For ninety-one consecutive issues, the private publication of arguably the most famous man in the world pounded away at the corrosive "Jewish influence" in practically every aspect of life, from finance to politics. One article, by way of example, addressed "Jewish Supremacy in the Theatre and Cinema":

> The Theater has long been a part of the Jewish program for the guidance of public taste and the influencing of the public mind. Not only is the theater given a special place in the program of the Protocols, but it is the instant ally night by night and week by week of any idea which the "power behind the scenes" wishes to put forth. It is not by accident that in Russia, where they now have scarcely anything else, they still have the Theater, specially revived, stimulated and supported by Jewish-Bolshevists because they believe in the Theater just as they believe in the Press; it is one of the two great means of molding popular opinion.
>
> Not only the "legitimate" stage, so-called, but the motion picture industry—the fifth greatest of all industries—is also entirely Jew-controlled; with the natural sequence that the civilized world is increasingly antagonistic to the trivializing and demoralizing influence of that form of entertainment as at present managed.
>
> As soon as the Jew gained control of American liquor, we had a liquor problem with drastic consequences. As soon as the Jew gained

control of the "movies" we had a movie problem, the consequences of which are visible.

It is the peculiar genius of that race to create problems of a moral character in whatever business they achieve a majority.

The man responsible for helping to crystallize Ford's somewhat muddled bigotry into a coherent attack on the Jews was his private secretary, a stern, colorless ex-bank clerk named Ernest Liebold, who in turn relied on the talents of an alcoholic wordsmith, William Cameron, a former editorial writer for the *Detroit News.*

"I am sure that if Mr. Ford were put on the witness stand, he could not tell to save his life just when and how he started against the Jews. I am sure that Liebold could tell," Pipp wrote after he resigned in disgust from the *Independent* in the spring of 1920, to be quickly replaced by Cameron.

Liebold was on Henry's private payroll, not the company's. The squat, bullnecked Prussian had insinuated himself into Henry's confidence the best possible way: by doing his bidding quietly, thoroughly, and without any questioning or much direction, tightening the nuts and bolts on whatever whims or unfinished business existed at the moment. "All Mr. Ford had to say to Liebold was, 'Do this, do that,' and he'd carry out the most ambitious projects," recalled Irving Bacon. James Couzens had hired Liebold to organize the bank Ford had established near the Highland Park plant to handle the work force's payroll. Liebold did so well that he was named president. Henry then handpicked him to reorganize a failing bank in Dearborn into the Dearborn State Bank, where he wound up handling the Fords' personal accounts. In 1918, Henry gave the trusted lieutenant power of attorney for himself and Clara. By the time Liebold was named general manager of the *Dearborn Independent,* he had successfully handled a multitude of private projects for Henry, including the design, construction, and staffing of Henry Ford Hospital. Ford didn't socialize with Liebold, who was twenty-one years his junior, and didn't particularly like him. But he respected his obstinacy. "When you have a watchdog," Henry said, "you don't hire him to like everybody that comes to the gate." Liebold's intimate dealings with Henry made him one of the most powerful men in the company.

Liebold was said to possess "a mind like a balance sheet." In much that fashion, Liebold interpreted his boss's broad swipes at the Jewish problem into something orderly, categorical, and digestible. And he

The *Dearborn Independent's* business manager was Ernest Liebold, Henry Ford's personal secretary.

wasn't above making leading suggestions or injecting his own opinion. According to Pipp, who started his own publication, *Pipp's Weekly,* to challenge the claims made in the *Independent,* the "door to the Ford mind was always open to anything Liebold wanted to shove in it, and during that time Mr. Ford developed a dislike for the Jews, a dislike which [grew] stronger and more bitter as time went on." Liebold, who always preferred to work behind the scenes, was careful to deflect "credit" to Cameron and Ford. "Everything that was being done was being done because of Mr. Ford's wishes in carrying out the idea of revealing to the public the facts pertaining to Jewish activities," Liebold insisted.

Because Ford dealers were heavily encouraged to sell a subscription to every person who bought a new Model T, circulation of the *Dearborn Independent* sometimes reached upward of 900,000 and more, giving the paper considerable clout.

Readers found no stereotype out of bounds. In one editorial, Ford offered $1,000 to anyone who could find an example of a Jewish farmer, a dig at Jews' supposed aversion to manual labor. No claim was too outlandish. If the *Dearborn Independent* was to be believed, Queen Isabella of Spain had been a "Jewish front" for the discovery of America, while Jewish bankers had been behind the assassination of Abraham Lincoln. Negro jazz—the "mush, the slush, the sly suggestion"—was of Jewish origin, as were the scandalous short skirts and rolled-down

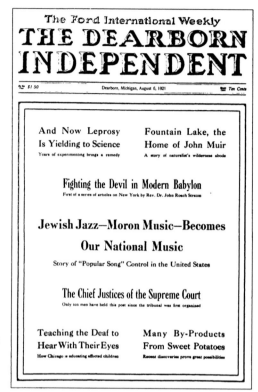

The Ford International Weekly

# THE DEARBORN
# INDEPENDENT

$1 50     Dearborn, Michigan, August 6, 1921     Ten Cents

And Now Leprosy
Is Yielding to Science
Years of experimenting brings a remedy

Fountain Lake, the
Home of John Muir
A story of naturalist's wilderness abode

### Fighting the Devil in Modern Babylon
First of a series of articles on New York by Rev. Dr. John Roach Straton

## Jewish Jazz—Moron Music—Becomes
## Our National Music
Story of "Popular Song" Control in the United States

### The Chief Justices of the Supreme Court
Only ten men have held this post since the tribunal was first organized

Teaching the Deaf to
Hear With Their Eyes
How Chicago is educating afflicted children

Many By-Products
From Sweet Potatoes
Recent discoveries prove great possibilities

A typical issue of the *Independent* "exposed" the Jewish influence in jazz, which the paper decried as "moron music."

stockings of the era's "flappers." No matter how preposterous the allegation, the paper could somehow trace it to the Zionist conspiracy that threatened public order and decency. The *Independent* even exhumed an old forgery known as the *Protocols of the Learned Elders of Zion,* in which senior Jewish leaders discuss their plot to overthrow Christian civilization. Many of the articles subsequently were bundled into a booklet titled *The International Jew.* Domestic versions of *The International Jew* sold poorly, but European sales were brisk.

Several biographies and a popular ghosted autobiography appeared during this period. In the 1923 book, *My Life and Work,* written with Samuel Crowther, the sage of Dearborn discussed "our work on the Jewish question." He was involved, he explained, because "there had been observed in this country certain streams of influence which were causing a marked deterioration in our literature, amusements, and social conduct; business was departing from its old time substantial soundness; a general letting down of standards was everywhere." At fault was "a nasty Orientalism which has insidiously affected every channel of expression." *Mein Leben und Werk* was a best-seller in Germany. A rabble-rouser named Adolph Hitler borrowed from it freely. He also kept a framed photograph of "Heinrich Ford" in his office.

There never was a formal boycott of Ford products by Jewish organizations, though an untold number of individuals and firms took their business elsewhere. Many offended Gentiles did so as well. National leaders such as former presidents Woodrow Wilson and William Howard Taft asked Ford to stop, to no avail.

The reaction from Jews close to Ford ran the gamut from bafflement to outrage. Rabbi Leo Franklin, a former neighbor who for years had gratefully accepted Henry's annual gift of a new Model T, returned his customized vehicle in protest. Ford was genuinely shocked. He naively assumed the "good Jews" would support his campaign against the "bad." Not quite comprehending his old friend's reaction, Ford phoned to ask: "What's wrong, Dr. Franklin? Has anything come between us?"

As a key member of the Anti-Defamation League, Rabbi Franklin had tried without success to reason with Ford. "Few thinking men have given any credence to the charges offered against the Jews," he told the press after turning in his car. "But Ford's publication has besmirched the name of the Jews in the eyes of the great majority, and especially in the small towns of the country, where Ford's word is taken as gospel. He had fed the flames of anti-Semitism throughout the world."

Albert Kahn, the architect of the Ford empire, was a "good Jew" who decided to take it on the chin. Although Ford's anti-Semitism was "a major strain on the relationship," Kahn continued to build for his longtime boss. "Let's be reasonable," said architect Bill Kahn in his uncle's defense. "You wouldn't turn down a commission for an entire firm because your nose was out of joint." Albert Kahn's compromise was not to personally meet with Henry Ford after the 1920s.

Where was Edsel during all this? While giving no visible support to his father's prejudice, he also was not about to openly criticize him over a public utterance or published editorial. He quietly resigned as a director of the *Independent,* a symbolic act that changed nothing. He tried appealing to the bottom line, protesting the attacks were cutting into vehicle sales. Henry's mule-headed reply was, "If they want our product, they'll buy it." Whatever else was said about the subject

Henry's definition of a "good
Jew" included Albert Kahn,
the brilliant and tireless
architect of the Ford empire.

between the two in private remains unknown, though one can easily
imagine the strain, anguish and frustration the liberal-minded Edsel—
who had many Jewish friends in Hollywood, New York, and Washington—must have felt in fighting yet another losing battle with his father.

∽∘∾

Beginning in January 1922 and continuing for the next two years, anti-
Semitic articles appeared only sporadically on the pages of the *Dearborn Independent,* a hiatus that coincided with Ford's brief flirtation
with national office. Then, in April 1924, the self-styled "Chronicle of
the Neglected Truth" went full-bore back on the attack. As always,
Liebold depended on detectives and stooges to provide dirt on prominent Jews, then left it to William Cameron and a band of talented staff
writers and freelancers (often writing under pseudonyms) to shape the
mass of innuendoes, half-truths, fabrications, and occasional facts into
some kind of story—the more sensational the better. Among the
paper's new round of allegations was the charge that Aaron Sapiro, an

attorney and the hard-charging organizer of agricultural cooperatives in the United States and Canada, had cheated and extorted some of the farmers he represented. "Sapiro is a shrewd little Jew" who "should be kicked out because he is trash," the *Independent* declared. After his requests for a public retraction were ignored, Sapiro sued for defamation, asking $1 million in damages.

The trial began on March 15, 1927. Because Sapiro sued Henry Ford personally, and not the *Independent,* defense attorneys were prepared to show a jury in Detroit that the carmaker had had no direct knowledge of what the paper had published in his name. Cameron spent a week on the stand propagating that fiction. One evening two weeks later, just hours before he was scheduled to testify himself, Henry mysteriously drove off the road near his home and smashed his Model T into a tree. A big Studebaker touring car with two men in it had sideswiped him, he explained. Bruised and shaken, the sixty-three-year-old Ford spent two days in the hospital before being sent home to recuperate. Meanwhile, Harry Bennett helped a *Detroit Times* reporter break the story of a female juror who had lied about being offered a bribe by an unknown Jew. A mistrial was declared and a new trial date of September 21 set.

Not long afterward, Ford met with representatives of the American Jewish Committee and threw in the towel. They drafted an apology, which he signed without changing a word.

Henry's sudden and unexpected capitulation was the result of a combination of factors, probably the least of which was genuine remorse over the harm he had caused. His time and money were tied up in a variety of activities, including his aviation and antiquarian pursuits and the changeover from the Model T to the Model A. The *Independent,* which would lose $4.8 million during its eight-year run of vitriol, was a drain on resources, and Ford had shown less and less interest in it as he became immersed in other activities. That he had alienated a good-sized portion of the car-buying public also had become more of a concern as the carmaker continued to lose market share to Chevrolet. But perhaps the greatest impetus was the prospect of repeating his abysmal witness-chair performance from the *Tribune* trial. The thought of suffering through such an ordeal again had clearly frightened him—enough to steer his car into a tree, many skeptics thought.

Ford's apology, dated June 30, 1927, was released worldwide on July 8 through one of his favorite newspapermen, syndicated columnist

Arthur Brisbane. Edsel, like Liebold and Cameron and everybody else, was caught completely by surprise by the lengthy recantation attributed to his father.

> For some time past I have given consideration to the series of articles concerning Jews which since 1920 have appeared in *The Dearborn Independent.* Some of them have been reprinted in pamphlet form under the title, "The International Jew." Although both publications are my property, it goes without saying that in the multitude of my activities it has been impossible for me to devote personal attention to their management or to keep informed as to their contents. It has therefore inevitably followed that the conduct and policy of these publications had to be delegated to men whom I placed in charge of them and upon whom I relied implicitly.
>
> To my great regret I have learned that Jews generally, and particularly those of this country, not only resent these publications as promoting anti-Semitism, but regard me as their enemy. Trusted friends with whom I have conferred recently have assured me in all sincerity that in their opinion the character of the charges and insinuations made against the Jews, both individually and collectively, contained in many of the articles which have been circulated periodically in *The Dearborn Independent* and have been reprinted in the pamphlets mentioned, justifies the righteous indignation entertained by Jews everywhere toward me because of the mental anguish occasioned by the unprovoked reflections made upon them.
>
> This has led me to direct my personal attention to this subject, in order to ascertain the exact nature of these articles. As a result of this survey I confess that I am deeply mortified that this journal, which is intended to be constructive and not destructive, has been made the medium for resurrecting exploded fictions, for giving currency to the so-called *Protocols of the Wise Men of Zion,* which have been demonstrated, as I learn, to be gross forgeries, and for contending that the Jews have been engaged in a conspiracy to control the capital and the industries of the world, besides laying at their door many offenses against decency, public order and good morals.
>
> Had I appreciated even the general nature, to say nothing of the details, of these utterances, I would have forbidden their circulation without a moment's hesitation, because I am fully aware of the virtues of the Jewish people as a whole, of what they and their ancestors have done for civilization and for mankind and toward the development of commerce and industry, of their sobriety and diligence, their benevolence and their unselfish interest in the public welfare.

Of course there are black sheep in every flock, as there are among men of all races, creeds, and nationalities who are at times evildoers. It is wrong, however, to judge a people by a few individuals, and I therefore join in condemning unreservedly all wholesale denunciations and attacks.

Those who know me can bear witness that it is not in my nature to inflict insult upon and to occasion pain to anybody, and that it has been my effort to free myself from prejudice. Because of that I frankly confess that I have been greatly shocked as a result of my study and examination of the files of *The Dearborn Independent* and of the pamphlets entitled "The International Jew." I deem it to be my duty as an honorable man to make amends for the wrong done to the Jews as fellow-men and brothers, by asking their forgiveness for the harm that I have unintentionally committed, by retracting so far as lies within my power the offensive charges laid at their door by those publications, and by giving them the unqualified assurance that henceforth they may look to me for friendship and good will.

It is needless to add that the pamphlets which have been distributed throughout the country and in foreign lands will be withdrawn from circulation, that in every way possible I will make it known that they have my unqualified disapproval, and that henceforth *The Dearborn Independent* will be conducted under such auspices that articles reflecting upon the Jews will never again appear in its columns.

Finally, let me add that this statement is made on my own initiative and wholly in the interest of right and justice and in accordance with what I regard as my solemn duty as a man and as a citizen.

The *Independent,* now benign, put out its final issue in December 1927. By and large, American Jews forgave Ford, who exhibited good will for a time by attending Jewish functions (he received a standing ovation from 2,000 people at one dinner) and by directing a sizable share of the company's advertising budget to Jewish firms. But damage had been done, particularly in Europe, where the synchronized footfalls of fascist jackboots grew disturbingly louder.

The extent of Henry Ford's impact, as both a publisher and a cult figure, on the rise of Nazism in Germany continues to be debated. Winifred Wagner, the daughter-in-law of the famous German composer, came away from a 1924 dinner at Fair Lane with the impression that "the philosophy and ideas of Ford and Hitler were very similar." Henry's admiration of Teutonic orderliness and technological efficiency was mirrored by what amounted to an Aryan adoration society. Hitler's inspiration for the Volkswagen ("the people's car"), the Autobahn, and arguably the death camps ("the mass production of hate," in historian Neil Baldwin's words) stemmed in whole or in part from the industrialist's work and writings. Ford was the only American mentioned in the U.S. edition of Hitler's *Mein Kampf*. Hitler Youth Movement leader Baldur von Shirach later testified at the Nuremburg war crimes trial that *The International Jew* had significantly shaped his racist views. "The booklets undoubtedly influenced many readers, all the more because they carried the imprint, not of a crackpot publisher in an alleyway, but of one of the most famous and successful men in the world," was one historian's judgment. In Ford's defense, it can be argued that the material under his imprimatur made up just a fraction of the anti-Semitic literature (much of it considerably more violent and obscene) flooding Europe during this period of social and political upheaval. And shared ideology did not necessarily translate into funding for fascist organizations. In early 1924, Henry agreed to see a charming promoter of the Nazi cause, Kurt Ludecke. After a few minutes of conversation, Ford abruptly ended the meeting and sent him back to Berlin empty-handed.*

Henry's bigotry remained cavalier and characteristically cryptic. "He made some remarks once in a while," recalled engineer Emil Zoerlein, who started his twenty-five-year Ford career about the time of the apology. "He said, 'Unfortunately we have the Jews around, but we have to have them.' He told me once, 'You know a Jew is an individual that kicks you down in the gutter but you've got to have them. He

---

* Journalist and historian Ron Rosenbaum, author of *Explaining Hitler* (1998), calls Henry Ford "one of the most vile and repulsive figures in American history . . . the spiritual godfather of mass murder." Rosenbaum contends that while Ford never advocated the extermination of Jews, the industrialist unknowingly played a key role in shaping Hitler's views, rhetoric, and policy. The conveyor belts at Highland Park and the Rouge led indirectly to the "industrialization of killing perfected in the death camps, the mass production of death by assembly line." The Ford Motor Company, anxious to remove the taint of anti-Semitism, later destroyed files relating to the *Dearborn Independent*. In 2000, after considerable internal debate, the company announced a $13 million contribution to a German fund established to compensate former slave laborers from the Nazi era, including those forced to work at Ford's manufacturing plant in Cologne. Most of the forced laborers at the Cologne plant were non-Jews from Eastern Europe. In making the donation, the company rejected all implications of guilt and responsibility, pointing out the Cologne plant had been seized by the Nazis and was thus out of the control of Dearborn from the spring of 1942 until the war's end three years later.

keeps the white man going.' He never explained that this was food for thought. He would make a remark like that just out of a blue sky, and leave you to put your own interpretations on it."

In the summer of 1938, as Detroit Tigers slugger Hank Greenberg was fending off vile anti-Semitic attacks from enemy dugouts and "radio priest" Father Charles Coughlin was denouncing Jewish bankers in his national broadcasts from Royal Oak, Michigan, Henry would celebrate his seventy-fifth birthday by accepting the Service Cross of the German Eagle from Detroit's German vice-consul. It was the highest decoration Nazi Germany could bestow on a noncitizen. To his detractors, his acceptance appeared to validate widespread charges that he was in some way an active conspirator in Hitler's rise to power—accusations that, while unsubstantiated, have never completely gone away.

How contrite was Ford when he issued his apology, reportedly the first public retraction of anti-Semitism in history? Not very, if at all. He was a product of his times, and his prejudices—buttressed by the bigotry demonstrated daily in the world around him—resisted easy enlightenment.

"I don't know as Mr. Ford ever apologized for anything," Liebold said later. "Of course, he was supposed to have apologized to the Jews, but I think everybody knows about that. He never even read that or never even knew what it contained. He simply told them to go ahead and fix it up."

# 12

⮎‿⮌

# The Little Man
# in the Basement

*We Nominate for Our Own Hall of Fame . . . Harry H. Bennett. Because
as head of the Personnel Department of the Ford Motor Company, he has
a more direct influence over the destinies of more men than anybody else
in Detroit. Briefly, his job might be described as that of "trouble shooter."
His specialty is preventing the tenancy of round holes by square pegs.*

—Detroit Athletic Club News

**M**ark Beltaire, the longtime "Town Crier" columnist of the *Detroit Free Press*, recalled a party he once attended at the fashionable Book-Cadillac Hotel in downtown Detroit.

"There was a lot of drinking going on up in the suites," he said. "When I went to the men's room, I stumbled over a body."

It was Harry Bennett, passed out drunk. That is, Beltaire and everybody else who gingerly stepped around the crumpled heap *thought* the legendary security chief of the Ford Motor Company was drunk. "I heard later that he had a habit of doing that so he could listen in on conversations," said Beltaire.

Any man who would play possum on the floor of a public lavatory deserves to be taken seriously. Bennett most certainly was. For the better part of a quarter-century, the stocky little man with the trademark bowtie and tattooed forearms flexed a muscle far out of proportion to his five-foot-five frame. "Do you really want to get rid of Hitler?" Henry

Harry Bennett
in 1932.

Ford asked an Englishman on the eve of World War II. "I'll send Harry over with six of his men. They'll get rid of Hitler for you in no time."

Bennett did all sorts of odd jobs for Ford, who liked his belligerence and his loyalty. "Many times in critical situations," Bennett recalled, "his attitude was: 'Harry, let's you and him have a fight.'" As corporate gangster, Bennett roamed the hallways and back alleys of the Ford empire practically at will, turning Henry's whimsy into policy with the kind of head-cracking efficacy the industrialist had found lacking in Edsel. "I became his most intimate companion," Bennett bragged years later, "closer to him even than his own son."

In a very real sense, Harry Bennett was the son Henry Ford never had. Bennett, two years older than Edsel, was an Ann Arbor native whose father had been killed in a fight when Harry was an infant. "I'd always wished I were a big man and all my life I took on jobs that were meant for a man bigger than I," recalled Bennett, who ran off and joined the navy when he was seventeen. He traveled the world, doing a little boxing, a little diving, a little illustrating for a service magazine, and lots of carousing.

Fittingly, it was a brawl that accounted for Bennett's introduction to Ford. One day in 1916, Arthur Brisbane came across Bennett battling another sailor at the customs house in New York. The Hearst journalist, master of the sensationalistic and the absurd, happened to be on his way to see Ford at the company's Manhattan sales office. He evidently saw the makings of a great story in bringing together the Flivver King and the pugnacious sailor, who was between hitches. A feature or column never materialized, but an odd relationship did: Henry, impressed by the way Bennett handled himself, invited him to Dearborn. He was looking for a tough guy to help with security at the Rouge plant, then under construction.

Bennett became Henry's "eyes and ears" at the Rouge, providing him with odd bits of information and gossip. "He wanted the lowdown on what was going on," said Bennett, who began accompanying Ford on impromptu factory tours. The big boss would approach workers at random, talking to each about his background, his job, and asking whether he had any complaints. "As often as not, the man had something to say," remembered Bennett. "When they were through talking, Mr. Ford would tell the man, 'Now, if you hear anything else, just call me on the phone.' I got a laugh out of that, because he was about as easy to reach on the phone as the President of the United States."

Bennett was placed in charge of the Rouge Employment Office in 1921, and he quickly abolished the Sociology Department. He also took over the Service Department. "Ford Service" had originally been created to provide plant security during World War I, when industrial saboteurs and spies were very real concerns. Under Bennett, the Service Department grew into the world's largest private security force: some 3,000 plug-uglies recruited from local gyms, college football teams, and prisons. Stooges were everywhere, peeping even into Edsel's design department.

Bennett was accountable to no one but Ford. This meant that not even Charlie Sorenson (who he got along with) or Ernest Liebold (who he didn't) could fire him. When the Rouge was shut down for several months to retool for the Model A, Ford and Bennett became daily companions; thereafter, Bennett would be one of Henry's top lieutenants. Ford would normally call Bennett at home early every morning to arrange a meeting for later that day, where they would talk over whatever was on the auto king's mind. Henry so rarely visited his own office in the Rouge Administration Building it was practically a movie set; he preferred going into the basement and hanging out in Bennett's office instead. Although Henry often met the press and visiting dignitaries here, more often it served as his hideaway. It had a private outside entrance near the garage, allowing him to slip in and out without being harassed by reporters, salesmen, autograph hounds, crackpots, and company executives. It also had a small gun range, giving Ford and Bennett—both dead shots—a chance to plink targets with their .32-caliber pistols while discussing that day's business. Occasionally Henry would tire of shooting at the box and fire at an overhead light fixture. "Let's wake Cowlings up!" he'd say, referring to the sales manager who occupied the office directly above.

The service chief pandered to Henry's fear of kidnapping, a crime as common in the 1920s as carjacking is today. Bennett's men shadowed Edsel's children when they went to school and also provided discreet protection for the adult members of the family. To keep on top of any potential threats to the family, Bennett forged links with different underworld types, getting involved in various escapades that Henry, relaxing inside Bennett's office, enjoyed hearing about. On one occasion, a shotgun blast blew out the windshield of Bennett's car as he drove home from the Rouge. During another attempt on his life, his car was rammed, sending him to the hospital with severe injuries.

Ford, the beneficiary of much positive publicity over the years for hiring and trying to rehabilitate ex-convicts, had "a profound morbid interest in crime and criminals," explained Bennett. "He also had a deep sympathy with them. He used to dream of a day when there would be no jails, and he was violently opposed to capital punishment. Whenever we hired a former criminal, Mr. Ford always wanted to come to my office and talk with him.

"He'd say, 'Now, how did you get into this?' And then, sometimes before the man would have a chance to answer, he'd say, 'I'll bet a woman got you into it.' That was his theory of crime—he always looked for a woman at the bottom of the trouble. He liked to say, 'I can tell a man who has a good wife by the way he's getting along.'"

According to Jo Gomon, who first met Bennett in 1931 when she was executive secretary for Detroit mayor Frank Murphy, the most important item in Bennett's austere office was not in sight. "It was a dictaphone," she said. "Every conversation was recorded. It was his chief source of information. Whenever a group asked him for funds or favors, it was customary for him to leave the room on one pretext or another. He then retired to an adjoining office and got the real lowdown on the situation later by listening to the recording of the group discussing it among themselves."

Bennett was undeniably colorful, once shooting a foul-smelling cigar out of the mouth of a visitor who refused his request to put it out. He kept lions and tigers as pets on his Ann Arbor estate, a medieval-looking structure with turrets and hidden stairwells known locally as "the castle." Once one of the big cats escaped and prowled Detroit for several nights before winding up in the Dearborn police station; inquiring about the animal's return, its owner was informed the lion had "hanged himself." Bennett was an above-average artist, a capable horseman, and he could play several musical instruments. Anne Morrow Lindbergh, taken with the service chief's charm, thought him "a troubadour." Aware of his position in the company, Bennett dressed fashionably but practically. He always wore long-sleeved shirts to cover up the garish tattoos—a ship, anchor, flowers, eagle, Indian head, and the inscription "Sempre Fidelis" among them—that he'd acquired in Cuba, New York, and Paris. And he always wore bowties because, as he explained, a four-in-hand could be grabbed in a fight. "I fought too much," he said as an old man, examining his misshapen knuckles in front of a visitor. All had been broken in brawls. "It's a wonder I didn't get killed in some of the fights I've had."

For most of his career with Ford, Bennett was not on the company payroll. In the absence of a regular paycheck, Liebold, Henry's personal secretary and financial watchdog, occasionally dipped into the office safe and unhappily extracted $10,000 or so for Bennett. It was never enough, and Henry dreaded Liebold's disapprobation, so every once in a while he quietly gave Bennett the title to one of the many farms he owned; the service chief would then sell the property for a healthy infusion of cash into his bank account. This form of compensation, while unusual, allowed Bennett to live—and entertain—in style. He owned several recreational properties, where he often threw stag parties for his cronies or company guests, including a 2,800-acre hideaway in Clare County, Michigan. He also had access to three Ford yachts.

As long as Bennett did Henry's bidding, he had the old man's complete backing. It took him several years, however, to get a handle on what Ford expected of him. "Harry," he once told him, "never try to outguess me."

"You mean I should never try to understand you?"

"Well," said Ford, "that's close enough."

"What he meant, I eventually realized, was that he expected me to carry out his wishes without probing for his motives," Bennett reflected

Bennett and his third wife, Esther, inside Bennett's office shortly after their marriage in December 1936.

years later. "Mr. Ford always had a motive for everything he did; usually he had two motives—the one he gave, and the real one. He didn't want me digging into that too far."

✧

Nowhere was the difference between Henry Ford's "good" son and "bad" surrogate son more pronounced than in the area of labor relations. As organizing efforts stepped up in the 1930s, Edsel favored a conciliatory approach. Bennett, with Henry's blessing, stressed intimidation.

"They were all rotten, no-good sons of bitches," exclaimed Al Bardelli, who despite his advanced age practically flew off the couch inside his Dearborn home when asked about Bennett's goons. Bardelli first entered the Rouge as a teenager in 1927. He recalled with bitterness how armed Service Department men used to follow him home, to the market, and to union meetings in hopes of intimidating him. "You couldn't go take a crap without one of the bastards following you into the rest room. No doors on the stalls. Take too long and you were out of a job."

"Everybody was just scared to death of Bennett," said manufacturing superintendent Albert Smith, who during his years on the shop floor saw Service Department men regularly usurp his and other supervisors' authority. "All [a service man] would do is turn in the guy's [badge] number to Bennett and Bennett would send an order out to fire the guy. That went on a lot. You would have no authority over it. . . . Actually, they were taking control of our personnel. Very often I would get names and numbers of men to fire from Bennett's office. There were times when the guy would ask me, 'What for?' And I wouldn't even know for what reason I was firing him. I was just following instructions."

Edsel had come to understand at the hand of his own father something of the petty tyranny Bennett's service men practiced on the shop floor. Henry loved his only child, but as the years slipped away he began to feel he'd had little success in molding a successor in his own crafty, hard-boiled image. He had great trouble accepting Edsel's urbane, sophisticated tastes, which ran counter to his in almost every way. Edsel liked reading *The New Yorker* and Kipling; Henry slapped his bony knee over *Little Orphan Annie* cartoons and cornball jokes. Edsel smoked Camels and drank highballs; Henry was a teetotaler who did not allow tobacco of any kind on company property. Edsel was a philanthropist; Henry didn't believe in charity. Other points of contention revolved around industry issues. Edsel, for example, wanted to develop an eight-cylinder car; Henry contended that "a motor car should not have more spark plugs than a cow has teats." Time after time, Henry thwarted Edsel, sometimes in humiliating and brutal ways. On one occasion, having disagreed with Edsel's decision to construct some coke ovens at the Rouge, Henry waited until they were built, then had them demolished. During an executive meeting in which Edsel argued the competitive need for modern hydraulic brakes, Ford shouted, "Edsel, you shut up!" before storming out of the room.

Sitting inside his well-appointed president's office on "mahogany row" in the Administration Building, Edsel understood who the *real* head of the Ford Motor Company was. That was fine with him. He typically deflected reporters' inquiries with "See Father." When he did speak, observed the *Detroit News*, "it was not with the picturesque flourish that would make a tale to be told and retold, but with quiet understanding and reserve." In twenty-five years as president of the company, Edsel did not conduct a single business press conference.

For all his natural reticence, Edsel had an impact on the company's fortunes, even if the public didn't know it and his father didn't always appreciate it. His accomplishments went beyond his exceptional taste in design, which resulted in some of the finest looking automobiles ever to come out of the Motor City. He deserved credit for overseeing the Rouge's massive and complicated expansion between 1919 and 1925; he also was responsible for the day-to-day administration of the company's far-flung business concerns. He personally approved every piece of advertising and was intimately involved in such nonautomotive activities as radio and aviation.

Unlike his father, Edsel was a democrat, not an autocrat, patiently hearing out associates and weighing options before making an informed decision. But his low-key, nonconfrontational nature frustrated many around him. He "submerged his own interests to a very remarkable extent," said Stanley Ruddiman, general manager of the Ford-owned Detroit, Toledo & Ironton Railroad during the 1920s. "He said that the company had been founded by his father and that the growth was entirely due to his father's genius. . . . Although he was president of the company, he did not try to assert his views. He said he would not do so as long as his father lived. I don't think Edsel would do anything contrary to his father's views. I feel that it would have been better for the Ford Motor Company if Edsel had asserted his own ideas, because his ideas were sound and fair. I think if Edsel had taken a firmer stand, the affairs of the Ford Motor Company would have been much smoother during the last years Mr. Ford lived."

Far too often for the good of his company or his son, Henry played the role of the unenlightened despot. He arbitrarily canned executives loyal to Edsel, countermanded his directives, and ridiculed or simply ignored many of his suggestions. This was his version of tough love. In his opinion, the heir to the Ford empire was "too soft." He hoped these kinds of cruel put-downs would put some steel into Edsel's backbone. Instead, battles over Ernest Kanzler, the Model T, and the *Dearborn Independent* often brought on nausea, hives, and headaches.

"He had a way of getting his work done through fear," one longtime engineer said of Henry. "The loyalty that you had, you had because of Edsel. It was not because of Henry Ford. You really worked here, hoping and praying for the day when Edsel could be in charge. . . . When things would come up where his father would put a stop to something Edsel had done, there would be sort of a woebegone expression come over Edsel's face as if to say, 'Well, what's the use.' There was a feeling of utter futility and a defeated attitude."

Despite the belittlement and frustration, Edsel remained loyal and respectful. Edsel "was a gentleman in the finest, fullest sense of the word," said Charlie Sorenson, whose attitude toward Henry's son softened over the years. "I never heard anyone who knew him speak of him except in the highest terms."

Unless, of course, the person talking was Harry Bennett.

Troubleshooter and troubadour, raconteur and racketeer, Bennett gradually consolidated his power. By 1930, the little man in the basement was widely considered to be among the half-dozen most powerful men at the company. Even Sorenson, Liebold, and others thought to be ahead of him on the organization chart (had the famously disorganized company actually had such a thing) thought it wise not to get on the wrong side of the service chief. Bennett, emboldened by his growing influence with Henry Ford, didn't try very hard to conceal his contempt for the person he viewed as the greatest impediment to his secret ambition of someday running the company himself. In conversations with subordinates, Bennett occasionally referred to the company's frail and sensitive crown prince not as Edsel but as "the weakling."

# 13

ᴄᴏᴏᴄ

## *Rearview Mirror*

# The Crown Prince
# at Work and at Play

*Jim Backus, a native Detroiter and an army veteran of the First World War, moved from the production line to a clerical position through the persistent pestering of his superiors and some evening classes in accounting. His twenty years inside Edsel Ford's office, beginning in 1923, gave him an intimate view of the heir apparent to the Ford Motor Company.*

Shortly after I started to work in Mr. Edsel Ford's office, he received an extortion letter threatening his sons, Henry II and Benson, with bodily harm unless a certain sum of money was left in a church. To my surprise, Mr. Harry Bennett called me to his office and asked if I would be willing to pose as Mr. Edsel Ford and deliver the ransom money demanded. I agreed and accordingly was instructed as to what I was to do.

A dummy box of money about the size of a shoe box was given to me, and with a chauffeur driving me in a big Lincoln I was driven to the particular church where I deposited the box on the pew as directed in the letter. Of course, detectives were planted all through the church and my every movement was carefully guarded. The writer of the letter was watching the events through the window of an adjacent bar and was apprehended. His name was Vaclac Simek. It was necessary for me to testify at this fellow's trial and I was complimented on being a good witness.

Harry Bennett is no champion of mine, but I do believe one thing: regardless of all the lousy things he may have done, he certainly must be given credit for protecting Mr. Edsel Ford's children to the extent that no harm came to them.

On numerous occasions I would meet Mr. and Mrs. Edsel Ford at the Michigan Central Depot in Detroit and they would have me accompany Henry II and Benson back to their school in New York. Whereas I would be keeping an eye on the children, Harry Bennett had his men on the same train watching all three of us. I distinctly remember one occasion when we left the Grand Central Station in New York by automobile and Henry II, looking back, remarked, "Here come those rats now." He was referring to Bennett's men, who were trailing our car.

This guy Bennett had ways of finding out anything he wanted to know. While I was in Florida with Mr. and Mrs. Edsel Ford at Ormond Beach, I decided to visit some of my relatives at St. Augustine one evening after Mr. Ford no longer needed my services. Well, as I happened to be carrying a money belt with considerable cash of Mr. Ford's, I packed a .32-caliber revolver. Upon returning to Detroit a month or two later, Mr. Ford called me in and reprimanded me for having a gun. How he knew I'll never know, but I'm sure Bennett had someone search my room because the gun was never in evidence.

Mr. A. J. Lepine was Mr. Edsel Ford's personal secretary and handled all the personal accounting, as well as correspondence. I was his assistant. A Mr. John Crawford had an office adjoining Mr. Ford's, and as I recall Mr. Ford gave him the title of assistant to the president during the Christmas season of 1923. Mr. Ernest Kanzler, Mr. Edsel Ford's brother-in-law, had an office adjacent to Mr. Crawford's. I can't recall whether or not he had a title, but he certainly had plenty to do with running the company, although Mr. Sorenson and Mr. P. E. Martin were Mr. Henry Ford's factory executives. Mr. Kanzler and Mr. Edsel Ford apparently got along well. They went places together, bought adjacent properties, they played tennis, squash rackets and golf together.

Everyone knew that Kanzler was Mr. Edsel Ford's brother-in-law and had obtained his job through Mr. Ford, or supposed to, and it was the consensus of opinion that this did not set well with the senior Mr. Ford. This is all conjectural on my part as I had never heard any comments from Mr. Edsel Ford to the effect that his father did not like Mr.

Kanzler. Everyone was also of the opinion that whereas Mr. Edsel Ford was president, any company decisions he might make were controlled by the elder Mr. Ford's rulings.

My first real exciting trip with the Ford family was in 1926. We went to Europe on the *Acquitania*. There were Mr. and Mrs. Edsel Ford and their friends from Connecticut, the Buell Heminways. On this trip Mr. Ford had me get calling cards printed, "Assistant Secretary." My duties were to take care of all Mr. and Mrs. Ford's personal wants, including twenty-six pieces of baggage, getting reservations, making dinner dates, paying all bills, etc. We went to France, England and Italy.

Mr. Ford's interest on this trip was to get furnishings for his new home in Gaukler Pointe, Michigan; also buying ancient rooms of paneling, Cotswold stone, slate, etc., for construction, as well as to inspect the various European plants.

Our tour started in London. From there we went to Paris, and from Paris we drove to Monte Carlo. I took the baggage on the train from Monte Carlo to Florence, Italy, where I waited about ten days while Mr. and Mrs. Ford and a Dr. Valentiner, curator of the Detroit Institute of Arts, drove up.

In Florence, Mr. and Mrs. Ford purchased several very expensive art objects for their new home. It was my duty to pay for them and I distinctly remember one amusing instance in carrying out this duty. It seems the taxi drivers in the cities on the continent get commissions from merchants for bringing foreigners into their establishments, provided a purchase is made. In paying for the particular sculpture which Mr. Ford purchased, our taxi driver tried to collect a commission but was informed that the merchant had already paid a commission to the art curator that had accompanied Mr. Ford on his shopping tour. I'm sure Mr. Ford never knew this. At least I never told him.

Mr. and Mrs. Edsel Ford were wonderful people to work for. At times Mr. Ford could be stern, but he was tolerant and seldom stayed cross for very long. I remember the night he asked me to buy adhesive tape so that he could tape up his back. It seems he had injured his back while driving one of his race boats and on occasions his back would pain him severely. I completely forgot this request and he called me on the telephone and asked me if I had the tape. This was during the early morning hours. Well, I just got dressed and scoured all Paris until I finally found someone who could understand English and knew what adhesive tape was. It was embarrassing to have to admit to

Mr. Ford that I had forgotten his order and he was certainly entitled to give me a damn good bawling out. However, gentleman that he was, he didn't even scold me. Believe me, I know now that adhesive tape in French is *taffeta anglais*.

Another instance when I deserved a bawling out and didn't get one was when Mr. Ford asked me on the *Acquitania* to get Mrs. Ford some white flowers. There just weren't any white flowers to be had so when I returned to his suite and rapped on the door, I understood somebody say, "Come in." Upon opening the door, I caught Mrs. Ford partially dressed. She hollered and ran through a door. The boss came out and just laughed like the deuce. He thought it was a good joke.

Yes, Mr. Edsel Ford was a swell individual and in my twenty-seven years with the Ford Motor Company I have never heard anyone say anything different. The only fault I could ever find with the man was that he did not understand the problems of his employees with reference to salaries. My criticism is based on the fact that clerical help in Bennett's office was receiving much larger salaries than I was and didn't have one-half the responsibility. Mr. Ford didn't seem to realize that, as his representatives, we had to dress better than average and entertain beyond our means.

At tax time each year beginning in January, we were required to work night after night to get out all Mr. Ford's returns and I can't remember an instance when we asked for an extension of time. There were about twenty or so returns to get out. There were income returns for all the family, fiduciary returns for all the children, gift tax returns, and hundreds of schedules to type up. I assembled all the figures, typed all the schedules, made all the extensions, after which I checked them with Mr. Lepine and then turned them over to a tax expert for further checking. Mr. Ford never knew about all this overtime or he probably would have done something about it. There were plenty of other occasions when I was required to work half the night and then got the dickens because I didn't get in by 8:30 A.M. That was when I had charge of some large party at the Ford residence and had to see that the entertainers got there on time and left after the party was over.

During my employment with Mr. Ford the unexpected was always happening. For instance, he had a new yacht built in Boston costing $300,000. During its trial run to New York the captain ran it on the shoals. It was a bad accident and Captain Anderson was brought before the Marine Trial Board and had his license suspended for awhile. One

Edsel and Henry share a laugh. "Yes, Mr. Edsel Ford was a swell individual."

man drowned and a representative from the New York firm that did the furnishings broke his leg.

On another occasion a burglar broke into the Jefferson Avenue residence and got away with a rope of pearls valued at around $80,000. The fabulous prices Mr. Ford had to pay for jewelry was always a wonderment to me. For instance, the above string of pearls was altered on one occasion. Four large pearls were added at a cost of $16,000 whereas Mr. Ford was allowed only a credit of $1,510 for the ones removed.

Concerning Mr. Ford's interest in the banks during the bank holiday, all I can say is that he was very much financially involved and was obligated to put up hundreds of thousands of dollars of his own securities to protect the Union Guardian Trust Company's solvency. I do know from personal experience that at the outset funds were poured in to try to keep the stock from going below $105 per share. That's when I got smart and bought what I could afford, as I assumed it was at the bottom and I would be able to make a nice profit. It didn't work and I lost all my investment.

Mr. Ford was very depressed and grumpy during this period. Like everyone else, he had to cut expenses at his various residences to the bone. At Gaukler Pointe, his year-round residence, a great number of employees were laid off. Normally there would be approximately twenty-five gardeners. As I recall, the number was reduced to four or five. Watchmen, boatmen, engineers and all the household staff were reduced to a minimum.

Mr. Ford had a very large home at Seal Harbor, Maine, where the family usually spent a month or so each summer. The help at this location consisted of a superintendent, a few gardeners, and a couple of maids. The watchmen, butlers, personal maids and cooks were taken from Gaukler Pointe each season. Riding horses were shipped from Haven Hill Farm either by railway car or sometimes by horse van, accompanied by Jim Lavender, the groom.

Of all the places Mr. Ford owned, I believe he got the most pleasure out of his Haven Hill Farm, where he would spend weekends in the summer and wintertime. Considerable effort was put forth to try to make this a paying farm, but with high salaries for farm managers, etc., and very expensive buildings, it didn't work out. There was a tax advantage, however.

Haven Hill was built of logs hauled down from the Ford Motor Iron Mountain plant in Michigan's Upper Peninsula. The shingles were hand-made and pine needles were bagged and brought down to spread on the paths around the cabin. A dam was built across a small stream on the property and formed a large lake, giving the 3,000 acres two lakes, there being an original one on the property called Teeple Lake. A friend of Mr. Ford's by the name of Robert Derrick built the buildings. Haven Hill was so well secluded that it was the one location where Mr. Ford wasn't bothered too much.

As a result of the depression, Mr. Ford acquired another place called the Book Estate, located at Wing Lake, Michigan. Mr. Ford's generosity with his friends got him into this deal, I am sure. Mr. Frank Book was hit quite hard by the depression and Mr. Ford gave him $200,000 for the place, which was in really bad condition. He also paid Book approximately $27,000 for the furnishings. I don't believe Mr. Ford was ever in the place after he bought it. A few years later he disposed of it for about the price he paid for the furnishings.

The last home that Mr. Ford built, I believe, was at Hobe Sound, Florida. Inasmuch as I was never there, I can't say much about it. Mr. Ernest Kanzler built a place adjacent. Prior to building at Hobe Sound, Mr. Ford would send his captain south with his houseboat, the *Onika*, on which they would live. On two occasions they tied up at Ormond

A 1930s postcard of the Edsel Fords' summer home in Maine, called "Skylands."
Its present owner is Martha Stewart.

Beach. I was fortunate enough to accompany Mr. and Mrs. Ford on one
of these winter trips and had wonderful accommodations at the Ormond
Beach Hotel. My duties did not include looking after the children. This
was done by either the watchmen or the governess. I would make
appointments for dinner dates, get reservations and run whatever
errands Mr. or Mrs. Ford desired. I also handled the correspondence.

During my entire employment with Mr. Ford, I got the biggest
kick out of handling his party arrangements. These parties were usually for the children, such as birthday parties, coming-out parties, etc.
Mr. Ford would book name orchestras and get entertainment, such as
singers, dancers, musicians, etc., through a booking agency. The orchestras were generally the ones that were the most popular at the time.
Once he had Glen Gray and another time Tommy Dorsey. On these
occasions I was required to wear a dinner jacket and was liaison man
for Mr. and Mrs. Ford, doing such things as getting the music started at
the right time and relaying messages for Mr. Ford.

The most elaborate event staged by Mr. and Mrs. Ford was the fiftieth wedding anniversary for Mr. and Mrs. Henry Ford. Entire buildings
were built temporarily to house huge ranges and kitchen equipment.
Walter Doran Teague of New York handled the decorations. A most
embarrassing moment at this party was the dripping of large candles

on all the guests' dinner clothes. Big fans had been installed in the art gallery to take off the excessive heat which the candles would create. However, somebody miscalculated, and the candles which were hanging from the ceiling in large candelabra bent double, even though they were made specially to avoid such a happening. It was finally necessary to put out all the candles, but only after a great many dinner jackets had wax on them. We ushered the unfortunate guests to the kitchen where the maids would take out the wax by a hot iron on paper. While it was always assumed that Mr. Henry Ford was much opposed to liquor, I recall Mr. Edsel telling me at this particular party, "I think I'd better give Grandfather a little wine."

Another interesting job Mr. Ford gave me was the time he and Mr. Phelps Newberry rented a private railroad car for themselves and friends to take them to Ann Arbor for the Michigan-Yale football game. J. Edgar Hoover, Harvey Firestone Jr., and Frederick Stearns were on the train as guests. All the seats were taken so I was forced to stand up all the way down and back. I spent my time leaning against the window near the washroom and Mr. Ford came back to visit me a couple times. On each occasion he asked me if I had a highball, so we had a couple together. He sure was one heck of a nice guy.

Phelps Newberry had brought a gross of two-ounce whiskey bottles aboard and it was one of my duties to hand them out so that everyone would be sure to have a drink during the game. It was an unusually cold day and Mr. Ford got a big laugh out of the fact that I had two overcoats on. Everyone else had fur coats or fur-lined coats.

I don't believe that Mr. and Mrs. Henry Ford attended very many of Mr. Edsel's parties. Usually the invited guests were friends from Grosse Pointe Shores and New York City. One thing that seemed surprising was that Mr. Ford did not entertain any of his Ford Motor Company executives. I do remember that on our trip to Europe he brought back about a dozen Dunhill lighters initialed with the various executives' names. For some reason or other they were never handed out and remained in his desk drawer at the office for years. It may be that upon arriving home he discovered that his father, through Harry Bennett, had discharged an executive without his knowledge, disturbing him to the point that he didn't care about handing out any gifts. I believe it was at the time Mr. Kanzler was released, but I am not too clear on this point.

Constant happenings like this, I am sure, affected Mr. Ford's health because we in the office could notice that he was more irritable.

I do know that Mr. Ford was very conscientious and thorough in his work. He usually got to the office about 9 o'clock after an hour's drive from Grosse Pointe. While riding he would look over his mail or company matters. His lunch period might have been a little longer than most of ours, but this was due to the fact that Mr. Henry Ford would invite several department heads to the Ford Laboratory for lunch. This invitation was actually an order, from what I could learn. Mr. Ford would return to the office after lunch and usually stay until 4:30 or later. There were plenty of times we had to stay past 5 o'clock until Mr. Ford left. He had considerable correspondence with the foreign plant managers, especially Lord Perry in England, and he didn't depend on his office executives to do this for him. His letters were concise and to the point and he certainly could express himself.

There were times when Mr. Ford would shut his door to the washroom, in which he had a leather couch, and would not wish to be disturbed. He was not too strong a man and probably tired easily. The first time he was away for illness and returned to the office, we were required to get crackers and milk for him from the cafeteria.

I don't recall Mr. Edsel Ford's reaction during the period of labor union problems nor did I ever hear him express his disapproval of Harry Bennett publicly or otherwise. Everyone had the idea that he did not care for Bennett and his group, but it was second guessing. He certainly must have resented the fact that Bennett had so much power with the elder Mr. Ford, but I am sure it was through the respect he had for his father that he just took it on the chin and said nothing.

What he should have done—and this is just my personal opinion—is to have taken his dough out of the company and quit. I am sure he would have lived a lot longer.

# 14

⤜∘⤛

# Airships and Time Machines

*The next time you come to Detroit you should bring your airship with you.*
—Henry Ford to zeppelin pilot Dr. Hugo Eckner, 1924

A viation was one of the few fields of interest outside automaking that bound Henry and Edsel in the years following the First World War. The pure romance of flight spoke to the artist in Edsel, who, along with his more practical father, also recognized a fledgling industry ripe with commercial possibilities. Both men greatly admired the personal courage involved in manned flight, an activity that was so precarious Henry discouraged his son and other important company officials from flying, even as he annually spent hundreds of thousands of dollars in advertising and promotions extolling its safety to the public.

Unlike the U.S. auto industry, which by 1920 saw most of its major players firmly based in Detroit, making the boom town of a million souls the undisputed motorcar capital, there was no logical center of gravity for American aviation. One could as easily make the case that St. Louis was the crossroads of flight as Long Island or San Diego. The Fords reasoned that Detroit could—and should—be the airship city. Certainly, much of what was needed was already in place: manufacturing expertise, facile mechanical and engineering minds, deep pools of investment capital. The only thing missing was corporate leadership, and Henry provided that in 1925 with the $1.3 million acquisition of the Stout Metal Airplane Company, a small-scale enterprise he and

Edsel (a shareholder and director) had been closely observing for several years.

William B. Stout, the head of Packard's aircraft division during the war, had already built the first successful all-metal commercial airplane in the country, the *Maiden Detroit*. Arguably a better salesman and idea man than engineer, Stout correctly foresaw the day when traveling by air would be as safe and routine as walking to the corner dime store. At the time, only barnstormers, crop dusters, air mail and military pilots regularly took to the sky, and they flew single-engine aircraft made of wood and canvas. The nascent use of lightweight metal and multiple engines promised to make flying safer and more reliable.

William Benson Mayo, a self-educated engineer who had been in charge of several large construction projects for Ford, including the Rouge complex, was made president of the Ford Motor Company's newest division. Mayo and Edsel had long been active members of the Detroit Aviation Society. They were close friends (Edsel is thought to have named his second son Benson after Mayo) and were instrumental in convincing Stout to sell his promising but chronically underfinanced company.

As part of the agreement that brought Stout into the fold, Henry built an airport on several hundred acres of land he owned near Oakwood Boulevard in west Dearborn (next to the company's new Engineering Laboratory) and a factory for the expected mass production of airplanes. A hangar capable of accommodating twenty planes—the biggest yet built—was constructed. (Anticipating a brighter future for dirigibles than actually materialized, he also erected the world's largest permanent mooring mast. The 210-foot-high steel tower wound up being used only twice, both by military airships in 1926.) Along one of the grass runways the 200-foot-high letters F O R D were spelled out with crushed stone and could be seen from 10,000 feet up. Over the winter of 1928–29, the airport became the first to switch from grass to concrete runways, an innovation that the Smithsonian Institute later called Ford's most important contribution to aviation.

It was Stout's impression that, of the two Fords, it was Henry who was most interested in aviation, though he often uncharacteristically deferred to Edsel. "Well, this is for the new generation, not for mine," Henry would say. "I'm too old to take this. You go see Edsel."

Edsel, who as a teenager had once built an experimental aircraft with a Model T engine, had a broad knowledge of aviation, but he didn't mind acquiescing to the experts. "Well, Father won't let me fly," he'd tell Stout, "so I have no basis to judge whether this is good or not and you have; so go ahead and do what you want."

Under the supervision of Stout and Mayo, a high-wing, corrugated metal aircraft with three air-cooled 1,260-horsepower Pratt & Whitney engines was designed, tested, and placed in production. The Ford Tri-Motor was extremely adaptable. It could be used to haul freight, passengers, or the mail. Twin floats made it into a seaplane, or it could be equipped with skis for work in snow and ice. Wags, taking their cue from Ford's similarly all-purpose Tin Lizzie, dubbed the Tri-Motor the "Tin Goose." At its peak in the summer of 1929, the aircraft factory employed more than 1,400 workers and upward of twenty-five planes were being built every month. The twelve-passenger planes were sold to airlines around the world for between $40,000 and $60,000 each. Trans World Airlines alone had twenty-five Tri-Motors in its fleet during the 1930s.

Ford Airport was for years one of the world's busiest airfields, open to any class of aircraft, civilian or military. Although no pilot flew in the dark by choice, the field was equipped with powerful floodlights for emergencies. For a while it was open seven days a week, until Clara complained to Henry one Sunday that the sound of aircraft over the Fords' nearby Fair Lane estate was disturbing what was supposed to be a day of peace. From then on, Ford Airport observed the Sabbath and planes were forced to use alternative landing sites. Beginning in 1925, the one-plane Ford Air Transportation Service made regularly scheduled round trips between Dearborn and Chicago, delivering company mail and auto parts. More Tri-Motors were soon added and service was extended to Cleveland and Buffalo. In early 1926, Ford planes started carrying U.S. mail to Chicago and Cleveland from Detroit, marking the first domestic airmail flights by a private carrier. To accommodate the growing number of air travelers, a passenger terminal was built in 1927. The Dearborn Inn, one of the first airport hotels, opened across the street in 1931. Symbolic of the generational strife that increasingly characterized their relationship, Henry and Edsel clashed over the decor of the buildings. Edsel argued that a cutting-edge industry such as aeronautics required modern design, while Henry stubbornly insisted on an early American motif, which was more in line with the historical museum he was building nearby. In a rare compromise, Henry got his way with the inn and Edsel was free to decorate the terminal as he saw fit.

Henry Ford and Charles Lindbergh at Ford Airport in August 1927.

Charles Lindbergh visited Ford Airport for three days in August 1927, three months after his solo transatlantic flight from New York to Paris in the *Spirit of St. Louis* had transformed him into an international celebrity on a par with the Flivver King himself. Like millions of others, Henry was inspired by Lindbergh's feat, an odyssey as fantastic and daring in its day as placing a man on the moon would be forty years later. "I am interested in large planes—real planes, planes that will carry 100 to 200 passengers, planes that will fly in any kind of weather, in any season of the year," Henry told the press shortly after Lindbergh's touch-down in Paris. "Planes that will go anywhere anytime. If one man can fly across the ocean, 100 men can be carried across the ocean with passenger planes."

Lindbergh was a native Detroiter who had learned how to drive in a Model T as a twelve-year-old on his father's Minnesota farm. With 75,000 worshippers at Ford Airport looking on, the "Lone Eagle" returned the favor, taking Henry and Edsel on their first airplane rides. The following year Lindbergh helped launch the first transcontinental air service, stocking the airline with Tri-Motors. It was the start of a long relationship between the Fords and Lindbergh and, with their famous names associated with commercial flight, the real beginnings of modern regularly scheduled airline travel in this country. The number of air passengers exploded from a mere 6,000 in 1925 to 450,000 six years later. Thousands of ordinary people, reassured by Ford's reputation

Cowboy-philosopher Will Rogers in the seat of an experimental "flivver" airplane.

for reliability, took their first commercial flight on a Tri-Motor. As Will Rogers, the era's most popular humorist and an unflagging booster of civil aviation, observed in his column: "Ford wouldent leave the ground and take to the air unless things looked good to him up there." Ironically, Henry went up in an airplane only three times during his entire life while Rogers, a frequent flyer, died in a plane crash in 1935.

Edsel's involvement with aviation shoved him into the spotlight for the first and only extended period of his life. In 1925 he donated $50,000 and a three-foot-high sterling silver trophy for an annual cross-country "reliability tour" that started and ended at Ford Airport. Looking to assist pilots, Edsel asked all Ford dealers to paint their garage roofs with a big northward-pointing arrow and the name of their town as navigational aids. The National Air Reliability Tour (which newspapers often called the Ford Reliability Tour) ended after seven years, but not before generating a tremendous amount of publicity for the company.

Edsel also was heavily involved in getting the polar flights of Admiral Richard Byrd off the ground. He donated $20,000 and a Tri-Motor to the 1926 expedition to the Arctic and $100,000 in cash and materials (including another plane) to Byrd's Antarctic venture three years later. Moreover, he convinced several influential friends, includ-

The cabin inside a Ford Tri-Motor seated a dozen passengers in cushioned wicker chairs.

ing John D. Rockefeller Jr., to open their wallets. "The whole thing would have been impossible without your backing and encouragement," Byrd wrote Edsel after the Arctic expedition. "I owe a great deal to a great many people, but I owe more to you than all the rest put together." Byrd was so grateful to his primary donor that, after the Tri-Motor slated for the 1926 flight to the North Pole was destroyed in a factory fire, he named the competing Dutch-built Fokker he was forced to fly the *Josephine Ford,* after Edsel's daughter. Following the expedition, Edsel then bought the Fokker to help erase the explorer's remaining debts. On Byrd's flight over the South Pole in November 1929, he named one newly discovered mountain range after Edsel and another mountain after Josephine. Edsel proudly displayed the American flag Byrd had carried over the Pole in his den at Gaukler Pointe.

Perhaps the most intriguing of all the Fords' aviation adventures was the unrealized dream of a "flivver plane," a reliable, affordable single-seat personal aircraft that Henry and Edsel thought might revolutionize travel in much the same way the Model T had. As aviation advanced in leaps and bounds during the period, it wasn't that far-fetched to envision a future when every house would come equipped with a garage and a hangar.

To that end a compact 35-horsepower monoplane, capable of reaching speeds of 85 miles per hour, was unveiled in the summer of 1926.

The experimental craft weighed only 320 pounds, had collapsible wings, and was just sixteen feet long. It was designed by a young engineer, Otto Koppen, who had been told by Henry he wanted a plane he could fit inside his office, and built by Jim Lynch, who in the past had made wooden speed boats for Edsel.

Four versions of the Ford flivver plane were built between 1926 and 1945, but the only men ever to fly one were Lindbergh (who took it for a spin during his 1927 visit) and the pilot who often was favorably compared to him, Harry Brooks. Brave, handsome, and unassuming, Brooks was one of Henry's personal favorites, rising from a $25-a-week riveter in his airplane factory to airmail pilot to $400-a-month chief test pilot in just two years. In many ways Brooks reminded Ford of his own background: a self-assured country boy with grease under his fingernails, one who didn't feel the need to smoke or drink to fit in with the crowd. Ford thought so much of Brooks he allowed him to use the flivver to fly every day between the airport and his suburban Detroit home.

One February day in 1928, Brooks took off from Ford Airport in the third version of the flivver, this one with a twenty-five-foot wingspan and weighing nearly twice as much as the original prototype. His goal was to reach Miami and set a new endurance record for class C light planes. Henry and a group of Ford dealers were waiting to greet him. But the planned celebration turned to ashes when Brooks, attempting to complete his flight after flying a record 972 miles nonstop from Dearborn to Titusville, Florida, crashed into the Atlantic. The wreckage was recovered but Brooks's body was never found.

Henry was shaken by Brooks's death. His interest in aviation sagged, though the degree to which the tragedy contributed to his subsequent withdrawal from the industry is usually overstated. By the end of the 1920s Ford's Aircraft Division had evolved into the largest manufacturer of commercial aircraft in the world. Then came the Great Depression and a corresponding nosedive in revenues. From a high of eighty-six planes sold in 1929, sales fell to just three in 1932. Henry, who had recouped less than half of the $11 million he poured into aviation, abruptly pulled the plug. He wanted to focus on his core business of making and selling cars, he said. In early 1933, the last of 196 Tri-Motors was built. Boeing and Douglas, two manufacturers who had been reluctant to challenge Ford's supremacy, quickly filled the void.

Ford Airport, with Tri-Motors in the foreground and the Edison Institute next door.

Today Ford Airport is the home of the company's test grounds; the hangar and airplane factory are devoted to experimental vehicles.*

The Ford Motor Company's contributions to aviation, while often overlooked, were significant enough to get Henry Ford posthumously enshrined in the National Aviation Hall of Fame in Dayton, Ohio. The assembly-line production of aircraft (to be perfected at Willow Run during World War II), the introduction of concrete runways, the perfecting of the radio beacon as a navigational tool, and the replacement of tail skids with brakes and tail wheels all had an impact on the industry. Although the company held numerous patents, Henry, anxious to

---

* According to William Stout, Charlie Sorenson's lack of enthusiasm played a key role in Ford's withdrawal from an industry the company was dominating. The man who kept cars spitting out of the Rouge "had little influence on it to start with. He came in and looked around, and I understand he took a little [airplane] ride one day and immediately was told not to come to the airport again by Henry Ford. He didn't like that, so since he couldn't have anything to do with the Airplane Division, he didn't want any Airplane Division. That's when the beginning of the end began to move in. . . . It's quite obvious that if the company had stayed in aviation and had pressed its advantage instead of quitting cold, they could have been in the highest position today in all of the aviation picture, both from operation and manufacture. I don't think the depression had anything to do with it."

advance the cause of aviation, directed that no royalties be collected on any of them. In William Stout's view, Henry's relatively brief but intense personal involvement was "more important than our building the Tri-Motor. I have often said that selling him on aviation was more valuable to the industry than the planes we assembled. It got America into the air industry and to see what was coming."

∽०∾

During the 1920s the "Colossus of Transportation" (as the *New York Tribune* dubbed Henry) began to earnestly pursue the re-creation of a past that his cars and planes were so instrumental in changing. At the same time Ford Airport was being laid out, 260 acres on the north side of the field were reserved for what would become an indoor-outdoor museum complex known as the Edison Institute (later renamed the Henry Ford Museum) and Greenfield Village. Over the course of the decade, and continuing well into the 1930s, he would spend several million dollars hunting down and buying relics of all types and sizes, from butter churns to entire buildings, and reassembling the fruits of his treasure hunt into an autobiographical homage to the candlelit America of his youth.

It was an interesting juxtaposition, the most modern private airport of the day adjacent to an irregular collection of early Americana. But the dichotomy of interests was entirely in keeping with Henry's split personality and evidence of an incessant internal tug-of-war. "If only Mr. Ford was properly assembled," mused Samuel Marquis, former head of the company's sociological program. "There rages in him an endless conflict between ideals, emotions and impulses as unlike as day and night—a conflict that makes one feel that two personalities are striving within him for mastery."

Henry was growing ambivalent about the changes modern machinery had wrought. The dream of providing personal mobility for the masses had had its unintended consequences, contributing to a gnawing sense of loss and melancholy in the sexagenarian tycoon. While the skies slowly filled up with flying machines, sales of the Model A, which reached their peak in 1929, added to the nation's increasingly congested downtowns and rural roadways. Between 1919 and 1929 the number of passenger cars in the United States jumped nearly fourfold, from 6,771,000 to a road-clogging 23,121,000. Roughly half of them were Fords. "And as [the automobile] came," observed journalist Frederick Lewis Allen in *Only Yesterday*, his 1931 book-length reflection on the 1920s, "it changed the face of America":

> Villages which had once prospered because they were "on the railroad" languished with economic anemia; villages on Route 61 bloomed with garages, filling stations, hot-dog stands, chicken-dinner restaurants, tearooms, tourists' rests, camping sites, and affluence. The interurban trolley perished, or survived only as a pathetic anachronism. Railroad after railroad gave up its branch lines, or saw its revenues slowly dwindling under the competition of mammoth interurban busses and trucks snorting along six-lane concrete highways. The whole country was covered with a network of passenger bus-lines. In thousands of towns, at the beginning of the decade a single traffic officer at the junction of Main Street and Central Street had been sufficient for the control of traffic. By the end of the decade, what a difference!—red and green lights, blinkers, one-way streets, boulevard stops, stringent and yet more stringent parking ordinances—and still a shining flow of traffic that backed up for blocks along Main Street every Saturday and Sunday afternoon. Slowly but surely the age of steam was yielding to the gasoline age.

A village "on the railroad" is precisely what Henry and his architect, Edward J. Cutler, wound up re-creating. Cutler was an artist and draftsman who worked on such varied projects as drawing illustrations for the *Dearborn Independent* and designing interiors for the Tri-Motor. For the mythical village of Greenfield (its name inspired by the community Clara Ford had grown up in), Ford acquired the 1858 Smith's Creek, Michigan, depot to service the private railroad he installed on the grounds. Greenfield Village was patterned after a typical New England town, with scores of transplanted buildings (and occasional reproductions) centered around a common green. The village green and Thomas Edison's Menlo Park complex (which had been moved there from New Jersey) became the anchors of the layout.

Ford was intimately involved with the design of Greenfield Village, modifying plans almost daily. "It was a relief for him to get down there," recalled Cutler. "For years he wouldn't let me have a telephone. When I would ask him about it, and I had a lot of running around to do, he would say, 'Oh, forget that stuff. I came down here to get away from that gang.'"

Henry's interest in historic preservation first became apparent in 1919, not long after his testimony during the *Chicago Tribune* trial held him up to national ridicule. When he learned that a road construction project threatened his Dearborn birthplace, he had the old farmhouse and barns moved 200 feet out of harm's way and restored. Looking to furnish his childhood home as accurately as possible, he and his aides fanned out, uncovering relics in attics, barns, and antique shops. He paid attention to the tiniest detail. Looking for the Starlight Stove Model 25 that had once heated the parlor, he and Edsel dug up old stoves buried all over the countryside. When, after an exhaustive search, he couldn't find an exact set of the family china, he had the dooryard excavated to a depth of six feet. Shards of broken plates were uncovered, allowing Henry to have the pattern custom matched.

Restoring his birthplace proved immensely satisfying to Ford, who had vowed to Ernest Liebold during the *Tribune* trial that he was "going to start up a museum and give people a *true* picture of the development of our country." His agents scoured every corner and crevice to satisfy what the papers called the "Ford craze" for technical and decorative objects. To dealers, Henry was that most valued of customers— an indiscriminate buyer for whom no price was too high. His shopping ultimately filled several warehouses. Scrubbing boards, milk bottles, saucepans, ploughs, and cigar-store Indians shared space with a $45,000 highboy, 500 spinning wheels, and one of every kind of shoe ever manufactured in the country.

He collected buildings like eight-year-old boys collected cigar bands. In 1923 he made headlines by buying and restoring the Wayside Inn in Southbury, Massachusetts, thus saving the storied 255-year-old structure. Eyeing the area as a potential site for the museum he was contemplating, he then bought up the surrounding 2,500 acres. That preservation effort alone cost more than $1.5 million. The following year he paid $100,000 for the Botsford Inn, sixteen miles outside Detroit, where he had danced as a young man. He spent an additional $336,000 renovating the 1836 structure, which he then used to host old-fashioned dance parties.

Those buildings stayed put. Once Ford had settled on his hometown as the place to erect his museum and village, others he bought were disassembled, each part carefully measured and numbered, then shipped to Dearborn, where they were just as meticulously pieced back together by Cutler's crews. The first of these was an 1854 general

One of Henry's early historical acquisitions was the old Redstone Schoolhouse of "Mary had a little lamb" fame. Ford had the 1798 building moved from Sterling, Massachusetts, to a site on the property he had bought surrounding the Wayside Inn in South Sudbury. The one-room schoolhouse reopened in 1927 with a reenactment that included a girl named Mary and a lamb.

store from Waterford, Michigan, which was raised off its foundation shortly after its purchase in August 1927, then re-erected the following winter. Next was an 1830s tavern from Clinton, Michigan, followed by Edison's Menlo Park research compound from West Orange, New Jersey, which had all but crumbled into dust. One by one, other structures that had figured in either national lore or Henry Ford's personal history were added. Here was the Illinois courthouse where Abraham Lincoln had once practiced law; over there was the jewelry store where Henry had once repaired watches. The one-room schoolhouse that Henry and his mother had attended was restored and became the cornerstone of a unique educational system on village grounds. Henry would visit the school nearly every morning for the rest of his life, listening to youngsters recite from the same *McGuffey's Eclectic Readers* he once had. Later he would import and restore William Holmes McGuffey's birthplace, just one more time machine that allowed him to exchange the pressures of the present for the pleasures of a less complicated past. Acquisitions would continue for several more years, bringing the total number of buildings to well past a hundred.

The Edison Institute, adjacent to the village, was the indoor component of the twin institutions. When completed at a cost of $5 million, the sprawling one-story museum featured fourteen acres of exhibition space given over to the most significant engines, tools, machines, and devices of the Industrial Age. The history of everything from cooking stoves and vacuum cleaners to baby buggies and banjo clocks was presented with a minimum of fuss. Even the lowly harrow received equal billing in this populist collection. Henry explained, "When I went to our American history books to learn how our forefathers harrowed the land, I discovered that the historians knew nothing about harrows. Yet our country has depended more on harrows than on guns and speeches. I thought that a history which excluded harrows and all the rest of daily life is bunk, and I think so yet." The installation of 350,000 square feet of teakwood flooring within would not be finished until 1938.

The exterior of the Edison Institute consisted of red-brick replicas of three of America's most recognizable historic landmarks: Independence Hall in the middle, flanked by Congress Hall and Philadelphia's Old City Hall. The facade had been suggested by Robert Derrick, a friend of Edsel's. The pace of hammering and sawing picked up when Ford announced he intended to dedicate his museum on October 21, 1929, the fiftieth anniversary of Edison's development of the incandescent lamp.

Henry Ford worshiped the very ground Thomas Edison walked on, going so far as to have seven railcar loads of clay shipped from the Menlo Park site to Dearborn. On one occasion prior to the village's opening, he gave a public relations official from General Electric a personal tour of the ongoing work. "That's Tom Edison's straight-shot privy from Menlo Park," he said proudly, pointing to the great man's outhouse.

Edison, the holder of more than 1,000 patents and the father of electric power, recorded sound, and moving pictures, had enthusiastically encouraged Ford to pursue his first automobile—a kindness Henry never forgot. In 1912 he commissioned Edison to design a battery, starting motor, and generator for the Model T (an order that, despite promised annual sales of $4 million, went unfulfilled). Away from the workbench, their conversations touched on common topics of interest: pacifism, reincarnation, the Jews. It was perhaps inevitable that the two men—self-taught Michigan farmboys and tireless tinkerers who embodied the practical American genius of technology—would become close friends despite the sixteen-year difference in age. Henry sent Edison a new Model T each year and took Clara to visit him at his home in Fort Myers, Florida. By then Edison and his wife, Mina, had already visited Fair Lane, where the inventor approvingly looked over the four-story power plant that Ford, disdainful of public utilities, had built on the property. Edison's free-spirited son, Charles, hit it off with Edsel and was the best man at his wedding to Eleanor Clay. For a while the two discussed going into business together. Edison was as irresponsible with his money as Charles was with his schooling, and from time to time Henry would find himself advancing money to the financially strapped inventor.

Each summer for several years after the war, Edison, Ford, naturalist John Burroughs, and industrialist Harvey Firestone—accompanied by a cadre of cooks, drivers, reporters, and photographers—embarked on a highly publicized camping trip in the Northeast. The self-styled "Vagabonds" didn't rough it in the traditional sense, wearing suits at breakfast and being chauffeured to rustic photo opportunities in a fleet of Packards and Cadillacs. But several days of communing with nature, however superficial, were restorative, especially for the chronically dyspeptic Edison, and strengthened bonds between the men.

As part of Ford's overall return to a form of rural primitivism during this period, he explored Edison's concept of "village industries," converting a score of old water-powered mills into small factories that employed local farmers during the winter. "Factory and farm should have been organized as adjuncts one of the other, and not as competitors," he explained. "With one foot in industry and one foot in agriculture, America is safe." Edison and Ford believed that cities—congested, unhealthy, and expensive to live in—had outgrown their original usefulness as manufacturing centers. Ford Farms, like the village industries, was a manifestation of that belief. About a hundred families lived and worked on small farms throughout southeastern Michigan, collectively working tens of thousands of acres of Ford-owned property. The company provided seed, livestock, and machinery and brought the resulting food products to market. Ford's village industries and farm collective were well-intentioned but impractical attempts at social engineering and, as was usually the case with Henry's nonautomotive interests, never came close to becoming self-supporting.

The "vagabonds" (*left to right*): inventor Thomas Edison, industrialist Harvey Firestone Jr., naturalist John Burroughs, and Henry Ford.

‿o‿

The Edison Institute and Greenfield Village were christened on October 21, 1929, in a ballyhooed event officially called the Celebration of Light's Golden Jubilee. The roster of guests included some of the most illustrious figures in politics, industry, science, and the arts: President Herbert Hoover, Albert Einstein, Orville Wright, Will Rogers, George Eastman, Madame Curie, Charles Schwab, Adolph Ochs, Gerard Swope, John D. Rockefeller Jr., and Henry Morgenthau, among others. They all descended on Dearborn on a wet, raw day and freely roamed the unfinished village grounds, which were a sticky paste of mud and manure from the steady rain and horse-drawn carriages. Henry and Clara, along with President and Mrs. Hoover, accompanied the frail eighty-two-year-old inventor and his wife on the circa-1858 wood-burning locomotive from Detroit to the Smith's Creek Station. The choreographed arrival was meant to recall Edison's work experiences as a youngster on Michigan's Grand Trunk Line.

That evening, following an extravagant candlelit banquet and speeches inside the Independence Hall section of the museum, President Hoover and Ford accompanied Edison to the restored Menlo Park laboratory, where he and his former assistant, Francis Jehl, prepared to reenact his successful lighting of the first practical incandescent bulb half a century earlier. Across the country, millions of Americans played along. They had already turned off lights and were now gathered around the faint glow of the family radio, listening to NBC announcer Graham McNamee's melodramatic description of the scene in Dearborn. His words were carried by 144 stations around the world, at the time the largest radio hookup ever.

> But, here is Mr. Edison again. While he was at the power house, Mr. Jehl sealed up the old lamp, and it is now ready. . . . Will it light? Will it burn? Or will it flicker and die, as so many previous lamps had died?
>
> Oh, you could hear a pin drop in this long room.
>
> Now the group is once more about the old vacuum pump. Mr. Edison has two wires in his hand; now he is reaching up to the old lamp; now he is making the connection.
>
> It lights!

A moment later, Edison threw a switch and the Menlo Park complex was awash in light. Bells pealed, car horns sounded, fireworks exploded, and electric lights burst back on in an unprecedented tribute to the deaf old man who had pulled the world out of darkness and put it on the brightly lit path to modernity. An airplane circled above in the rain, carrying an illuminated sign: "Edison, 1879–1929." Overcome with emotion, Edison could barely make it back to the banquet hall for his radio address to the world. "As to Henry Ford," he concluded in a trembling whisper, "words are inadequate to express my feelings. I can only say to you that, in the fullest and richest meaning of the term—he is my friend."*

The miserable weather, the cloying nostalgia, and the nagging illness that caused the quarantined Edsel Ford family to miss the festivities all proved portentious. Although none of the celebrants that rainy Saturday evening was aware of it, good times, like Edison's cotton-filament lamp, would soon become a thing of the past.

---

* Edison collapsed and was taken to Ford's Fair Lane estate, where he recovered in the company of his benefactor. The sickly inventor died in West Orange, New Jersey, on October 18, 1931. Many of the same dignitaries who had been at the jubilee two years earlier attended his funeral, including Ford and President Hoover. Greenfield Village later was extensively used for the 1940 film, Young Tom Edison, starring Mickey Rooney in the title role.

# 15

∽o∾

# An Invitation to Organize

*The idea that Ford is adored by his men has certainly never existed except outside Detroit. It is probably true that the lay-offs and speed-up due to the present depression have made them at this time particularly bitter; but one heard more or less the same story back in 1917, when the first blush of the high wages was beginning to fade. Today the Ford workers complain not only of being overworked, but also of being spied on by Ford's secret police and laid off on trumped-up pretexts. The Ford plant is infested with "spotters" looking for excuses to sack people. Mr. Cunningham tells of an old man who had been working for Ford seventeen years but who was discharged for wiping the grease off his arms a few seconds before the quitting bell, and of an office boy sent into the factory on an errand and fired for stopping off, on his way back, to buy a chocolate bar at a lunch wagon.*

—Edmund Wilson, 1931

Just days after Henry Ford dedicated his new museum, the stock market, a runaway train stoked by years of overspeculation, easy credit, and paper profits, finally flew off the tracks. On "Black Tuesday," October 24, 1929, millions of shares were dumped, touching off a panic that would soon affect every American, investor or not. Detroit, perhaps the city that benefited most from the boom times of the 1920s, was devastated by the resulting economic depression, which came quickly and would linger for most of a decade. Between March 1929 and August 1931 (when Ford closed his factories for five months to change over from the Model A to the V-8), the Ford work force shrunk from 128,000 to 37,000 people. Other businesses that did not go under slashed their payrolls just as dramatically to survive. By 1933, an estimated 46 percent of Michigan's workers were unemployed. Those lucky enough to have jobs collected only a fraction of what they had been earning just before Wall Street's derailment. Men who made 92 cents an hour at the Rouge in 1929 were paid 59 cents an hour in 1933—when they worked.

Suddenly, the "City of Tomorrow" held no future. "Dynamic Detroit," once a bright and shining exemplar of industrial might, became a slag heap of misery, impoverishment, pessimism, and hopelessness. The country's fourth largest city actually lost 150,000 people during the Depression, as hollow-eyed workers and their families abandoned a metropolis now branded sadly "stalled" and "out of gear" by national publications reaching for automotive metaphors to describe its plight. "I have never confronted such misery as on the zero day of my arrival in Detroit," social worker Helen Hall wrote of her visit to the Department of Public Welfare in early 1930:

> There we came upon muffled men and women at the entrance. They crowded the lower corridors and we had to push by. They were on the stairs and filled the upper halls, standing, waiting their turn. I wanted to look at them and see what type of men and women they really were, but I was ashamed to look. I felt suddenly conscious of the fur lining of my coat and the good breakfast I had eaten. Perhaps it was the bitter cold I had come in from and they had come in from that gave me the impression that they were congealed into one disconsolate lump.

At the time of Hall's visit, Detroit's welfare rolls included some 48,000 families. Within two years, 211,000 dependents were on the dole. Among their number was a family of Scotch immigrants eking out a living in a predominantly Polish neighborhood on the city's west side. "People don't realize the frustration of people who are ready, willing, and able to work, but can't find jobs to support their families," said Doug Fraser, whose father lost his job at Studebaker. "My dad was such a proud man. The devastating fact is that you lose your sense of dignity."

Fraser, a teenager in the early 1930s, recalled the shame of being evicted. "I can still remember lying in bed and hearing my mom crying. I suppose my first social action was when I moved the furniture back into the house from the curb. It was just a temporary victory because, of course, the landlord had it moved out again.

"We survived those years, though," continued Fraser, destined to serve as the sixth international president of the United Auto Workers from 1977 to 1983. "We used to grow onions in our backyard, and I would go to the Taystee or Wonderbread plant and buy two- or three-day-old bread. My ma used to take the bread, soak it, and mix it with onions. When you're hungry it sure tastes good."

 ‌

Automobile manufacturing, an industry not even listed in the 1900 census, was by 1929 one of the chief driving forces—literally and figuratively—of the U.S. economy. That year saw an unprecedented 3,848,397 new cars sold, a level not to be reached for another two decades. Thanks to the Model A, Ford's share of the market was 34 percent, well ahead of Chevrolet's 20 percent piece of the action. Henry Ford, flush with $90 million in profits for 1929, felt good enough about the future that, just a month after the stock market crashed, he announced price cuts for the Model A, a $25 million expansion, and a new $7 day for his workers (though the wage increase was more than offset by yet another "Go like hell, boys" speedup of the assembly line). In 1930, the first full year of the Depression, Ford managed to rake in another $40 million in profits. Although General Motors (GM) would continue to eat away at Ford's dominance, passing its rival in 1931 by claiming 31 percent of the market (to Ford's 28 percent), it was thought that the Dearborn automaker was probably in the best overall shape to ride out the Depression.

The "Dirty Thirties" would prove to be catastrophic to carmakers. With credit dried up and a customer base barely able to afford groceries, much less a new vehicle, sales plummeted and assembly lines ground to a halt. From a high of more than 5.5 million cars and trucks built in 1929, overall production bottomed out at less than 1.4 million three years later. Between 1931 and 1937, such well-known nameplates as Essex, Franklin, Reo, Pierce-Arrow, Auburn, Cord, and Duesenberg ceased production and GM dropped the Oakland and LaSalle brands. Although smaller automakers such as Nash, Studebaker, Packard, and Hudson managed to survive, the industry shake-out ultimately resulted in GM, Chrysler, and Ford emerging as automaking's "Big Three."

Henry Ford's public response to the deepening crisis, while certainly in character, was far less than hoped for by his longtime admirers. "It's a good thing the recovery is prolonged," he said in September 1930. "Otherwise the people wouldn't profit by the illness." The following March he observed that "these are really good times, but only if you know it" and that "the average man won't really do a day's work unless he is caught and cannot get out of it." Ford's folk-hero status and reputation as an advocate of social justice were irreversibly damaged by these and similarly callous pronouncements, all of which underscored his belief that charity was debilitating and simple self-reliance was the key to recovery. From about 1930 on he would increasingly be viewed as no friend of the working man—the "little guy," the "two-by-four," that in the past he had always seemed to champion.

Edmund Wilson, the truculent author and critic, visited Detroit in 1931 and came away with the impression that Ford's "immunity to social ambitions and to the luxuries of the rich has evidently been the result rather of an obstinate will to assert himself for what he is than of a feeling of solidarity with the common man":

> It has already been too difficult for Henry Ford to survive and to produce the Ford car and the River Rouge plant for him to worry about making things easy for other people, who, whatever disadvantages they may start with, can get along very well, he is certain, if they really have the stuff in them as he did. Has he not helped to create a new industry and made himself one of its masters—a boy from a Western farm, with no education or training, and in the teeth of general ridicule, merciless competition and diabolical conspiracies of bankers? Let others work as hard as he has. What right have the men in his factories to complain of the short eight hours that they are paid good money to spend there?

The problem, of course, was that few men in his factories were spending *any* time there, much less eight hours a day, five days a week. The changeover to the V-8 temporarily doubled the number of Ford unemployed from 45,000 to 90,000, placing an almost insurmountable strain on Detroit's already overburdened welfare rolls. Even when production resumed in early 1932, the good money was a memory: the $7 day announced to considerable hoopla in late 1929 was quietly scaled back until by 1933 it had even fallen below the old standard of $5 a day. To further squeeze profits out of his work force (and to help pay for the $50 million design and retooling costs of the V-8), Ford continued his practices of laying off higher-paid skilled tradesmen, revving up the assembly lines to near breakneck speeds, and farming out certain operations to low-cost suppliers.

Contributing to Ford's deteriorating public image was his refusal to follow other automakers in endorsing the National Industrial Recovery Act (NIRA), a piece of New Deal legislation that, among its several objectives, looked to promote harmonious relations between management and labor. Section 7(a) gave workers the right to organize and collectively bargain with employers without interference, though there were no provisions for punishing the recalcitrant or belligerent. Ford had a deep personal dislike of the new president, Franklin D. Roosevelt, who took office in March 1933 and who the tycoon considered just another meddlesome "Jew." Edsel, on the other hand, had been friends with FDR for many years and could see the benefits—"progress through unity"—of following the Blue Eagle, the symbol identifying companies cooperating with the National Recovery Administration (NRA), the department established to administer the act. Henry derisively referred to the NRA's seal as the "blue buzzard" and gloated when the Supreme Court declared the NIRA unconstitutional.

When Ford did come around, ever so slightly, he did so in signature style. Whereas New Dealers such as Detroit's liberal mayor Frank Murphy believed that increased government involvement was needed to correct social and economic ills, and offered an "alphabet soup" of new taxpayer-supported programs to that end, Henry, as always, espoused simple homilies, preached the gospel of self-reliance, and served up folk remedies. Publicly criticized by Murphy that the Ford Motor Company employed many of the Detroiters now on relief while the company itself paid no taxes to the city, Ford shot back with unfounded accusations that Detroit's relief measures were being sabotaged by incompetence and welfare cheats. In the midst of the rancor, newspapers reported the possibility of the city—one of the few consistent payrolls remaining—missing payroll because New York banks were calling in $15 million in loans. Using intermediaries, Ford arranged an emergency $5 million loan to the city. When Murphy found out, he laughed and said, "Ford hates the New York bankers worse than us."

Meanwhile, flashing the old paternalism, Ford also bailed out Inkster, a community of mostly black Ford families that had been devastated by layoffs. He hired back every man in the village at the rate of four dollars a day, three of which were used as a credit to bankroll the city's commissary and welfare program. He craftily circumvented the city of Dearborn's plan to levy a special tax to fund welfare assistance— a tax that would have hit Ford particularly hard—by creating a company program that provided laid-off workers with sixty cents a day in groceries from the Ford commissary (though grateful recipients who later returned to work found the cost of this benevolence deducted from their paycheck).

Most revealingly, perhaps, Ford also established a program that provided workers with plots of land, including some on the grounds of his Fair Lane estate, to grow their own vegetables. Sounding hopelessly out of touch with the true depths of the country's despair, the now nearly seventy-year-old paterfamilias of American industry used one of his full-page ads to publicly express hope that these "family gardens" would allow people to "recover some of the old security which the land gave its cultivators."*

∽o∾

Ironically, the city known far and wide today as the cradle of the modern labor movement was for decades a notoriously open-shop town, a reputation that helped attract fledgling automakers and comforted their financial backers in the early years of the motor car. The open shop— and the advantages it gave industrialists—owed much to the Employers' Association of Detroit (EAD). The organization, formed in 1902, offered member firms a citywide employment agency that recruited strikebreakers and blacklisted "quarrelsome" workers.

"The blacklist in Detroit was such that if a man was fired as an 'agitator,' that was what they marked on his card—'Agitator,'" recalled one union man. "Word went out all over the city. It was relayed from plant to plant and these men could not get jobs anywhere in Detroit. The

---

* If Ford's garden program seemed vaguely familiar to older Detroiters, it was because it resembled a plan hatched by Hazen S. Pingree, Detroit's progressive reform mayor of the 1890s. "Potato Patch" Pingree became a national figure during the country's last prolonged depression by allowing starving families to grow vegetable gardens on vacant lots, both publicly and privately owned. A trust-busting populist Republican in the mold of Theodore Roosevelt, Pingree even auctioned off his prize horse to raise money to buy seed and tools. The innovative public works program became a model for other cities all over the country and appears to have inspired Ford.

blacklist was spread throughout all of industry. Many men lost their homes, their jobs, everything, because they had the nerve to be in the forefront, perhaps not even as organizers. Maybe they had just joined early in a plant. The blacklist was such a tremendous weapon over the heads of people, that they were scared to death of joining an organization. The blacklist lasted for many, many years in Detroit. All the time that they were bragging of the 'great open shop City of Detroit,' that was how they kept it open. Many, many times people changed their names. They worked under brothers' names and completely phony names."

The EAD also planted spies inside factories and unions to help identify troublemakers. The climate became so hostile toward unions that by 1911, a year after Ford joined the EAD, only one in eleven Detroit workers carried his lunch pail into a closed shop. In this balmy environment the Motor City quickly became recognized as an employer's paradise, with major firms such as the Burroughs Adding Machine Company and the Packard Motor Car Company relocating from other states to take advantage of the antiunion atmosphere. Nationally, whatever gains organized labor did enjoy during the Progressive Era were rolled back after World War I, the result of a succession of Republican presidents, a conservative Supreme Court, and the pro-business tilt of Congress. President Calvin Coolidge spoke to the prevailing mood of the country when he famously said in 1925: "The business of America is business."

Throughout the postwar boom, factory hands were viewed as little more than disposable cogs in the great wealth-making machinery that was America. To Ford's credit, his factories were always clean, spacious, orderly, well-lit, and well-ventilated. Injured workers could count on immediate, top-notch medical treatment, either on-site or at the hospital that bore their benefactor's name. But this wasn't capitalism with a human face as much as an attempt to wring the last drop of productivity out of each shift.

Management's lash took many forms. Supervisors demanded production competition between shifts and within shifts. Time-study men set unattainable production standards for each job. Workers who protested there was no time left for a break were simply told, "Too bad, that's your problem." Anyone who couldn't keep up the killing pace was let go. There were plenty of men milling around the hiring gate who were ready to take his place. "We used to drive our men pretty hard in those days," admitted production supervisor W. C. Klann. "It was nothing to call a man a dirty name and tell him to keep on going. . . . We used to have every man learn how to say 'hurry up.' It was *putch-putch* in Polish; *presto,* Italian; *mach schnell,* German; and *hurry up* in English. That was all a fellow knew, just drive, drive, drive."

"It used to be a saying around Detroit that you could always tell a Ford employee," said a veteran of the line, Martin Jensen. "When he walked in a street car, the first thing he did was look for a place to sit down and his eyes would be closed the moment he sat down. I mean, you walked out of that plant after a day's work completely dejected, exhausted. . . ." Joe Glazer captured the draining, dispiriting essence of auto assembly work in his 1930s ballad, "You Gotta Fight That Line":

> They put me to work on the assembly line;
> My clock-card number was 90-90-9.
> Those Fords rolled by on that factory floor,
> And every fourteen seconds I slapped on a door.
>
> Those Fords rolled by all day and all night,
> My job was the front door on the right.
> Foreman told me the day I was hired,
> "You miss one door, Mr. Jones . . . you're fired."
>
> I slapped those doors on always on the run
> Every fourteen seconds, never missed a one.
> And I staggered home from work each night,
> Still slappin' 'em on—front door right.

Foremen and supervisors ruled as miniature Napoleons. For amusement, a manager accompanying a visitor through the plant might whisper, "Watch this speed-up." There was no need to flip a switch. "He would walk into a department and just stand and look and every man would try to increase his momentum just from fear," recalled Jensen.

With workers subject to getting fired for any reason, currying favor with the boss was an essential element of maintaining steady employment. A foreman might go around to the men in his department, collecting a dollar or two from each as a "loan" for the weekend. Or a supervisor might arrange to take a worker's wife out on a "date." Hiring was as corrupt and capricious a process as firing. "There were a number of jobs that were considered good jobs," said Jensen, "but they were always given out to either the fellow that drove the boss to work or the one that went out and cut his grass or he was a relative of a big boss of some kind."

Shelton Tappes remembered how he got his job as a machine molder in the foundry, where most of the several thousand black workers at the Rouge were relegated. He was told to approach a certain man at the hiring gate with twenty-five dollars in hand. "I didn't have $25, but I went to see him anyway," said Tappes. "He would never let you know he wanted any money, so I said, 'I thought if I bought a car through you, maybe I could get a job.' He says, 'Yeah,' and he told me where to go buy the car. Then I told him I wouldn't be able to go until I'd earned enough money to make a down payment. He looked at me with a funny smile, and said, 'You're a smart fella,' and he wrote his name on a card and I took it into the employment office."

"The ordeal that I hated most about going to work," said John Zaremba, "was when we got there in the morning we would find the foreman or superintendent standing at the clock. Before you could grab your card to punch, he would say, 'Well, you can go home, you are not wanted today.' You had a lunch packed. You had paid your streetcar fare. You are paying another streetcar fare just to present yourself to the superintendent or foreman. You would spend all that money, then get home and wait for the next day. Maybe he would let you work and maybe he would not. God knows, it all depended on his highness if he liked the way your hair was parted."

Fear, tension, and intimidation characterized life inside a Ford factory. "It's worse than the army, I tell ye—ye're badgered and victimized all the time," one Ford worker, an English veteran of World War I, complained to a reporter. "You get wise to the army after a while but at Ford's ye never know where ye're at. One day ye can go down the aisle and the next day they'll tell ye to get the hell out of it. In one department, they'll ahsk ye why the hell ye haven't got gloves on and in another why the hell ye're wearing them. If ye're wearin' a clean apron, they'll throw oil on it, and if a machinist takes pride in 'is tools, they'll throw 'em on the floor while he's out. The bosses are thick as treacle and they're always on your neck, because the man above is on their neck and Sorenson's on the neck of the whole lot—he's the man that pours the boiling oil down that old Henry makes."

The work pace and hectoring drove many men to the breaking point. An oft-told story from this period had Charlie Sorenson coming across a machine tender who was doing his job while sitting on a crate.

"Get up!" yelled the bull-necked production chief, who was known to punctuate such orders with his fists. When the man refused to budge, Sorenson kicked the box out from under him—at which point the aggrieved worker punched Sorenson square in the jaw. "Go to hell!" he yelled. "I don't work here—I'm working for the Edison Company!"

Apocryphal or not, the factory hand that popped Cast Iron Charlie on the button actually was an anomaly during good times. What most auto workers of the 1920s struck instead was a Faustian pact with their employer: high wages in return for mind-numbing routine, nerve-wracking speedups, arbitrary firings, dangerous working conditions (Detroit was known as "the eight-finger city" because of the large number of digits lost to moving belts and punch presses), frequent layoffs with no unemployment benefits or guarantee of callback, and whatever whimsical demands a boss might entertain—all without the collective redress of grievances.

"The working conditions were dehumanizing," said Paul Boatin, an Italian immigrant who followed his father into the Rouge in 1925. "You couldn't talk to another worker, couldn't even say hello without getting fired. There was no laughing, no smoking. You had to get permission to get a drink of water or go to the toilet. You'd sit and eat your lunch by your machine because the servicemen wouldn't allow any groups."

Hard times caused a backlash, however, with chronically abused workers starting to exhibit a long-suppressed crusading spirit. As the 1930s wore on, wildcat strikes and picket-line violence in all sectors of American industry played out before an increasingly sympathetic public. No longer were malcontents automatically dismissed as "Communist agitators" by their neighbors, friends, and co-workers, all of whom were likely to be in the same soup. And very thin soup at that, as the average annual wage of an auto worker plummeted 40 percent in four years: from $1,600 in 1929 to about $1,000 in 1933.

With a young wife and a newborn child to provide for during the depths of the Depression, Richard Frankensteen knew that he could never get ahead on the 49 cents an hour Chrysler paid him. "I knew there was something wrong with a system where, working every minute you could work, never missing a day, you still could not eke out a living," explained Frankensteen.

In his free time, the idealistic college graduate prepared an elaborate chart showing what it took the average family in Detroit to maintain a decent standard of living. On it was everything from the cost of housing

A Detroit bread line in the early thirties.

to the price of eggs. His plan was to present his well-documented argument before the Works Council, one of the company-sponsored unions that carmakers created to satisfy the collective bargaining provisions of the National Recovery Administration's automobile code. "Dick, you are really a dreamer to think that anything you might say can persuade these people about wages and economic conditions," his father told him. "And it is not a question of convincing them. It is a question of what they want to do."

Nonetheless, Frankensteen went ahead with his lengthy presentation, which was politely received. After he finished, another man took the floor to speak for the corporation.

"We do not control the cost of living," the spokesman said. "We have nothing to say as to what the price of butter, eggs, or meat may be. We do not regulate rents. We cannot tell if your wife is as frugal as some other wife, or whether someone else's wife is more frugal. We cannot control the spending habits of people. All we know is that we pay a going rate, comparable to those of our competitors. We are in a competitive market. We cannot pay more than our competitors if we hope to sell cars and stay in business and provide jobs."

"There was nothing wrong with his answer," Frankensteen, who was to play an important role in the rise of the United Auto Workers, reflected years later. "It was true. It certainly made obvious the fact that if men who were working wanted to improve their conditions, the only way they could do so was to organize the competitors and force their wages up. In effect, remove wages from the category of raw materials. The company's answer was so callous and so hard that it offered no out, except to organize. It was, in effect, an invitation to organize."

# 16

⌘

# Bullets and Frescoes

*Edsel resented me for being treated like Mr. Ford's son. . . . One time Mr. Ford asked me if I was afraid of Edsel. I told him I'm not afraid of him. I can lick him. But I've got principle. "Don't start that principle stuff again," Mr. Ford said.*

—Harry Bennett

With a management style better suited to the back alley than the boardroom, Harry Bennett's star climbed in a trajectory directly paralleling the rise of labor militancy. As the rest of the country followed Detroit's miserable march into the abyss, a workers' revolution, akin to those that had toppled governments in Russia and Europe, was in the air. Soapbox radicals preached it, the chronically laid-off discussed it, and executives hunkered inside boardrooms feared it.

Dave Moore's nine-member family shared four pairs of shoes. Whoever was working or looking for work that day got priority for the valued footwear. Like many other dispossessed Detroiters, Moore was drawn to the Unemployed Councils. Its members, many of whom were Communists, ran soup kitchens, staged rallies, and mobilized neighbors when landlords evicted the unemployed from their homes. "One day they were setting a family out in my block," recalled Moore. "And I just got together with a bunch of guys and said, 'Let's put it back in.' We chased hell out of the bailiff across the old Brewster playground and we put the furniture back in."

American "Reds" such as Moore were much more interested in a steady job and a square meal than in overthrowing the government. But if marching under a Communist banner meant he was that much closer to his goal of having his own pair of shoes, he was all for it. As one Ford worker said of the American Communist Party: "They were the only game in town. They were the only people doing anything."

On the cold, gray morning of March 7, 1932, an estimated 3,000 demonstrators assembled under the aegis of the Unemployed Councils as they prepared to march to the gates of the Rouge plant. There they planned, in a symbolic gesture, to deliver a petition asking Henry Ford for jobs, medical care, and emergency relief for the unemployed.

The demonstrators, peacefully escorted by Detroit police, were in high spirits as they set off from Fort Street and Oakwood in Detroit. "The marchers were heterogeneous," reported the next day's *Detroit Free Press*. "All were not Communists, although faces of familiar agitators were in the ranks. In line were known radicals, habitual demonstrators, former Ford workers, professional paraders, and jobless men hoping somehow to obtain work by parading. The line-up, however, was a good three-quarter Red." Trouble began when the raggedy bunch crossed into Dearborn, whose city council had refused to issue a permit to march. The marchers swept past a skirmish line of Dearborn policemen, who lobbed tear gas at them, and surged up Miller Road to Gate 4 of the Rouge.

As the police fell back, fire hoses were turned on the marchers. Some picked up pieces of slag and rocks and hurled them at the large knot of police and Ford service men. At some point in the confusion shots were fired. Marchers fell to the ground. Suddenly, in the midst of the chaos, Bennett brazenly drove through the gate.

"Who are the leaders here?" he called out. "I want to talk to them."

"We're all leaders here," retorted Joe York, a nineteen-year-old organizer for the Young Communist League.

As Bennett tried to make sense of the situation, angry demonstrators continued to throw slag and rocks. "You're stoning your own fellows up there," he said, referring to the fact that Ford executives were at that very moment working with Soviet engineers on a $30 million Russian order. A woman yelled, "We want Bennett, and he's in that building."

"No, you're wrong. I'm Bennett," said the service chief, climbing out of the car.

The announcement was met with a fresh shower of slag, a chunk of which struck him in the forehead. Bleeding profusely, Bennett grabbed hold of York and fell to the pavement. As more slag rained down, York struggled to his feet—just as policemen and guards let go a volley. "I would guess that hundreds of shots were fired into the mob," said a press photographer on the scene. Bullets ripped through the crowd, striking scores of unarmed marchers. As the great army of the unemployed scattered, the bodies of the fallen were dragged off. As many as sixty marchers were wounded. Four others, including York, were dead; a fifth would die later from gunshot wounds. "Dearborn pavements were stained with blood," reported the *New York Times,* "streets were littered with broken glass and the wreckage of bullet-riddled automobiles, and nearly every window in the Ford plant's employment building had been broken."

At least two dozen policemen were injured by missiles during the melee. Bennett was knocked unconscious when another rock hit him in the back of the neck. While some of the wounded demonstrators were held in hospital rooms under police guard (at least two were handcuffed to their beds), Bennett mended at Henry Ford Hospital. "The newspaper stories that came out in rapid succession got more and more fantastic," he recalled. "At one time the papers had me out there facing the crowd with a gun smoking in each hand; another time they had me wading into the mob hurling tear-gas bombs."

The hyperbolic stories gilded Bennett's already substantial tough-guy reputation, while the company's violent response marked it as one that brooked no nonsense when dealing with disaffected workers.

That summer, the Wayne County prosecutor conducted a grand-jury investigation that was later characterized by one of its members as "the most biased, prejudiced and ignorant proceeding imaginable." The prosecutor's office, like many local and county agencies, was basically "owned" by Ford. (Dearborn's mayor, for example, was Henry's cousin, while the five-member Dearborn Safety Commission was comprised entirely of Ford service men.) Therefore its conclusions were no great surprise. The Dearborn police, whose corrupt chief was on Bennett's payroll as a "special investigator," came in for some mild official criticism. But the Ford Motor Company was found to be without blame. In the eyes of many, the lack of criminal culpability in what became known as the "Ford Hunger March massacre" meant that the company could literally get away with murder.

Communist "agitators" were blamed for touching off the deadly confrontation outside the gates of the Rouge on March 7, 1932.

As for the victims, four were buried in a common grave at Woodmere Cemetery, in the shadow of the Rouge. Fifteen thousand people attended the funeral as hundreds of policemen—their nightsticks discreetly shoved under their uniform coats—nervously stood watch. The fifth victim—a black man barred from joining his comrades in a "white" cemetery—was cremated and his ashes spread by plane over the plant.

❧

Diego Rivera was an avowed Marxist, but he was not an agitator—unless one considered his art. The dumpy Mexican muralist with the froglike features was known for his controversial works, many of which

Mexican muralist Diego Rivera
at work on *Detroit Industry* in
the courtyard of the Detroit
Institute of Arts.

depicted scenes that could be interpreted as being unkind to the capitalist system. One panel in the mural he had painted for the Ministry
of Education in Mexico City in the 1920s, called "Capitalist Dinner,"
depicted J. P. Morgan, John D. Rockefeller, and Henry Ford at a table,
munching on ticker tape.

Edsel thought he was a genius. As the president of the Arts Commission at the Detroit Institute of Arts (DIA), he not only approved of
the idea of bringing Rivera to Detroit to decorate the walls of the
museum's garden court, but he agreed to pay the $22,000 stipend.

Such outlays were not unusual for Edsel, even as the economy hit
rock bottom in 1932. Through the years he and Eleanor were steady
but quiet contributors to a variety of causes. In addition to such large
donations as $4 million to Henry Ford Hospital and $750,000 to the
Detroit YMCA, they also gave generously to the arts. They donated
$1 million to the Detroit Symphony Orchestra and annually wrote a
check for $5,000 to the New York Museum of Modern Art, on whose
board Edsel sat. But the DIA, which had opened on Woodward Avenue
just north of downtown in 1927, was Edsel's pet cause.

Rivera hit it off immediately with his corporate benefactor. He
found Edsel to be sincere, plain-spoken, and unpretentious, which was
not always something he could say about many of the leaders in the

Marxist movement. "They had a mutual interest in art, engineering and design," said Linda Downs, former curator of education at the DIA. "Rivera was fascinated with the Rouge complex. Edsel opened up the plant completely to him." The middle-aged artist had loved machinery since he was a boy, so to see the creation of an automobile from its raw material stage to final assembly was a process that totally absorbed him. He sketched and pored over photographs and read manuals. In his view, engineers were the new artists of the new industrial age, and Detroit provided the prefect muse. "I have found in Detroit the typical American city which I have sought for so long," he told a reporter. "Here is the machine and the man united in the production of one object—the motor car. Here is a chaotic unity that gives me the subject I most love to paint."

Rivera and his wife, the painter Frida Kahlo, came to Detroit in late April 1932, on the heels of the Hunger March massacre. His political sympathies became apparent as work started that June. After a month of preliminary designs, he began painting on July 25. Work progressed through the fall and winter and into 1933. On the panels completed for the north wall, the unsmiling workers are straining at their tasks, watched over by the omnipresent service men. "Rivera knew, he identified with the workers," said Paul Boatin, one of several Ford workers who posed for the murals.

Lucienne Bloch assisted Rivera. She remembered Edsel observing the cigar-smoking artist and his helpers at work. "I had the feeling he was a little confused about what we were doing," she said.

Edsel was no poseur. Looking to expand his knowledge, he had taken private tutorials with DIA director William Valentiner and visited museums around the country and throughout Europe. He eventually became one of the most respected self-educated art experts in the country. He was able to appreciate the talent of such artists as John Carroll (with whom he took lessons every Saturday morning for years) and Charles Sheeler early on. The museum not only benefited from his and Eleanor's largesse (they contributed more than $1 million and paid the entire staff's salaries for a spell during the Depression), but it profited from their discerning eyes. Among their many donated master-pieces were works by Donatello, Corot, Verrocchio, and Titian. The Fords' private collection of paintings represented a range of styles and periods: Van Gogh, Renoir, Cezanne, Matisse, Titian, Hans Holbein, Degas, and John Gilbert Stuart.

The mighty Rouge, pictured in the late 1930s. In the right foreground is the Ford Rotunda, originally built for the 1934 World's Fair in Chicago and subsequently removed to Dearborn, where it served as a reception center. Across Schaefer Road is the Administration Building.

Edsel's sophistication, so at odds with his father's rustic tastes, impressed those around him. Said one associate: "He was far above the rest of us in this monkey-shoe society of ours. At the time he hired Diego Rivera to paint a mural for the Detroit Institute of Arts, Rivera could have been an outfielder for the Washington Senators for all we knew. Where he got his refinement is something of a mystery. Both of his parents were simple farm-bred people who never changed after they became wealthy. They kept Edsel pretty much under their wing when he was growing up, yet by the time he was 18 he was wearing the right clothes and he knew the right fork. Still, he was never a stuffy highbrow. Always kind and generous and warm-hearted."

Fresco mural painting has a long, storied history in Mexico, with artists like Rivera each practicing their own method. Rivera's "was the closest to the Renaissance painters," said Stephen Pope Dimitroff, one of several assistants who prepared and plastered the wall surfaces. He recalled the process by which the murals called *Detroit Industry* came about:

> On an existing wall or a newly constructed one, three coats of rough plaster were applied with a wait of a week between each coat. On the third coat, using a sketch which had been approved by those who had commissioned the mural, Rivera selected the assistants to enlarge the sketch in proportion to the wall. For example, his sketch might

be in inches, to the wall's dimensions in feet. The sketch was in squared inches. The wall was squared in feet, using a chalk line with corresponding numbers to guide us. With charcoal sticks we drew the sketch in its new proportions, so large that we had to work square by square.

Next, Diego climbed the scaffold and outlined the charcoal sketch with red ochre pigment mixed with water. This was when he made changes and corrections, for sometimes what looked fine on a sketch might not be right on the wall. When he had completed the red outlines he selected the area he wanted to paint the next day, marking it for the plasterer. This was the section to be plastered with the fourth and fifth coat. This final coat was very fine—the intonaco layer on which the artist painted. Rivera insisted on this method of preparation for durability and strength. All these five coats of plaster added together were not more than ¾ of an inch thick.

"Diego was a glutton for work," said Dimitroff. "When we thought he had finished after 18 hours, when the painting looked great, he was still going back to work, sometimes for more than two hours." On March 13, 1933, after seven months and eighteen days of painstaking labor, Rivera announced he had finished. The scaffolding came down and Edsel formally unveiled *Detroit Industry* a few days later.

Covering all four walls of the interior courtyard, Rivera's frescoes were complex in composition, brilliantly executed, and are today considered his finest work. "The machines look like Aztec monsters," said Bloch. "He saw the feeling of those machines he studied and of those conveyor belts going back and forth."

"Rivera successfully captured the clutter, the chaos, the heat, the noise and the monumentality of Detroit's automotive industry," wrote Laura Rose Ashlee, a frequent visitor to the museum. "Bulbous, gigantic machines dwarf the multiracial mix of laborers scurrying and straining to accomplish their tasks. . . . Several smaller panels frame the doorways and the automotive scenes and contain allegorical images that symbolize the relationship between the land, from which industry draws its raw materials, and man. Large mythical-looking figures represent the races that made up North America's labor force. These images remind us of the dangers and benefits of technology, the latter's impact on man and the people who make the machines work."

Critics saw something completely different. The idea that industry was deemed a subject worthy of display inside a leading museum was astonishing—and offensive—to many art patrons. Civic leaders and clergy

A detail of one of the panels of Rivera's *Detroit Industry* on the north wall. The likeness of auto worker Paul Boatin, wearing overalls and a fedora, can be seen at lower right.

members were shocked by the murals' supposedly irreligious and anti-capitalistic themes. Other alarmed citizens considered the nudes pornographic. "Senor Rivera has perpetrated a heartless hoax on his capitalist employer, Mr. Edsel Ford," declared the president of Marygrove College. A city councilman called it "a travesty on the spirit of Detroit [that] completely ignores the cultural and spiritual aspects of the city." Boycotts were threatened and whitewashing was demanded. Despite the outcry, said Bloch, their patron "courageously" rode out the storm of protest.

This time Edsel (whose likeness can be spotted in the lower right corner of the south mural) refused to be bullied. "I admire Mr. Rivera's spirit," he said. "I really believe he was trying to express his idea of the spirit of Detroit." He arranged classes for visitors to be educated in Rivera's work, and in time the howling became a whisper.

Henry, who had once proclaimed, "I wouldn't give five cents for all the finest art in the world," largely ignored the goings-on at the museum, but one day his curiosity got the better of him and he went over to see what all the fuss was about. Rivera had met the old tycoon several times during his stay in Detroit and liked him. They had talked of the artist's trip to Russia, where he'd seen portraits of Ford hung on admirers' walls.

Henry looked over the murals and was impressed—not so much by what Rivera was trying to convey, but by his draftsmanlike accuracy. Harold Wills could not have done a better job. This Rivera fellow, he told Edsel, has "fused together, in a few feet, sequences of operations which are actually performed in a distance of at least two miles, and every inch of his work is technically correct. That is what is so amazing!"

# 17

⚜

# A Matter of Style

*So gradually has Edsel come up in the industrial world that he has attracted little attention in the world at large. The towering character of his father has had much to do with it, but that is not the only reason. It would be difficult to find a person who has greater love, respect and admiration for a father than does Edsel, and he has purposely kept himself in the background. But Edsel has not lost thereby. With him deference is not a weakness. It has given him many opportunities to quietly establish himself against the day when he alone will carry on the Ford traditions. In the inner executive circle of the Ford company there is complete agreement that Edsel is the answer to all questions about the future of the business.*

—*Detroit Saturday Night* (1936)

At the time Edsel was publicly standing up to critics of Diego Rivera's murals at the Detroit Institute of Arts, he was emerging from a financial mess that had privately caused him to become weak-kneed with worry and dread. Along with several Grosse Pointe friends, most notably Ernest Kanzler, he had become deeply involved, as a director and its major shareholder, in the Guardian Group, a syndicate of banks and trust companies whose number included the Universal Credit Corporation. Kanzler had spearheaded the creation of the UCC in 1928 to handle installment loans for the Model A. UCC's partnership with the carmaker resulted in more than 400,000 loans in its first year and helped make the Guardian Group the largest financial syndicate in the state. Flush with money and optimism, the conglomerate built the Guardian Building on Griswold Street, a gaudy thirty-six-story tribute to high finance and even higher expectations.

"Edsel Ford's involvement in the Guardian Group represented a bid for freedom," Robert Lacey would write. "It was an attempt to do something as a businessman in his own right—and it also represented, in just about the most direct fashion that Edsel could manage, a gesture of defiance towards his father. In financing Ernest Kanzler, Edsel was publicly backing a man who had dared question the great carmaker's judgement; and by becoming a director of the Guardian Group, he could scarcely have registered a clearer disagreement with his father's well-known views on bankers, moneylenders, and financial speculators."

During the high-flying twenties the Guardian Group borrowed money to expand and to invest. Just months after the Guardian Building opened, however, Wall Street crashed and the cash flow quickly dried up. Few new loans were written and existing borrowers were either slow in making payments or simply defaulted. Suddenly, the Guardian Group was struggling to honor its own onerous financial commitments. In the fall of 1929, in an attempt to bid up the value of Guardian stock, which had plummeted more than 80 percent in just a few weeks, Edsel and the rest of the directors of the various Guardian companies agreed to buy an aggregate 60,000 shares and to hold onto them for a year until the economy recovered. Junior employees of the member firms were encouraged to invest as well. Guardian banks lent many of their own directors and employees millions of dollars to do so. In most cases the collateral pledged was practically worthless.

As the Depression deepened, Edsel pumped dollars into the Guardian syndicate in an attempt to keep it afloat. In 1930–31 he personally lent $6 million to the Union Guardian Trust Company, then guaranteed a 1931 loan using $5 million in Ford Motor Company municipal bonds as collateral. In 1932 he arranged a direct loan from the carmaker to the trust company, this time for $3.5 million. Meanwhile, the newspapers were filled with horror stories of other banks failing left and right, leaving depositors penniless. On the radio, the Reverend Charles Coughlin railed against "criminal banksters," further eroding public confidence. Panicky men and women closed out accounts and hoarded their money, adding to the illiquidity of already troubled banks.

In January 1933, the Guardian Group applied for a $50 million loan from the Reconstruction Finance Corporation (RFC) to keep its trust company solvent. The federal agency, which had previously lent Guardian $15 million, agreed to another $37 million, but only if Edsel and other major shareholders chipped in with the balance, $13 million. Just as the financial package was coming together, an old adversary threw a switch in the track. The Guardian was "Mr. Ford's baby," declared James Couzens, and he was dead-set against using taxpayers' dollars to bail out a Ford-financed bank.

Henry, who had $32 million of company cash deposited in a Guardian bank, the Guardian National, had never thought in those terms. After all, as much as he distrusted bankers, he couldn't very well stuff all that money in his mattress, so why not place it in an institution his son was involved with? He had tens of millions of dollars on hand at several other banks. However, the cries of protest from Couzens, now a U.S. senator and head of a Senate subcommittee investigating irregularities in banking practices, caused Ford to pay closer attention to the looming crisis. He first learned the extent of his son's misery from Ernest Liebold, who had been shocked to see the desperate and depressed Edsel walk into his office with tears streaming down his face.

"Well, I'm cleaned out," Edsel told Liebold. "All that has to happen is for the Continental Bank to call on me for that five million and I'm cleaned out."

Liebold repeated the whole story to Ford. The father of eight couldn't resist adding a rebuke: "You don't take very good care of your son."

Ford looked into the matter, then got back in touch with Liebold.

"Go ahead," he said. "Fix it up." Several million dollars in Ford funds were immediately deposited in Edsel's personal account.

However, Kanzler and his associates were on their own. When outgoing President Herbert Hoover sent high-ranking representatives to Fair Lane to ask Ford to put up more money to secure the RFC's loan, Henry refused. Warned that Guardian's failure might bring down the entire state banking system, Ford exploded. "Let them fail! Let everybody fail! I made my fortune when I had nothing to start with, by myself and my own ideas. Let other people do the same thing. If I lose everything in the collapse of our financial structure, I will start in at the beginning and build it up again."

Three days of meetings between the state's leading bankers and industrialists on the top floor of the Guardian Building accomplished nothing. In the early hours of February 14, 1933, Governor William Comstock reacted to the growing threat of a run on the banks by jittery depositors. After consulting with national and state authorities, he declared an eight-day bank holiday "for the preservation of the public

Edsel with
Ernest Kanzler.

peace." All banks, trust companies, and other financial institutions in the state closed, tying up an estimated $722 million in Detroit alone. Business was paralyzed. Checks were not honored and transactions of any type had to be in cash. Although a follow-up proclamation by Comstock allowed depositors to withdraw up to 5 percent of their balances, for the most part the only money to be found was what had been inside pockets, cash registers, and safe deposit boxes before the governor's shocking (and questionably legal) announcement.

In the days that followed, Ford offered to put up the cut-rate figure of $8.25 million to take over the city's two principal ailing banks, igniting a short-lived wave of "Bank with Hank" hysteria. The move was blocked, however, by self-interested financiers. They knew Ford's first action would be to clean house of all managers and directors. They also were alarmed by Henry's announced policies, which included low-interest, and possibly even *no*-interest, loans. Meanwhile, the city, one of the few remaining sources of a regular paycheck during the Depression, was forced to issue paper scrip to pay municipal workers.

As feared, a chain reaction followed, with bank holidays proclaimed in state after state as federal agencies worked out stabilizing plans. The banks in Indiana shut their doors on February 23, those in Maryland two days later. On February 27, the governors of Arkansas, Kentucky,

Nevada, and Tennessee ordered all financial institutions closed. The dominoes continued to fall: Arizona, California, Louisiana, Mississippi, Oregon. As more states followed, there was talk of incoming president Franklin Roosevelt nationalizing the banks. On March 6, two days after taking office, FDR declared a week-long national moratorium to give the government additional time to sort through the mess and install emergency measures.

On March 13, most banks across the country were finally allowed to reopen. Some were reorganized and others placed in receivership. In Michigan, depositors whose accounts had been frozen eventually got back an average of ninety-six cents on the dollar. The 116,000 depositors in Guardian National with individual balances of $1,000 or less did even better, getting back every cent. At this point, there were no federal regulations insuring depositors' holdings in case of a bank failure. Thus bank owners and stockholders, legally obligated to make good out of their personal holdings, were the ones who most often took it on the chin. In addition to the Fords, this included small-time players such as Jim Backus, Edsel's secretary, whose modest investment was wiped out, and would-be masters of the universe such as Kanzler, who saw the Guardian empire liquidated and all business ties to Ford severed. Out of the debris came a new slew of federal banking regulations that guaranteed the safety of deposits, as well as a new local bank, Manufacturers National, which Henry and Edsel organized with $3 million of their own money.

A chunk of Edsel's personal fortune was lost in the Guardian fiasco—perhaps as much as $12 million or more. Afterward, Henry's only known comment to Edsel about the entire mess was, "Well, son, I see they took you to the cleaners."

✎∽

Detroit and the rest of the country recovered from the banking crisis of 1933, though afterward an unknown number of people would always prefer to bury their money in a jar than to risk it in a bank again. By the middle of the decade the economy seemed to be on the mend, thanks chiefly to an unprecedented infusion of cash from the federal government. About $4 billion of it went into building and repairing streets and highways around the country, a major expansion that literally paved the way for the bigger, faster, and more technically advanced cars coming out of Detroit each year. The modest recovery collapsed in

1938, however, and auto industry production tumbled 40 percent from the previous year. The New Deal could accomplish only so much; ultimately it would take a world war to finally pull the United States out of the Depression.

Edsel worked harder than ever. In 1936, Ford topped Chevrolet in model year output but still suffered the ignominy of finishing third among the Big Three in market share, its 22 percent slice of the pie trailing Chrysler's 25 percent and General Motors' 43 percent. What success the Ford line enjoyed was due in part to the subtle facelift that Edsel's design team performed on a tired line of sedans and roadsters. It certainly wasn't due to the technology. As late as 1938, no Ford offered such features as hydraulic brakes—what Henry derisively rejected as "air in a bottle"—or a column-mounted shift lever.

In 1939, however, the company took the wraps off the Mercury 8, a medium-priced product that featured a distinctive aerodynamic shape, a more powerful V-8 engine than the Ford, and—at long last—hydraulic brakes. With a sticker price of $930, it was meant to compete with a crowded field of similarly priced makes, including Pontiac, Hudson, Nash, Dodge, Buick, DeSoto, and Oldsmobile. The Mercury finally gave the company something to position between its high-end (Lincoln) and low-end (Ford) offerings.

The Mercury's styling borrowed from the Lincoln-Zephyr, which was first put into production in 1936. Although the first new Lincoln model since Ford bought the company in 1922 was around for only six years, it was notable for being "the first successfully streamlined car in America," opined the Museum of Modern Art in a 1951 show devoted to the esthetics of automobile design. The museum called attention to the Zephyr's "impeccable, studied elegance, enhanced by such small decorative details as the thin, linear grille and sharp, prow-like leading edges."

It was Edsel's good fortune that Henry had no interest in styling, for that was an area in which he excelled and thus could make a unique contribution. Although he possessed a fine mechanical mind, Edsel had always preferred designing cars to tinkering with them. As a boy he kept a scrapbook filled with pictures of automobile styling. When he was seventeen he created his own speedster, a modified Model T that saw limited production as the "Torpedo," and later drove around town in a bright yellow Stutz Bearcat. These were the first in a long line of exotic automobiles that overflowed Edsel's garages during his lifetime. In 1939 he added a new custom-built Lincoln to his

The 1939 Continental was a classy collaboration between Edsel and chief designer Bob Gregorie.

collection. The "Continental," its name evocative of European elegance, was the result of a collaboration with design chief Bob Gregorie.

Gregorie, a tall, brash protégé of GM's legendary Harley Earl, had joined Ford in 1931. He worked inside the styling department set up four years later in the abandoned terminal at Ford airport. This became Edsel's playground and refuge, a haven for young stylists hoping to overcome the resistance of Henry's old-school body engineers, crusty types such as Joe Galamb with no patience for clay models and styling bridges. Long, low, and sleek, and featuring a V-12 engine, the Continental was created as a one-of-a-kind land yacht for Edsel's personal use. Wealthy friends, however, soon persuaded Edsel to put the car into production. Frank Lloyd Wright called the Continental the most beautiful car ever built.

According to Gregorie, the simple, clean, and graceful lines of the cars he and other designers created under Edsel's watchful eye were a reflection of his dignified but self-effacing personality. "He had his own way of determining whether something met with his taste and his taste was very conservative. I don't know if he just did not care for anything spectacular, or just did not dare stick his neck out toward anything that was spectacular. That was just his nature. I believed he always felt on safe ground by following a good middle ground."

✤

If Henry's confidence in his son's fitness to take over the company's reins was shaken, it was at least partially restored by Edsel's work in finding a solution to the "wealth tax" that Congress passed in 1935.

The act imposed a tax of as much as 70 percent on estates worth more than $50 million. This meant that the death of either Henry—already the country's largest single taxpayer—or Edsel would force the Ford family to sell stock in the company just to be able to pay the staggering inheritance tax. Henry detested accountants, once clearing out an entire floor of them just on general principle, and he hated attorneys, whom he considered all "Jews" even if their names happened to be O'Brien or Lopez. But he absolutely despised FDR and, more than that, feared the idea of losing control of his company to outsiders, so he approved of the strategy arrived at by Edsel and a battery of legal and financial experts to outflank Washington's "soak the rich" legislation.

The result was the creation of the Ford Foundation, a benevolent organization that separated Ford money from Ford management. Existing stock in the company (Henry had held 55 percent, Edsel 42 percent, and Clara 3 percent since the buy outs of James Couzens and the Dodge brothers) was converted into two classes. Ninety-five percent of the shares became Class A "nonvoting" stock and were earmarked for the foundation, while the remaining 5 percent was classified Class B "voting" stock and was retained by the Fords. Henry and Edsel had wills drawn up bequeathing all Class A stock to the charity and all Class B shares to the family. The Ford Foundation, officially established on January 15, 1936, to "receive and administer funds for scientific, educational, and charitable purposes, all for the public welfare," would wind up saving the family an estimated $321 million in taxes upon Henry's and Edsel's deaths.*

Throughout this period of personal and professional upheaval, Edsel continued to draw on the restorative powers of Eleanor and the kids. Gaukler Pointe provided an expansive playground for the children as they grew. The boys' famous grandfather built them miniature motorized cars, which they joyfully maneuvered around (and occasionally through) the hundreds of meticulously pruned trees and shrubs.

---

* The death of Clara Ford in 1950 transformed the initially small-scale charity into an international philanthropy of unprecedented size. By 1955 the Ford Foundation's 95 percent stake in the Ford Motor Company was worth an estimated $1 billion. Trustees of the foundation, however, sought a more diversified portfolio and by 1974 had sold the last of its Ford stock. Since its inception the Ford Foundation has provided more than $10 billion in grants and loans.

Lest Josephine feel slighted as an only daughter, the family had Albert Kahn build a $15,000 miniature playhouse, complete with scaled-down furniture and a fireplace, for her seventh birthday. Edsel doted on his children, organizing a baseball or football game with them when he got home, or taking them down to Navin Field, Olympia Stadium, or Dinan Field to cheer—and often chat with—Mickey Cochrane, Dutch Clark, Ebbie Goodfellow, and the other sporting heroes that made Detroit the "City of Champions" during the mid-1930s. A civic booster when it came to professional sports, Edsel was part of the syndicate that brought the current Red Wings hockey franchise to town. He also unsuccessfully tried to buy a National League baseball team with the idea of relocating it to Detroit. In 1938, Henry II became the first of the four children to reach the landmark age of twenty-one. To celebrate, Edsel shelled out several thousand dollars to bring in Tommy Dorsey, tap dancer Paul Draper, and an up-and-coming crooner named Frank Sinatra to perform at a lavish birthday party.

The Edsel Fords, now entering their forties, remained socially active, often stepping out to the theater, charity balls, and concerts. Whether sailing, playing tennis, riding horses, or attending the opera, both were always impeccably attired. Edsel was named to various "best-dressed" lists over the years, putting him in the same sartorial class as actors Fred Astaire and Gary Cooper. "All the Ford executives dress neatly," *Fortune* magazine observed in 1933, "but Edsel is the only one you may notice is wearing the green-and-white tie today, was wearing the brown-and-white tie yesterday." Many years later, Edsel Ford II was so taken by one of the photographs used to accompany an article about his grandparents in a period magazine that he tracked it down and had a print of it enlarged and framed. "That's the Edsel Ford that I think of," he said one day inside his World Headquarters office, smiling at the fashionably attired couple striding confidently down some Manhattan street, circa 1932. "And look at my grandmother—look at how stylish. It shows through everything they did as a couple, it shows through to his design—the kind of flare he had and the sense of fashion."

The couple regularly entertained at home, with the guest list at 1100 Lakeshore Drive featuring the best-connected names. After guests assembled in the drawing room filled with eighteenth-century French furniture, everyone would move into the dining room, softly lit by the warm glow of candles. To ensure atmosphere, Edsel had instructed Kahn

Edsel and Eleanor with children Henry, Benson, Josephine, and William, c. 1936.

not to install electrical outlets in the room. After a leisurely dinner, the ladies retired to the intimate morning room for coffee (and a look at van Gogh's *The Postman Roulin*), while the men gathered in the Elizabethan oak-paneled study for cigars and liqueurs.

Henry and Clara were, of course, by choice never part of this scene. They were basically homebodies, anyway. As time passed and the grandchildren grew they found themselves missing the younger Fords' once regular weekend stays at Fair Lane, where years earlier Henry had built a fantasy hut deep in the woods for the kids' amusement. Nonetheless, father and son stayed in near-constant touch. A direct telephone line in Edsel's study connected him to Henry at home, and the two usually spoke each night even though they had typically just spent several hours together during the day. Henry's ear would perk up at the sound of clinking ice on the other end of the line. He remained openly disdainful of social life in Grosse Pointe, and the thought of his son, miles beyond his reach, decadently sharing highballs with the likes of the Kanzlers and the Newberrys rankled him no end.

Perhaps because he'd had no success in prying Edsel away from that crowd, Henry felt the continued need to assert his authority during the workday. Asked to evaluate the sweeping curve of a fender that Edsel's design team was working on, he could issue a withering remark that left no doubt how he felt or—most important—who was in charge. Henry was "bitterly sarcastic, of course," said Harold Hicks, who brainstormed with Edsel on a variety of aviation and automotive projects. "That was part of the treatment every designer had to take if he wanted to work here." As the introductions of the Lincoln-Zephyr, Mercury 8, and Lincoln Continental during the 1930s demonstrated, there existed the potential to do some wonderfully creative work, thanks to one man.

"That is naturally why you stayed. I often thought no one would have stayed here as long as they did had it not been for Edsel Ford," said Hicks. "It was people who were loyal to Edsel that had an awful lot to do with the success of the Ford Motor Company. Very little was ever said about the excellent moral influence Edsel had on the people that worked here."

# 18

⌘

# The Overpass

*That one incident—the sheer stupidity on the part of Bennett and his men—did more to build the UAW in the auto industry than any other incident in the history of labor organizing.*

—Richard Frankensteen

In the wake of the Hunger March massacre, Henry Ford regularly stated that he did not believe in labor unions or collective bargaining. "I have never bargained with my men, I have always bargained for them," he insisted in 1933. "I think we have made better bargains for them than any stranger could, or than they could make for themselves."

Once in the vanguard of labor-management relations, the father of the Five-Dollar Day now vowed to do everything possible to keep the union out of his plants—even after Congress passed the National Labor Relations (Wagner) Act in 1935. This piece of legislation gave workers the right to collectively bargain with their employer for better pay and treatment. Henry turned up his nose at it. "Labor union organizations are the worst thing that ever struck the earth," he declared, "because they take away a man's independence."

Workers, of course, saw it differently. Although the espionage and intimidation employed by companies kept its numbers small at first, the United Auto Workers (UAW), affiliated with the Congress of Industrial Organizations (CIO), soon emerged as the greatest threat to Ford and other automakers. By law, companies could no longer thwart elected worker organizations and were required to bargain in good faith with them. The National Labor Relations Board (NLRB) was created to enforce the Wagner Act and to adjudicate any disputes.

Ordinarily, Edsel Ford and Charlie Sorenson, as company president and production boss, respectively, should have been the point men in dealing with any organizational attempts by the UAW. But Henry ordered both men not to personally meet with any union officials or to discuss labor issues with the press.

"I've picked someone to talk with the unions," Henry announced after the Wagner Act was passed. "I want a strong, aggressive man who can take care of himself in an argument, and I've got him. He has my full confidence and I want to be sure that you, Edsel, and you, Charlie, will support him." To the disgust of Edsel and Sorenson, the man Henry selected turned out to be his service chief, Harry Bennett.

From 1935 on, Bennett drew on an ever-expanding network of informants and underworld ties to squash all attempts to organize Ford. Inside the Rouge, perhaps as many as one in five workers was a stooge. "They were called 'gallopini,' which in Italian is loosely translated as 'runarounds,'" said Paul Boatin. "They were the eyes of the company on the production line. Busybodies. They ran around looking for troublemakers that they could report to Bennett. They'd deliver their co-workers so they wouldn't be let go themselves." Bennett had service men take down the license plate numbers of cars parked outside houses and halls holding union meetings, planted spies in the UAW ranks, instructed plant guards to ransack workers' overcoats and lunch pails in search of union literature—all in a comprehensive campaign to weed out any present or potential union members. Harassed workers, who could be fired for such minor infractions as talking on the job, mastered the "Ford whisper"—talking out of the side of one's mouth.

The UAW made its first big move in the final days of 1936, when workers at General Motors plants in Detroit, Cleveland, and Flint, Michigan, sat down on the job, paralyzing the giant automaker. This was the beginning of "sit-down fever," as disgruntled factory hands physically took possession of their workplaces. The innovative tactic, which originated in France, gained extensive coverage in national publications such as *Life* magazine, whose January 18, 1937, issue featured a cover photo of Henry and Edsel, with the Rouge plant as backdrop. Inside, on seven oversized pages, the magazine juxtaposed pictures of

In January 1937, Henry and Edsel were pictured in front of the Rouge for a *Life* magazine article about sit-down strikes in the auto industry.

auto kingpins Walter P. Chrysler and Alfred P. Sloan Jr. ("The lords of Detroit are men of strength and pride in their achievement") with shots of bored strikers in Flint washing laundry in company paint pails, shaving with the aid of a car mirror, but mostly sitting around waiting for something to happen ("Sit-down is a literal word for what the workers do").

According to Victor Reuther, one of three brothers active in the UAW, during previous short-term strikes "the workers had been promised concessions, only to find, when they returned to the plant a few days later, that everything was just as before, and as likely as not the ringleaders of such a strike would be discharged. Such betrayals had made the sit-down strike the only recourse." Staying inside the plant, instead of marching outside in picket lines, also kept strikers out of the reach of local police and company-hired vigilantes.

The union found it had a powerful ally in the state's new governor, Frank Murphy. The former Detroit mayor refused to call in the National Guard to oust the sit-downers, even though the seizing of private property was obviously illegal. Prior to the Depression and FDR, Michigan had been a staunchly Republican state. Now, with nearly every elected office of consequence occupied by New Dealers, industrialists such as

Sloan and Chrysler could read the writing on the wall. On February 11, representatives for GM and the union met inside Murphy's office and signed an agreement whereby the company recognized the UAW as bargaining agent. Chrysler, its nine Detroit plants taken over by workers on March 8, also quickly capitulated. Only Ford remained unorganized. *Life* had handicapped the UAW's chances of organizing each of the Big Three automakers. Henry Ford's "vast River Rouge Plant," the magazine decided, "is apparently impenetrable by any union."

&infin;

In the early afternoon of May 26, 1937, after eight months of secret meetings, UAW organizers Richard Frankensteen, Walter Reuther, John Kennedy, and Robert Kanter drove out to Gate 4 of the Rouge to oversee the distribution of union literature by some sixty union members. This was the UAW's first attempt at cracking the Rouge, and so the event was widely publicized. Clergymen, reporters, photographers, and investigators from the U.S. Senate Civil Liberties Subcommittee were present, as were scores of Ford service men.

As the 2 P.M. shift change neared, Frankensteen and his three lieutenants climbed the stairs of the Miller Road overpass. The organizers might not have been up there at all except that a photographer, looking for something for his paper's five o'clock "red-line" edition, persuaded them to pose with the Ford sign in the background. As they tried to look busy for the cameras, grinning and making small talk amongst themselves, a group of unsmiling service men strode purposefully toward them.

"What are you doing here?" one of them demanded.

"The next thing I knew," Kanter told an interviewer many years later, "somebody had socked me in the jaw":

> I had a pair of glasses and they were hanging by one ear like this. Then somebody grabbed them and threw them, and I could see them sailing through the air. At the same time somebody kept clobbering me and I fell and hit the side of the overpass, which was metal. I remember only vaguely that there was a lot of turmoil and fighting going on, and then somebody grabbed me by the legs and under the arms. I was being carried part of the way, and then the next thing I knew I was sailing through the air and I landed on the ground. I guess they threw me off the second level of the overpass which was

On May 26, 1937, union activists (*from left*) Robert Kanter, Walter Reuther, Richard Frankensteen, and Jack Kennedy watch Ford service men approach them as they oversee the first major leafletting of the Rouge.

about eight feet or ten feet high. They threw me over the rail. Then I only vaguely remember people screaming, yelling and running. I got up and started to stagger in the direction of the road.

The burly Frankensteen, a former football standout at the University of Dayton, decided to fight back—and paid the price. He was given a thorough and professional going-over. His jacket was pulled up over his head, rendering his arms useless, and once knocked to the ground, his legs were kicked apart, leaving his groin and stomach open to scores of strategically placed kicks and heel grinds. "My head was like a piece of raw beef steak," he said later. "I remember I was nauseous from the beating. My stomach felt like it had nothing to cling to." Meanwhile, Reuther "was being rolled, literally rolled, down the stairs," said Kanter.

On the street, servicemen pushed, kicked, and slapped the women who had gathered to distribute leaflets and pounded their male counterparts, all while Dearborn police went through the motions of trying to break up the assaults. Photographers had their box cameras snatched from them and the incriminating glass plates smashed at their feet.

The Battle of the Overpass. Richard Frankensteen is pounded by Ford service men as photographers train their cameras on the mayhem. Most press photographers had their plates seized and smashed by Harry Bennett's men, but a handful of incriminating glass negatives survived.

"There were ten photographers there," recalled Kanter. "If all the pictures that had been taken had been printed, there would have been some dillies there."

As it was, though, the few photographic plates that did survive were enough to document the mayhem. Clearly identified in the pictures were such characters as Joe "Legs" Laman, a convicted kidnapper and rumrunner; Charles Goodman, a thug with a string of twenty-one arrests; ex-prizefighter Sam Taylor, who the Moulders Union had expelled for embezzlement; former downriver gang boss Angelo Caruso; and former "Black Sox" pitcher Eddie Cicotte, who'd been banned from baseball for life for helping to throw the 1919 World Series. Splashed across the front pages of newspapers and grouped inside the glossy weekly news magazines, the photographs of what came to be known as the "Battle of the Overpass" graphically illustrated Ford's "Gestapo tactics" and helped turn public opinion against the company. Ford's rebuttal was to yank all advertising from *Time, Life,* and *Fortune* magazines. It would be eighteen months before the company advertised on their pages again.

In the aftermath of the beatings on the Miller Road overpass, Richard
Frankensteen receives support from Robert Kanter and Walter Reuther.

Hours after the incident, Bennett, evidently unaware of the damning photographs to come, issued a statement reflecting the company's
view of what had happened on the Miller Road overpass. "The affair
was deliberately provoked by union officials," he charged:

> They feel, with or without justification, the La Follette Civil Liberties
> Committee sympathizes with their aims and they simply wanted to
> trump up a charge of Ford brutality that they could take down to
> Washington. . . . I know definitely no Ford Service men or plant
> police were involved in any way in the fight! As a matter of fact, the
> Service men had issued instructions that the union people could
> come and distribute their pamphlets. . . .
>
> The union men were beaten by regular Ford employees who
> were on their way to work on the afternoon shift. The union men
> called them scabs and cursed and taunted them. A Negro who works
> in the foundry was goaded and cursed so viciously by one union
> organizer that he turned and struck, and then the workmen and
> union men milled around a few minutes, punching at each other and
> the union men withdrew. I would be glad to testify before any offi-
> cial . . . committee and I would have no trouble convincing them
> that the union cold-bloodily framed . . . today's disturbance.

Bennett got his wish, testifying in a hearing that dragged through the steamy summer and which saw 150 witnesses take the stand. To the company's contention that the battle had occurred on Ford property, the NLRB board responded: "Technical trespass has never been recognized in law as a fortification for extreme brutality. It was clearly unnecessary for the respondent in protecting its property to blackjack and otherwise maltreat defenseless men and women.... Within the vast River Rouge plant at Dearborn the freedom of self-organization guaranteed by [the Wagner Act] has been replaced by rule of terror and repression." Ford was ordered to "cease and desist" from all antiunion activities, an instruction that was ignored.

As the fight for representation heated up in Ford plants across the country, thugs armed with rubber hoses, brass knuckles, blackjacks, and pistols were organized into so-called terror squads. Subsequent NLRB investigations would disclose their bloody history. In Dallas alone, two squads commanded by a character named "Fats" Perry kept organizing efforts at bay, one inside the plant, the other cruising the city. Organizers and their supporters were singled out for beatings and whippings that led to at least one death. Several union sympathizers were driven out of town, including one man who was beaten and stripped naked before being tarred and feathered. Whether it was Long Beach, Kansas City, Buffalo, St. Louis, or Edgewater, New Jersey, the NLRB found what it called "organized gangsterism" in every Ford factory. Local police typically cooperated with Ford management in breaking up picket lines and escorting strikebreakers in and out of plants. A county sheriff once arrested a Kansas City terror squad caught with an arsenal of fourteen pistols, a dozen shotguns, and scores of other weapons, but the local prosecutor, aligned with the corrupt Pendergast machine, refused to press charges against the twenty-eight men.

The sheer scale of the terror inside Ford plants warranted more attention from the federal government than it actually received. However, Bennett understood that influence was as important as intimidation. He had carefully cultivated ties with J. Edgar Hoover, director of the Federal Bureau of Investigation, providing the agency with names of suspected Communists and using his underworld connections to help solve crimes. In appreciation, the FBI never cracked down on Ford's nefarious union-busting activities.

"What made Bennett so powerful," said union activist Harry Ross, "was he could call you in his office and he could make you a millionaire in three or four months. He could call you in and if he liked you, he would say, 'Okay, from now on you have got the contract to sell powdered soap or lead pencils to the Ford Motor Company.' You sit down and figure out the potentials of selling a product to an empire such as Ford and its affiliates. It is limitless. You could be made a millionaire. It was through this patronage that Bennett always ran his business. It was always this screwed-up sense of power through this patronage that he depended on."

The NLRB repeatedly cited Ford for violations, which had no effect on its behavior. Company lawyers used every stalling tactic legally available to them, delaying cases for years. Meanwhile, the violence mounted on both sides. Bennett was the target of attacks, including an incident where gunmen, firing through the front door of his fortified Ann Arbor home, shot one of his daughters in the leg.

At the end of 1938, Bennett used a combination of charm and bribes to dupe UAW president Homer Martin into accepting a tentative agreement that would have resulted in the withdrawal of all NLRB lawsuits against the company. Hard-core activists such as Walter Reuther and Frankensteen were outraged: anticipated victories in these cases represented the union's best hope of organizing Ford. The resulting uproar created a split in the ranks, with Reuther's loyalists aligning themselves with the CIO and Martin's supporters setting up a separate department within the American Federation of Labor. Bickering between the two factions stalled organizing efforts for more than a year.

Edsel was conflicted by all that was swirling around him. Privately, he identified with the humanistic ideals of most New Deal legislation, including the Wagner Act. "If there was anyone who was concerned about the injustices to workers that were then prominent in the Ford organization, Edsel was," said Ross. "He was a good guy, in my opinion." Always pragmatic, he also knew the company's labor policy was causing it to lose car sales and could potentially wind up costing the automaker hundreds of millions of dollars in government defense contracts as the country moved from depression into war. Yet, as the loyal son of one of the most obstinate antiunion bosses in the land, he could hardly go public with his true feelings.

Suffering from what was assumed to be ulcers, he literally had little stomach for fights with his father. These sessions often ended with him breaking down behind closed doors in despair over Henry's intransigence. Bennett's machinations sickened him all the more and once caused him to blurt out to a friend, "The hurtful thing is that Father takes Harry's word for everything and he won't believe me. Who is this guy anyhow? Where did he come from?"

On more than one occasion in the late 1930s Edsel declared out of frustration that he was going to resign, but each time he was talked down from the emotional window ledge he had climbed out on. There was no telling what would happen to the company if he left, loyal executives told him, and besides, Henry could not go on forever. He was in his seventies and obviously slipping. Soon he would have to give up the reins, and then the company would be Edsel's to run as he saw fit. Weighing everything, the sickly and disillusioned crown prince felt he had no choice but to stay on, while leaving the critical issue of labor relations to his unbending father and his volatile henchman.

"It is pathetic," said Ross, reflecting on the pitched battles still to come, "that such a man of the character of Edsel was not able to fit into the Ford picture instead of this guy Bennett."

# 19

⌬

## *Rearview Mirror*

# Battling "Fordism" in 1937

*On May 26, 1937, Bill May was a twenty-four-year-old wire service reporter new to the labor beat when he innocently hitched a ride to history with several top union organizers. May later became a reporter and photographer for the* Muskegon Chronicle *and retired in 1974 as the paper's managing editor.*

I remember one day in the spring of 1937 when I went down to the River Rouge plant, looking for workers to ask what they thought of the UAW. I'd ask questions, but mostly I got silence and a look that clearly indicated suspicion. I could hardly blame them. Most of them were too frightened to talk to reporters. They just wanted to hold onto their jobs.

But there was one fellow not far from the plant. He was sitting by some rail tracks, eating lunch from a brown paper bag, and he let me sit down by him. He spoke with a heavy accent, in English I could hardly understand, and he, too, didn't feel like talking much. I explained to him how Henry Ford had warned his employees about joining the union, and how Ford had praised the benefits of working in a non-union company.

He listened to me and then he was quiet for a minute. Then he said, "Well, if Meester Ford say that, eet mus' be so. Meester Ford—he's all right man."

This conversation took place shortly before the "Battle of the Overpass," when Richard Frankensteen, Walter Reuther, Robert Kanter and

Reporter Bill May in 1937. "I look for open gun fighting when they go out again," May wrote his wife a few hours after the Battle of the Overpass.

Jack Kennedy were darn near killed in front of me. I wonder if that fellow changed his mind about "Meester Ford" after that.

I was new in Detroit at the time. I'd come to the International News Service [INS] on January 25, 1937, after spending six years at the *Owosso Argus-Press* as a reporter and telegraph editor. I'd spent a year in New York as a darkroom technician while studying photography in Manhattan, and I liked the city. I thought I'd like Detroit. As it turned out, I discovered I didn't have the necessary grit or determination to be a big-city reporter and I soon left Detroit. But while I was there, I happened to experience one of the seminal moments in labor history.

Although there were quite a few reporters and UAW-invited observers on or near the overpass that day, the number certainly wasn't what it might have been had there been a widespread expectation of violence. I was there because of a hunch felt by Jack Vincent, the INS bureau chief. He decided that morning that it might be worth the time and effort to see what would happen when the union attempted to distribute leaflets to workers at the 2 P.M. shift change.

I was a $35-a-week newsman without a car. I took a street car to the UAW's organizing office, where I found Frankensteen and the others getting ready to go to Gate No. 4, the Rouge plant's principal gate, where they were to oversee the scheduled distribution of leaflets by

The United Auto Workers distribute leaflets during a shift change at the Rouge.

about sixty UAW members, mostly women. It was either get a ride or walk, so I asked Frankensteen if I could bum a ride with them.

"Of course," he said, and told me to hop into the car.

It was about a two-mile ride from the UAW office to the gate. I remember Frankensteen's mood as being almost jaunty, but there was some apprehension. After all these years, I can't relate the conversation. Yet I'm sure there was some talk of possible trouble, because I can remember sitting in the back seat, wedged between Frankensteen and Kennedy, and joking about the fact that I was so "well-protected" by union officials.

Frankensteen was in charge of the Ford organizing drive. Reuther, of course, is so well known today that little more need be said of him. Robert Kanter helped Reuther organize Local 174. Kanter was considered the "intellectual" of the four in the overpass battle. His father was a pacifist and his mother knew twenty-one languages. Jack Kennedy came to Detroit in the late 1920s as an organizer for the Carpenters Union, then joined the UAW in 1933. Kennedy was the first president of Chrysler UAW Local 7, which met for the first time in March 1937 at the Chrysler Kercheval plant. He and Reuther, along with Morris Fields, were named assistant district organizers in the drive to organize Ford. According to UAW headquarters, they had obtained permission from the Dearborn City Council to pass out the leaflets. Harry Bennett, Henry Ford's chief of security, had told the press there would be no effort to stop the distribution, but he also said he couldn't predict what might be the reaction of the men, the Ford workers.

Once we arrived at the Rouge, we climbed a long flight of stairs to an overpass above a street and rail tracks. The four moved close together to pose for some pictures. There were broad smiles on their faces for a moment, but their facial expressions were changing to a look of inquisitiveness as a group of some twenty to thirty unsmiling, husky men moved towards them in a fearsome stride. It was obvious these toughs were not there to greet or shake hands with the union leaders. Within seconds, three to five of them surrounded each of the UAW organizers and began to inflict a brutal beating. Amidst the flying fists you could hear shouts of "Get the hell out of here!" and "This is Ford property!"

Because Frankensteen was in charge of the operation, and because I knew him better than the others, I tried to watch him most during the "battle." It was clear to me that he had been singled out to receive the worst of it—or he got the worst of it because he tried to make a fight of it. One of his assailants behind him grabbed his jacket and pulled it up to his head, locking his arms so he couldn't break free. Two men in front of him were methodically flailing him with crisp, hard punches to the face and stomach, doing the job like professional fighters. Frankensteen dropped to the cement floor of the overpass. They kicked him, lifted him to his feet, and gave him some more of the same. As he went down again, they kicked him in the kidney area of the back and in the groin.

Meanwhile, another squad of Bennett's servicemen was giving the same kind of a beating to Reuther, who was too small to put up much resistance. By not trying to defend himself, he explained later, he had hoped it would end sooner and his beating wouldn't be as severe. But he didn't get off easy. He was punched in the face without mercy. When he fell to the concrete floor, he was grabbed by the shoulders, lifted up and beat some more. Several times he was lifted from the concrete and then slammed to the ground. He was kicked, over and over.

Being so close to the action, I heard an exchange of words between two of the servicemen which was not generally reported. The men had Frankensteen, already bleeding from his nose and mouth, backed against a guard railing of the bridge. One of them, it appeared to me, was attempting to roll him over the railing, onto the street below. I heard the other serviceman protest. "No, no, don't push him over," he said. "It'll kill him."

While all this was going on, other teams of Bennett's men were giving similar beatings to Kennedy and Kanter, neither of whom was capable of putting up any effective defense. I lost sight of them. There was violent fighting almost everywhere on the bridge.

After one of the servicemen said, "That's enough!" a couple times, Reuther was kicked down the steel stairway with the admonishment, "This is Ford property. Get the hell out of here. And don't ever come back!" As he fell—or rolled—down the steps, servicemen in pursuit would lift him to his feet and then kick him down again.

Frankensteen got the same treatment, if not worse, on the stairs. They bounced him, slugged him, helped him to his feet, and kicked him down again until he finally fell to the ground at the bottom of the stairway, beaten to a condition of near helplessness.

Precious few of the leaflets—urging "Unionism, not Fordism"—got into the hands of the Ford workers that day. Below the overpass a near riot erupted as the army of ex-cops, bouncers, prizefighters, ex-convicts and gangsters violently put a halt to the distribution. UAW women, wearing berets and arm bands, arrived just as the beatings began on the overpass. Kicking and screaming, the women were forced back into the autos or street cars which brought them. Many were injured. Of the union men who tried to pass out the leaflets, one was reported to have received a skull fracture; another was hospitalized with his back broken.

It was all over in about five minutes.

Back at the UAW organizing office after the battle, Frankensteen—battered and bleeding—said, "If Mr. Ford thinks this is going to stop us, he's got another think coming."

Was I frightened? I certainly was! After all, I had climbed those stairs along with Frankensteen and the others. I wore no press identification. I stood no more than fifteen, twenty feet from Frankensteen throughout the beating. Yet, while I got shoved and pushed, no one struck me. How did they know I was not a UAW man? Or would they have cared?

That night I wrote a letter to my wife, Emily. "I was in the riot this afternoon," I wrote. "I look for open gun fighting when they"—meaning the UAW—"go out again. And I can't see how the union is ever going to organize Ford, although sentiment will be with them more after today's rioting." I underestimated the determination of the UAW. Nevertheless, the next few years saw much terror and violence in all of the Ford plants.

After the Battle of the Overpass, I asked Frankensteen for a letter of recommendation. A ruptured appendix had caused me to miss almost a year of work. He graciously wrote one, jokingly asking that I please don't show it to Henry Ford. "Other than that," he said, "use it wherever it will do you the most good." He also accepted my offer of a Rotary engagement.

See, having been a newsman in Owosso prior to joining INS, I was quite well-acquainted with many businessmen and industrialists. And it was my home town. George C. Reineke, an officer of the Estey Manufacturing Company, the once-famous furniture maker, knew from a conversation that I was well-acquainted with Frankensteen. He asked me if I could get Frankensteen to speak at one of the Owosso Rotary meetings.

Considering the era, this was a rather daring venture for both Reineke and Frankensteen. Owosso was strongly nonunion in almost all of its industries. Reineke didn't want to be in the position of suggesting unionism to the Rotary Club members, but he did believe Frankensteen had a good message to sell. Frankensteen did come and speak. His speech, of course, was about the UAW, problems of the auto workers, and why he was dedicating himself to the UAW's cause. He got a rather cool reception from the Rotarians, though they did politely applaud him after he had spoken.

All four of the UAW leaders who were brutalized that day are now dead, one of them—Reuther—dying at age sixty-two with his wife, May, in a plane crash in 1970. He was flying to the UAW's Family Educational Center near Onaway in northern Michigan. The center was one of Reuther's cherished projects during his twenty-four years as president of the UAW.

Jack Kennedy died at age forty-nine on August 18, 1937, only eighty-four days after the beating he took at the overpass. His death, however, was not due to injuries sustained in the Ford battle. Bob Kanter died in Connecticut in 1977, his death being related to rheumatic fever he had as a child and that had damaged a heart valve. That same year Dick Frankensteen died in Detroit, at age seventy. Although his death was attributed to natural causes, UAW people who had been close to him believed the beating he took in 1937 damaged his eyesight and contributed to the breakdown in his health which eventually claimed his life.

I was amazed at how little was made of the Battle of the Overpass when the UAW had its fiftieth anniversary in 1985. I remember at the time asking one person working on the UAW staff if he knew the story of Richard Frankensteen.

"Frankensteen?" he said. "I recall hearing the name, but I really don't know who he was."

I dropped the subject. I figured it'd be useless to ask him about Kanter and Kennedy.

# 20

❦

# A New Social Order

*The day they walked out of Ford, one of the Italian company guards who was an ex-convict, pulled out a gun in the machine shop and he went to the guys. He said, "If you leave the machine, I'll blow your brains out." Another Italian boy, who was a union man, appeared from somewhere between the machines and he pulled out a knife and cut this company guard's belly wide open. His guts came out and they had to take him to the hospital right away. Now the guys could walk out. I mean, the thing got so bad. Finally, we succeeded.*

—Nick DiGaetano, recalling the climactic 1941 strike

F oundry worker Shelton Tappes, called back to the Rouge after a layoff, made the mistake of marching in the 1939 Labor Day parade in downtown Detroit without attempting to disguise his identity. "I didn't wear a mask like I was supposed to, because I thought, 'This is a free country,'" Tappes remembered.

When he reported to the Ford employment office the following day, he was told: "Oh, you like to walk, don't you? Well, you walk yourself out that door, and you just keep on walking, 'cause you don't work here anymore."

With that, Tappes's name was added to the ever-lengthening list of arbitrarily fired Ford employees petitioning the National Labor Relations Board to get their jobs back. While waiting for his case to wind its way through the legal system, he worked full-time for the union, receiving $15 a week in car fare and 60 cents an hour when he distributed handbills.

No employer in America was cited more often for NLRB violations than the Ford Motor Company, which remained defiant years after other carmakers had come to terms with organized labor. In 1940 the NLRB determined that at least nine Ford plants were guilty of unfair labor practices. For Edsel, this was an embarrassing distinction for the company and threatened defense contracts with the federal government, which required all contractors to adhere to the provisions of the Wagner Act. But his crotchety father's intransigence only grew as walkouts and sit-down strikes interrupted production at his regional assembly plants. "All wars, labor unions, strikes, by an insidious conspiracy group of war mongers and mongrels," Henry scribbled in one of his jot books.

Several months after the Battle of the Overpass, when the NLRB wrapped up hearings with an order to Ford to reinstate twenty-nine discharged workers, Harry Bennett had spoken for his boss: "They'll have an awful fight over that one. We won't take those men back."

And they didn't. If anything, the intimidation inside many Ford factories grew worse. Men suspected of union affiliation were searched when they entered the plant, harassed as they worked, and spied on after they left for home. Sidewalk sluggings and arbitrary firings remained the cornerstone of the company's Neanderthal labor policy. Ford's control of Dearborn (the city council hastily passed an antihandbill ordinance after the Battle of the Overpass, for example, to curtail leafletting) made the Rouge a particularly tough nut to crack. In 1938, two men armed with revolvers and blackjacks broke into an apartment and worked over Walter Reuther during a family gathering. In the resultant trial, they admitted to the beating and to being hired by Bennett but were acquitted by a stacked jury.

"I'd come home so tired and irritated I'd take it out on my wife and my kids," said Al Bardelli, curling his gnarled hand into a fist at the memory of those days. "What I really wanted to do was beat the shit out of Bennett. That's what we all wanted to do."

∽∘∽

Although the Rouge was the real and symbolic epicenter of the sprawling Ford industrial empire, and thus the logical focus of the union's principle organizing efforts, it can hardly be said that auto manufacturing and its attendant problems occupied all or even most of Henry's waking moments during the latter part of the 1930s. He admitted the place had become so big, so unwieldy, that it had long since ceased to be fun. He still ate lunch with Edsel and the heads of the various departments inside the executive dining room at the Engineering Laboratory every day, a long-standing ritual that allowed him to keep up with what was going on. Occasionally, a special guest, such as Charlie Chaplin, Will Rogers, or Mickey Rooney, was invited to break bread with them. (Bennett, not being a "car guy," never was. He had his own private dining room inside his basement office.) Away from the Rouge, Henry spent his time in a variety of idiosyncratic but personally satisfying pursuits, secure in the knowledge that—unlike General Motors and other monolithic multinational corporations—the operations and policies of the Ford Motor Company still were dependent on the whims of one man.

Bruce Simpson often saw more of Henry than his father did. Howard Simpson was one of the few engineers at the company who held a degree and was Ford's point man on many tractor and transmission design projects. In 1929 eight-year-old Bruce was part of the first class of thirty-two students enrolled in the Greenfield Village school system, sitting at the very desk Henry had occupied half a century earlier. "It still had his initials carved into it," said Simpson. By the time Simpson graduated a decade later, the village schools had expanded into the museum and several historic buildings. Lovett Hall, a new recreation and education center, opened in 1937. Before the village schools closed in 1969, as many as 300 children from kindergarteners to post-high school technical students were enrolled in the unique educational system, which, like its founder, stressed "learning by doing."

Every morning when school was in session, Ford would join students at the nondenominational prayer service at the Martha-Mary Chapel, the small church he built and named after his and Clara's mothers. Afterward he often joined the children in class, folding his lanky legs into a cramped seat and "just sitting back and listening to our lessons," said Simpson. He would sometimes join them on the frequent "hands-on" field trips to the surrounding buildings and museum.

Simpson, who demonstrated some musical ability, managed to get his adolescent hands on an antique Italian violin. Still active in the local orchestra today, Simpson estimates the current value of the instrument to be $500,000. "Mr. Ford just pulled it out of his vault in the

Engineering Laboratory and let me use it for four years. I played it at our graduation ceremony."

The young Simpson also came across the great man at the monthly formal dances the Fords started in the 1920s in their effort to revive old-fashioned dancing. Henry and Clara were shocked and distressed by the sudden appearance of "sex dancing" after the war, whirlwind numbers such as the Charleston, Black Bottom, and lindy hop. So they imported a stern, self-educated instructor named Benjamin Lovett from Massachusetts to teach the calls and steps of the more civilized waltzes, cotillions, and quadrilles they had enjoyed in their youth. With the Fords' backing, it wasn't long before dancing became an integral part of the curriculum in local school systems. Simpson described Ford as "a very agile, very spirited dancer." One of his favorite partners was Simpson's mother, Gertrude. As dancing was his and Clara's principal social activity, Henry would tolerate nothing but excellence. "It was Lovett's responsibility to rescue Ford from a clumsy dancer," observed one executive.

The dances originally were held in the "Blue Room" of the Engineering Laboratory before moving to Lovett Hall. A small band played for the 200 or so invited guests, who danced at arm's length and with perfect deportment. Sorenson never showed up and Edsel only rarely, but scores of other executives regularly attended because they felt their jobs depended on it. To get through the ordeal, many periodically retired to the restrooms for a nip of "rejuvenator." Their subterfuge often backfired as the "dancing billionaire," his nostrils flaring over a wanton whiff of alcohol, would wait until the offending parties took the floor before ordering the band to increase the tempo.

When he wasn't demonstrating the proper use of a nineteenth-century farm implement to wide-eyed seven-year-olds or spinning Clara around a polished dance floor, Henry often could be found inside various experimental laboratories (including one on the upper level of the Fair Lane powerhouse). He searched for ways of converting common agricultural products into innovative commercial uses, finding his greatest success with soybeans. Beginning in 1935, several of the parts in each Ford car, including the paint, door handles, horn, accelerator, and timing gears, were made of soybean-based materials. In 1940, a soybean research center was established at the Rouge, and on separate occasions the following year Ford unveiled a handmade plastic car and wore a "soybean suit" to demonstrate alternative uses for the versatile legume. He even picked up an axe for the cameras and took a few whacks at the car's trunk to show its superior resiliency as compared with metal. An amused press, noting that soybeans, wheat, flax, ramie, and hemp had gone into the making of the plastic, called the new vehicle "part salad and part automobile" and wondered why Ford didn't add spinach into the mix for increased strength. But once again, Henry was ahead of his time: in 1953, General Motors took the wraps off the Chevrolet Corvette, the first mass-produced plastic-bodied car.

Ford's immense wealth allowed him to transform casual interests into large-scale projects. An example was the socioeconomic revolution he engineered in Richmond Hill, Georgia. In the process of building a winter home on the site of an old plantation overlooking the Ogeechee River, Henry became concerned that the local economy revolved around moonshining and not much else. During the 1930s he bought up some 75,000 acres of land, a heavily wooded tract he called Ford Farms. Starting in 1936, scores of buildings—including a sawmill, ice plant, chapel, commissary, post office, fire station, bakery, health clinic, schools, and housing—were constructed on the property, all with the goal of lifting the chronically depressed community out of its doldrums. While acknowledging the legal right of Georgia to segregate its facilities, Ford also knew the Southern claim of "separate but equal" was a myth for blacks. He took a look around the dilapidated schools that black children struggled to be educated in and said, "All they need is a chance, and we are going to give them a chance." Then he built a first-class school named after the famed agricultural scientist, George Washington Carver (with whom he tried to develop edible weeds). At the same time, a comprehensive health campaign helped eradicate such diseases as malaria and hookworm, while lumbering and farming operations provided jobs for hundreds of men and women, including many physically handicapped. All told, the Richmond Hill project cost Ford more than $4 million in depression dollars.

Ford's experiences with radio provide another case study of how a fancy could quickly turn into a major involvement when he got excited. One day in 1919, intrigued by the newest phenomenon, he approached the business editor of the *Dearborn Independent*, Fred Black.

"Say Fred, what do you know about wireless?"

"I don't know anything, Mr. Ford," replied Black. "Just the stories published in the newspapers."

Students of the George Washington Carver School in Georgia pose with their benefactor (*top row, second from left*). To the left of Ford is the school's teacher.

"Well," said Henry, always happy to turn to a rank novice instead of some fancy expert when he wanted something done, "I think it would be a damned good idea to learn. You make me one of these wireless receiving sets."

Within a few years the new wireless station Henry built in Dearborn was arguably the biggest in the world, its long-wave and short-wave frequencies carrying as far as Siberia and the waters off of Japan. Henry, not accustomed to thinking small, envisioned his own network of 400 stations. Federal legislation soon made Ford drop out of the communication business as a carrier, but as a sponsor he continued using the airwaves to reach the multitudes. During the 1930s the company was the largest radio advertiser in the automobile industry. In 1934 it paid an eye-popping $100,000 to underwrite the broadcast of the World Series between Detroit and St. Louis, the first commercial sponsorship of the fall classic.

That same year the *Ford Sunday Evening Hour* began broadcasts over the entire CBS network. Its soothing "long-hair" music, originating from Orchestra Hall and then the Masonic Temple in Detroit, featured the top musicians and conductors of the day and reached upward of 13 million listeners each week. Edsel introduced the first show by telling the audience that "our program will not be interrupted by irritating sales talk." What listeners got instead was a six-minute essay written and delivered by William Cameron, the man who had once penned Henry's anti-Semitic rants in the *Independent*. Cameron occasionally went on the air drunk but always managed to convey Henry's folksy observations on "certain matters of national interest and importance" in a calm, righteous voice. In the aftermath of the Battle of the Overpass, Cameron's "sermonettes" typically involved some aspect of business-government relations. The man in the White House took a verbal pounding while the spirit of free enterprise was praised. Each show closed as it had opened, with a playing of "The Children's Prayer" from Hansel and Gretel.

The union, in the midst of processing the legal claims of thousands of discharged workers, wasn't having any of Ford's dressed-up "propaganda," as a ditty in *The United Auto Worker* made clear:

> Now the music dies out in the distance,
> They announced a lovely old hymn,
> Giving all glory to God
> And singing their praises to Him.
> Do you think, Henry Ford, you exploiter,
> You can buy with this kind of stuff
> The thanks and goodwill of thousands
> Who haven't nearly enough?
> So you might as well keep your music
> And shut old Cameron's yap
> For while we enjoy your music
> We haven't time for your crap.

⁖◦⌣

On February 10, 1941, Ford's last best hope—the U.S. Supreme Court—upheld the findings of the NLRB. This meant workers were free to organize as they wished. The CIO faction of the UAW, its Ford organizing drive now led by Walter Reuther and Mike Widman, a former coal miner and a top aide to labor legend John L. Lewis, cranked up its efforts several notches. Harry Bennett had already been preparing for this day, insinuating himself with Homer Martin (through the bribe of a fully furnished house and a couple of lucrative concession contracts) and financing the organizing drive of the renegade AFL faction. Bennett envisioned a scenario where he would have Martin in his hip pocket and thousands of flunkies filling the union ranks, allowing the company to keep de facto control of its work force.

On April 1, 1941, eight members of the union's grievance committee were given permission by their foreman to see the division superintendent. The manager instructed the men to report to the employment office, where they were told, "You left your jobs. You're fired."

News of the firings and the company's refusal to arbitrate "spread in the plant like wildfire," Widman later told Studs Terkel. "We called the strike for 12:15, just after midnight. . . . What everybody said was impossible was about to happen."

> We had surveyed the fourteen highways that led into the plant. It would take at least two thousand cars on each of 'em as a picket line to tie things up. One of the boys got the idea: We'll pull the trolley pole off the first streetcar coming in from Detroit. So we had the streetcars clear downtown for about six miles all stopped. The boys stacked up rubbish and cars and anything they could find. Everything was tied up.

A tense standoff between Dearborn police and union workers who had seized control of several departments ended when the men marched out. By then thousands of pickets and vehicles squeezed the Rouge like an enormous boa constrictor, locking Bennett and a small army of service men inside the plant and preventing scabs from entering. Henry was not about to capitulate. "He told me to arm everyone we had in the plant, and use tear gas if necessary," said Bennett. "I felt the same way Mr. Ford did." Bennett stationed men with machine guns on rooftops. He had already recruited several hundred black workers, who had historically been shunned by unions, to act as strikebreakers. Armed with homemade weapons and paid their hourly wage around the clock, their controversial presence inside the plant added a racial dimension to an already explosive situation.

While Bennett refused to even talk, preferring to have his service men pelt strikers with screws, bolts, and washers, flying squadrons of union toughs kept order on the sidewalks and streets outside "the fort." Al Bardelli, a picket captain, gleefully recalled several workers picking up a car containing half a dozen service men and turning it back in the direction from which it came. Skirmishes broke out between black

The 1941 Ford strike. Ford's "fascist" policies were equated with those of Hitler.

workers loyal to Ford and union men. Pickets assaulted anyone foolish enough to try to enter the plant. The photograph of one such beating, "The Picket Line," ran on front pages across the country and graphically illustrated the UAW's resolve. At Fair Lane, just four miles west of the Rouge, Clara Ford followed the unfolding drama through newspapers, the radio, and her husband's fumings.

Governor Murray Van Wagoner refused Ford's request to send in the National Guard to end the strike. Instead, he visited Henry at home, hoping to mediate a solution.

"Well, you've got a plant," said Ford by way of greeting, "what are you going to do with it?"

The crisis caused Edsel to cut short a recuperative holiday in Florida. Henry told Edsel to stay out of this latest showdown, that Bennett would handle it, but the son argued his case for a peaceful compromise so passionately, so persuasively, that the elder Ford finally caved in and reluctantly gave his blessings to a truce. On April 10, in exchange for a promise that the plant would remain closed while both sides talked, the union took down its barricades. "Mr. Ford gave in to Edsel's wishes,"

Striking union members swarm all over a worker trying to cross the picket line on April 3, 1941. The photograph won a Pulitzer Prize for Milton E. (Pete) Brooks of the *Detroit News*.

said Bennett in his memoirs. "I don't think the CIO would have won out if it hadn't been for Edsel's attitude."

Ford agreed to a government-supervised election to determine which, if any, union would represent Rouge workers. The men voted on May 21. Of some 78,000 ballots cast, 51,868 of them (69.9 percent) indicated they wanted Reuther's hard-core CIO to be the plant's bargaining agent, as compared with just 27.4 percent for the AFL. In yet another sign of his creeping senility, Henry had convinced himself that his workers would somehow forget years of abuse and vote instead to keep the company an open shop. But only 1,958 men—2.7 percent of voters—marked their ballots "no union." Ford was bewildered and devastated, Sorenson would subsequently write, calling it "perhaps the greatest disappointment he had in all his business experience. . . . He was never the same after that."

Contract negotiations followed. On June 18, 1941, a formal agreement was shown to Henry. In it, the union was given everything it had desired—plus some. In fact, the terms were so one-sided that Henry, who had left contract talks in the hands of a team of negotiators supervised by Bennett, initially refused to agree to them.

"I'm not going to sign this contract!" he shouted during a meeting the following day with Edsel and Sorenson. "I want you and Edsel to understand that as far as I am concerned the key is in the door. I'm going to throw it away. I don't want any more of this business. Close the plant down if necessary. Let the union take over if it wishes." When Sorenson, playing to Ford's hatred of FDR, suggested the federal government would probably get involved to assure the timely fulfillment of defense orders, Henry retorted, "Well, if the government steps in, it will be in the motorcar business and it won't be me."

For the longest time, Clara had watched from the sidelines as the relations between her son and husband became increasingly strained by labor strife. At one point she had confronted Sorenson at his office. "Who is this man Bennett," she demanded to know, "who has so much control over my husband and is ruining my son's health?"

Now she could no longer restrain herself. That evening, when Henry came home, she put her foot down. She had had enough of the violence and the turmoil and the family quarreling that had taken so much out of everybody, she frantically told her husband of fifty-four years. If he did not agree to the contract, what she tellingly referred to as a "peace agreement," then she was going to pack up and leave him.

Henry could not believe what he was hearing. Feeling betrayed by his workers and convinced most of the rest of the world had turned its back on him, he could not bear the thought of the Believer, the one constant source of support and comfort throughout his long life, abandoning him as well. The next morning, radio reports revealed the old tycoon still had the ability to surprise. Henry Ford had done a complete about-face and agreed to terms with the union.

"What in the world happened?" Edsel asked the equally stunned Sorenson.

"I was just about to ask you the same thing," said Sorenson.

A few days earlier, Bennett had insisted that union representatives "can bargain till hell freezes over but they won't get anything." Now the union was practically partners with the company. Ford agreed to match the highest wage rates in the industry, to reinstate discharged workers with back pay, to install a shop steward system to handle grievances, and to require service men to wear identifying uniforms. Furthermore, workers were to be given two hours' pay when called to work and then sent home; and they were to receive time and a half for overtime and double pay for Sundays and holidays. Ford also agreed to the checkoff, whereby the company was responsible for deducting union dues from workers' paychecks. The remarkable pact affected 130,000 Ford employees below the foreman level.

Why the abrupt change in direction? Union officials had their own theory about Bennett's unexpected largesse, said Richard Frankensteen:

> Now, it was our conjecture that the reason for . . . Bennett's change of heart was because he was on shaky ground, figuring that Henry Ford, Sr., would be logically the first to die, knowing that he was on the out list with Edsel Ford. I think he figured that his best security in the Ford Motor Car Company was to be the man who could deal with labor . . . that if they had a contract, he would again enhance himself as he had in the days when he controlled the hoodlums who were hired into the plant, and when he protected the grandchildren from kidnapping and so forth. This was a new medium for Bennett to proclaim himself.

Whatever the motives of the principles involved, the union was as ecstatic as Ford's fellow industrialists were outraged, for the historic and hard-fought accord became the template for all future labor agreements. "We have decided to go the whole way," Edsel declared. "No half-measures will be effective."

The upshot of a suddenly enlightened workplace was a freedom that bordered on giddiness. "It was a little tough for some of the fellows to accept at first," said Mike Widman. "They were suspicious. There was a rash of wildcat strikes. I think it came out of this newborn freedom. Each little thing, they'd pull the pin in that department until the grievance was settled." Bennett, naive to the mindset of the rank and file, even suggested allowing workers to elect their own foremen (an invitation to shop-floor anarchy) and once offered to provide Widman with a company ride to a meeting. "That's all I needed was a car with a chauffeur, provided by the Ford Motor Company," Widman recalled with a laugh. "From a very tough anti-union position, the company now tried to get along," he added. "In the old days, every time we saw a Ford go by, we'd say, 'There's another tin lizzie.' After the strike, we said, 'Doggone, isn't that a nice little buggie?'"

Henry was just happy to hold onto his beloved Callie. Describing the circumstances of his capitulation later to Sorenson, he warned, "Don't ever discredit the power of a woman."

# 21

⌇⌀⌇

# You Know How Father Is

*"You're lucky to have such a son," someone remarked to the father in the presence of the son at a reception this spring.*

*"Yes, I am," laughed the father, "and Edsel is lucky to have me as a father—to bring him up for the job that's ahead of him."*

*He put his arm around his son and they both laughed at their little family joke.*

—Detroit Free Press (1943)

Ford's battles with organized labor foreshadowed a much deadlier global conflict between the forces of fascism and democracy. On December 7, 1941, Japanese warplanes attacked Pearl Harbor, transforming America's foot dragging on the issue of Japan's and Germany's bellicosity into instant resolve to smash the enemy on two fronts. One day a few months later, with U.S. industry frantically retooling for this monumental task, Edsel presided over a paratroop demonstration at Ford Airport. A reporter, noticing Henry and Clara off on their own across the field, asked the aging automaker why he wasn't with the high-ranking company and military brass.

"Edsel is over there," said Henry, "that's his job from now on. I'm getting too old. I'm relieving myself of all my responsibilities as fast as I can. I feel my years."

"Any regrets?" Ford was asked.

"None!" exclaimed Henry. "Everything is in good hands. Edsel has grown into a fine man and when my time comes I'll know that everything will go on as I've planned it."

Although the press kindly refrained from describing his condition, the Flivver King finally was looking his age. A lifetime of fad diets, daily exercise, and abstinence from alcohol and tobacco had kept Ford physically strong and mentally alert through his middle seventies. "You can live as long as you want," he announced about this time, "as long as you only eat cracked wheat." But a mild stroke in 1938, when he was seventy-five years old, followed by another stroke two years later, took their toll. By the time of America's entry into World War II, his gray hair had turned white and his skin, normally colored by activity, had the appearance of rice paper. Equally fragile was his mental capacity. Henry was prone to bouts of senility, though displays of odd or irrational behavior often were diplomatically dismissed as being part of his well-known contrariness.

Those closest to the throne knew better, however. A year and a half prior to the attack on Pearl Harbor, when President Franklin Roosevelt was positioning the still officially neutral country as the "arsenal of democracy," Edsel went to Washington to discuss ways of getting the Ford Motor Company involved. He met with William Knudsen, who had given up the presidency of General Motors to serve as FDR's Commissioner of Industrial Protection. Edsel, whom Knudsen liked and respected from their days together at Ford, left with an agreement to build 6,000 Rolls-Royce Merlin engines. These were earmarked for England's air force, whose Spitfires were involved in a death struggle with Germany's Luftwaffe. Although Henry initially approved of the contract, he changed his mind three days later. After unsuccessfully trying to reason with him, Edsel was forced to call Knudsen and tell him of the company's about-face.

Knudsen was flabbergasted. The contract had already been publicly announced. "Aren't you president?" he asked.

"Yes, I am," said Edsel, sadness and resignation in his voice. "But you know how Father is."

Knudsen certainly did: it was one reason he had left Ford's employ a couple of decades earlier. He hurried to Dearborn to argue the government's case. "Mr. Ford," he said at the climactic point of their meeting inside Edsel's office, "we have your word that you would make them. I told the President your decision, and he was very happy about it."

Henry's moral oscillation over his company's proper place in time of war had originally caused him to give, and then rescind, his permission. It was possible he could change his mind again. But bringing

Roosevelt into the conversation made him dig his heels into the carpet. "We won't build the engines at all," he barked. "Withdraw the whole order. Take it to someone else." Knudsen left Dearborn outraged, while Edsel felt helpless and embarrassed. It was a classic display of Henry Ford the bully.

The fiasco resulted in severe public humiliation for Edsel, as well as for Knudsen, and helped labor unions, then engaged in their own war to organize Ford plants, to more credibly paint Henry as a Nazi sympathizer. Picket signs and pamphlets regularly equated Ford's "fascist" policies with Hitler's, with a swastika usually employed to drive home the point. Up until Pearl Harbor, Henry did, in fact, openly side with isolationists such as Charles Lindbergh (who also had received the Service Cross of the German Eagle from Nazi Germany). His contradictory thinking—that it was all right for Ford subsidiaries in England and Germany to profit from producing vehicles and armaments for their respective governments but immoral for domestic factories to manufacture the same for sale to foreign powers—was the kind of illogic Edsel was accustomed to dealing with even before his father's descent from reason. A few months later, Edsel was able to persuade him to take on a defense contract to build Pratt and Whitney engines by stressing that the job benefited the United States and not a "belligerent" nation. For all of his ethical objections to war, after the United States officially entered the fray Henry became a "fighting pacifist," just as he had in the previous world war. The Ford Motor Company ultimately would become the country's third largest defense contractor, its $5.25 billion in government sales trailing only General Motors and Curtiss-Wright.

Henry could still be persuaded by the sheer grandiosity of a project, which is how Willow Run, the largest aircraft factory in the world, came to be built in the soybean fields outside Ypsilanti, Michigan. Henry named the $200 million superplant after a stream that wound through the woods. Charlie Sorenson cockily promised to pump out B-24 "Liberator" bombers as regularly as his boys at the Rouge pumped out cars. Never mind that nobody had ever built thirty-ton warplanes in bulk before and that four-engine bombers, each requiring 1.5 million parts and 700,000 rivets, were quite different from V-8's and Model A's.

With its sixty-seven-acre main building and goal of 500 bombers a month (more than twice the number the plane's designer, Consolidated Aircraft Corporation of San Diego, was capable of producing in a year),

The bomber plant at Willow Run.

Willow Run was audacious in scope and purpose. It was designed by Albert Kahn (who was to die shortly thereafter) and fully operational in mid-1942. It was larger than the prewar factories of the three major domestic aircraft companies combined and easily the largest factory in the world under one roof. Columnist Westbrook Pegler, in a comment typical of the gushing over Henry Ford's newest manufacturing marvel, proclaimed it "the damndest colossus the industrial world has ever known." Charles Lindbergh, hired by Ford as chief aviation consultant, considered Willow Run "a sort of Grand Canyon of the mechanized world." At its peak almost 30,000 men and women worked there, including James Sterner, who later described the "roar of the machinery, the special din of the riveting gun . . . the far-reaching line of half-born skyships growing wings under swarms of workers, and the restless cranes swooping overhead."

Some observers commented on the plant's L shape, an unusual configuration when one assumed Ford would take advantage of the wide-open countryside to lay out what Kahn was calling "the longest room ever built." But the ground that steam shovels bit into when construction began lay in Washtenaw, a Republican county. Unwilling to have the plant cross into bordering Wayne, a Democratic county, with all that suggested in terms of FDR and higher taxes, Henry had Kahn give the building a "hard left" short of the county line.

✨

With auto manufacturing suspended for the duration of the war, Willow Run consumed nearly all of Edsel's waking hours. It also helped to break him physically. Original production estimates proved embarrassingly optimistic in the beginning, when only an occasional bomber managed to make its way down the mile-long final assembly line before being taxied to the adjacent airfield. After an initial rush of laudatory news stories, the high absenteeism, low morale, and seemingly endless production problems caused some national publications to criticize the plant and prompted wags to label it "Will It Run." Even someone as robust as Sorenson fainted twice from the long hours needed to get the bomber plant on track.

In Edsel's case, the workload aggravated a preexisting medical condition. He had suffered from stomach problems since the late 1930s. However, a jammed calendar and the intrusive nature of the tests caused him to put off treatment until the pain became almost unbearable. In January 1942, he underwent an operation for ulcers. What doctors found was cancer. They removed half of Edsel's stomach. "I'm making fine progress," the patient insisted in a letter to Irving Bacon, "and am fully confident of the outcome." By March he had recovered sufficiently to resume work, but a few weeks later he suffered a relapse while on a trip to Washington with Sorenson. Gaunt and weak, yet afraid of what might happen if his father and Harry Bennett were not at least partially held in check, Edsel soldiered on. "The war won't wait," he told friends concerned over the pace he was keeping. Painkillers, sedatives, and a bland diet helped him get through each day.

Henry blamed his son's decline on his "high living" and "ear piddlers," his term for gossipmongers. He thought drinking unpasteurized milk from Ford Farms would help settle Edsel's stomach. Instead, a bad batch of unsterilized milk caused him to come down with undulant fever. The chills, aching joints, and high temperatures aggravated his condition. Today, antibiotics would be used to treat the fever. But in 1942 all that the best doctors at Henry Ford Hospital could really do was prescribe rest and monitor his condition. When Edsel failed to show any significant improvement, Henry threatened to get rid of them and place his son under the care of his personal chiropractor.

On September 18, 1942, President Roosevelt visited Willow Run. Henry, a vacant look in his eyes, joined FDR and Edsel in a jeep tour. "Will It Run" seemed to come to life in the wake of the presidential inspection. By the end of December a meager total of fifty-six planes had been built. But thanks to the unflagging efforts of Edsel and Sorenson, the retooling, assembly, and manpower difficulties that made the bomber plant a national disgrace in the first full year of the war were being resolved. One key decision was to move subassembly work to other Ford shops and subcontractors, freeing up workers to concentrate on final assembly. Monthly production steadily mounted, from thirty-one Liberators in January 1943 to 190 in June. By early 1944 one bomber was coming off the line each hour, which worked out to a rate of about 700 a month. With the kinks in mass production ironed out, the price per plane dropped—from an original cost of $238,000 to $137,000. By war's end a total of 8,685 B-24's had rolled out of Willow Run.

⌇⌇

In October 1942, at the height of public criticism of the bomber plant, Edsel had his most violent confrontation yet with Bennett. The argument arose when the service chief informed Edsel he was going to provide armed guards for Gaukler Pointe and the residences of his adult sons, Henry II and Benson. "Stop this talk!" Edsel shouted. "Leave the boys alone! I don't want protection for myself or my sons!" Edsel then angrily accused Bennett of making up most of the kidnap stories that had simultaneously titillated and frightened his father all these years. Bennett reacted in typical fashion: he ripped off his jacket and balled his fists. Only Sorenson's intervention stopped Bennett from punching out the ailing president of the Ford Motor Company.

Several days later Bennett challenged Sorenson himself to a fistfight, this time after the production chief, uneasy with Bennett's ever-growing presumptions of authority, had countermanded one of Bennett's instructions. "For two cents I'd punch your face for you," Bennett threatened. When Sorenson turned away in disgust, Bennett punched Sorenson's aide in the jaw, knocking him to the floor. Lindbergh watched these kinds of episodes with bemused awe. This was how one of the world's greatest corporations handled its internal affairs? "Oh, we had some experiences those days at Ford," he later wrote, recalling fistfights and buffoonery. "There was never a dull moment."

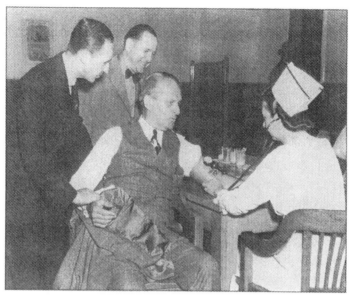

Charlie Sorenson gets his blood pressure checked one day in December 1942. Looking on is a bemused Harry Bennett and a gaunt Edsel Ford, just out of the hospital. Sick with cancer, he had just six months left to live.

Edsel could have done without the excitement. In November 1942, he underwent a second stay in the hospital for what doctors were publicly insisting was undulant fever. It was either at this time or the following spring, when Edsel entered the hospital yet again, that doctors discovered the cancer had spread to his liver. It has never been clear exactly when Edsel was told he had cancer.

During this period, remembered his private secretary, A. J. Lepine, Edsel "became quite a sick man. He was carrying on normally, however, at the office, and I had no idea, seeing him almost every day . . . that he was seriously ill or would die. At the time he died, I didn't expect it. That would reflect something of his makeup to this effect, that if he was at the office, he was there to continue doing business, and he never would complain or say anything even if he felt poorly."

Despite his debilitating illness, Edsel still had enough strength of character to challenge the firing of another longtime employee. For years, A. M. Wibel, vice-president in charge of purchasing, had butted heads with Bennett over his awarding of lucrative contracts to cronies such as local mob boss Chester LaMare, who'd been given the Rouge's fruit concession as well as a Ford agency. In the spring of 1943, as

Edsel was in Florida trying to regain his health, Bennett took advantage of his absence to sack Wibel. On his return in April, Edsel reinstated Wibel and ordered Bennett to "keep his nose out of purchasing," whereupon Bennett prevailed upon Henry to take his side in the dispute.

On April 15, 1943, just as Sorenson was getting ready to leave on his own Florida vacation, he received a phone call from Henry. The old man told Sorenson that Wibel was through. According to the notes Sorenson hastily jotted down, Henry would "support Bennett against every obstacle." Handling labor relations was Bennett's job alone, Henry added, despite the union's desire to deal with Edsel. Furthermore, Edsel needed to change his attitude toward Bennett.

Edsel broke down when shown the list the following morning. Physically worn out and emotionally beaten to a pulp, he told Sorenson he was going to leave the company. He did, in the manner many had feared—by leaving life itself.

∽०∾

After a surgeon opened him up a few days later and discovered his cancer had advanced too far to treat, Edsel was moved into the third-floor infirmary at Gaukler Pointe. There his pain was eased by morphine. In May, as his children were called home from college or the service, he slipped in and out of consciousness. Benson, for one, had no trouble identifying the root of his father's illness. "Grandfather is responsible for Father's sickness," he raged after learning that it was terminal, "and I'm through with him!" Henry, in denial over his son's pending death, remained at Fair Lane, where he tramped the woods in agonizing solitude. Neither Henry nor Clara was present when the end finally came.

Edsel passed away in the early hours of May 26, 1943. He was forty-nine years old. The irony in the date of death escaped the press. It was sixteen years to the day that he and Henry had ceremoniously driven the last Model T off the assembly line together, and exactly six years since Harry Bennett's goons had so brutally enforced the senior Ford's wishes on the Miller Road overpass.

Even in death, Edsel was overshadowed by Henry. Many of the obituaries focused more on the dynamic auto tycoon than on his quietly admirable son. "When word was flashed that Edsel Ford had died, editors emptied their files of Ford lore and turned up only the countless anecdotes that have studded the life of the inventor-father," observed the *Detroit News.* Nonetheless, Edsel received kudos for his personal qualities—his modesty, his philantrophy, his loyalty to family, firm, and country—as well as credit for many of the company's successes of the last couple of decades, especially in the areas of automobile styling, aviation, and defense manufacturing. "In his official capacities," stated the *Detroit Free Press,* "it was estimated that Edsel Ford had handled more money and had been responsible for more of the manufacture and distribution of automobiles than any individual in the automobile business, including his father." It was noted that, despite years of ill-ness, Edsel had successfully administered the complicated coordination of the sprawling Ford empire—glass factories, steel plants, mills, coal and iron mines, coking ovens, ships, timberlands, rubber plantations, auto manufacturing and subassembly plants, village industries—as the carmaker switched over to war production. Despite Henry's meddling and muddleheadedness, Edsel had managed to keep the firm's myriad defense contracts on schedule.

The community, from the top on down, mourned Edsel's passing. Hundreds of factory hands, ordinary workmen who might have stepped out of a certain museum mural, came to the William Hamilton Funeral Home in downtown Detroit to pay their respects. Funeral services were held two days later at Christ Church in Grosse Pointe Farms. Thousands of white flowers and the cream of Detroit society overflowed the stone Episcopal chapel. Bennett, refusing to be a hypocrite, did not attend. "I knew that Edsel had despised me," he later explained, "and felt that the honest thing to do was to stay away."

Henry, weeks from turning eighty, sagged with grief. Perhaps he sensed what the judgment of historians would be. "In retrospect, Edsel emerges as one of the most tragic figures in American business history," decided David L. Lewis. "He was more than talented; he was creative. He was more than hard-working; he had an extraordinary sense of responsibility to his company and community. He was an excellent administrator, and he commanded the affection, respect, and loyalty of his associates. Unfortunately, his father, far from rejoicing in and making constructive use of these qualities, restricted and nullified them in his unceasing effort to remold his son into a tough, hard-hitting executive." Henry already knew what the judgment of his family was. Clara, for one, would shun him for the next two months. The Believer, like most others privy to the closet dramas involving the Fords, believed he had killed their son.

Henry and Clara emerge from the chapel following their son's funeral service. Two days later Henry reassumed the presidency of the company.

The old man, encouraged by Bennett to reassume the presidency of the company, ordered the entire organization to observe a spell of silence on the day of the funeral.

Ford R. Bryan was working inside the Rouge plant's magnesium foundry, next to the powerhouse, the afternoon Edsel was laid to rest at Woodlawn Cemetery, about four miles north of the Highland Park plant. At precisely 2:30 P.M., every Ford factory around the world shut down. "My recollection is that it was very strange," said the Dearborn resident, who in retirement has written several Ford-related books. "Everything stopped. Having been accustomed to hearing all the banging, all the machinery roaring all the time, the silence was eerie. The only sound was the boiling of the furnaces, which were kept on."

Industry can wait only so long for any man, regardless of station. After five respectful minutes, the Rouge and the rest of the Ford empire roared back to life.

For several months following Edsel's death, Henry alternately mourned and raged. He blamed the cows, the doctors, himself. He sought solace in his long-held conviction that all living beings are rein-carnated. "Well, Harry," he'd say hopefully to Bennett, "you know my belief—Edsel isn't dead."

But he was, and Henry couldn't shake the feeling that he bore the brunt of the responsibility. Regret flooded out. He brooded constantly on the nature of their relationship, once asking Bennett whether he thought he had been cruel to Edsel.

"Well, cruel, no," Bennett answered. "But unfair, yes. If that had been me, I'd have got mad."

"That's what I wanted him to do," said Henry. "Get mad."

# 22

࿊

# Running on Empty

*One time Mr. Ford came into the shop in the evening and no one else was there. He pulled out his wallet, which had loose leaflets in it with pictures of Edsel and the grandchildren. He paid me and said, "Joe, look. This is Edsel when he was a little child and I was very proud of him. Here are the grandchildren, Benson, Henry, Billy, and Josephine. My son had everything to live for but he worked too hard and now he is gone." I looked at his face and he had tears in his eyes. He was a lonely old gentleman.*

—Joseph Zaroski, Henry Ford's barber

On May 30, 1943, just two days after burying his son, Henry Ford officially reassumed the presidency of the Ford Motor Company. At the same board meeting, Henry appointed Harry Bennett the company's administrative director and a member of the board of directors. Edsel's grieving widow and children were insulted by the insensitivity of the timing. Their outrage was tempered by a sense of dread. How could the already drifting company hope to survive with Henry, a man born just days after the battle of Gettysburg, at the helm?

Henry was increasingly showing signs of confusion. He would be completely lucid one day, but then on the next, his attention would wane and his memory would often fail him entirely. Rufus Wilson, his chauffeur for many years, was in a position to trace the old man's rapid decline. "I'm pretty sure that Edsel Ford's death and the war shortened Mr. Ford's life by five or six years, maybe a little bit longer. I daresay Mr. Ford showed signs of failing both physically and mentally. He was forgetful and he knew it, because he remarked about it. But he always put it to me that he wanted to forget. He said, 'I put these things out of my mind so I won't have to worry about them.'"

Ford's daily itinerary remained as casual and haphazard as it had been for years. He would routinely join the children at Greenfield Village for morning service at the Martha-Mary Chapel and join the department heads for lunch at the Engineering Laboratory, but beyond that he simply had his driver take him around to whatever person or project piqued his interest at a given moment. "I wouldn't know where I was going next but I would just drive along until I got the idea that I should go to some other office or shop and drop in and see somebody else," he told engineer Howard Simpson.

Such a desultory approach was fine, even preferred, when Edsel was conscientiously and expertly tending to the details of the company's many affairs. But with his son gone, Henry's rudderless leadership and rattlebrained meddling promised nothing but disaster. For example, he impulsively killed two of Edsel's ongoing projects, both of which had potential for the postwar market. One was the creation of a small, fuel-efficient car, perfect for returning servicemen with growing families. The other was an experimental vehicle with front-wheel drive and independent suspension, technological advances that had Henry shaking his head. "Joe, we've got to go back to Model T days," he told Joe Galamb. "We've got to build only one car. There won't be any Mercury, no Lincoln, no other car."

Bennett accompanied Ford on his daily rounds. The two men were almost inseparable—and it quickly became a question of whether the orders coming from the boss reflected Henry's views or those of a certain bow-tied Svengali. It didn't take long for the newly empowered Bennett to purge the company of potential threats. Within a few months of Edsel's death, his machinations were behind the dismissals or forced retirements of longtime executives Ernest Liebold, Charlie Sorenson, and Fred Black, engineering head Laurence Sheldrick, and design chief Bob Gregorie.

The departures of Liebold and especially Sorenson were significant because they were among Henry's oldest and most loyal lieutenants. Liebold had suffered an apparent breakdown during the banking crisis and, thanks to Bennett, had afterward seen his once considerable influence diminished. By the time he was finally forced out, his duties as

Henry and Clara's personal secretary had already been assumed by Frank Campsall, one of Bennett's men.

The ouster of Sorenson, an executive vice-president on the company's board since 1941 and generally considered the best qualified man to serve as president, benefited Bennett's aspirations much more than Liebold's departure. Years of stress and overwork had taken their toll on Sorenson, but it was Bennett's manipulations that did him in. Just three weeks after Edsel's death, Bennett had appointed himself Sorenson's administration assistant; he then installed one of his cronies, Ray Rausch, as Sorenson's production assistant. The squeeze play, combined with Henry's ingrained suspicion of any executive receiving the kind of widespread publicity Sorenson did for the success at Willow Run, resulted in Cast Iron Charlie's premature departure for Florida in December 1943. Henry and his production boss of four decades' service briefly shook hands, then never saw each other again. Bennett named Rausch to replace Sorenson, who a few months later emerged from his forced retirement to take over the presidency of Willys-Overland Motors of Toledo. "The whole official structure of the company was turned topsy-turvy," remembered Gregorie. "Things were in complete turmoil."

The man who had given the world such wonders as the Highland Park plant, the Rouge, and Willow Run was himself a puzzle factory. Jo Gomon, hired to be the head of labor policies and working conditions at the bomber plant, remembered that Henry typically wore a look of detachment or bemusement at meetings.

"By the time I knew Mr. Ford all contacts with him were made through Harry Bennett's whim or discretion," she said. "I sat in on some of these conferences and watched Mr. Ford, who seemed to be enjoying every minute. He was at ease and relaxed, his erect figure fitting comfortably into a hard, straight-backed chair. He would show a lively interest in what was being said without taking any part in the conversation. Many a visitor came away with the impression that he had talked with Mr. Ford and was confused later when he tried to recall what Mr. Ford had said. If he said anything, he had told an amusing story which probably had nothing to do with the business at hand."

Although Henry's mind wandered, certain prejudices remained strong. One summer day in 1944, Ford had his driver take him to the Dearborn home of longtime company photographer George Ebling, who was recuperating from an operation. Ebling's son, George Junior, was in the service, so his daughter-in-law Virginia and new grandson were living with him for the duration. Henry visited for a while, at one point going upstairs to see the three-week-old baby. He sat on the edge of the bed where little George Ebling III lay.

"Your daddy should be home with you," said the frail old tycoon, idly stroking the pink-cheeked infant with his long bony fingers. "And he would be—if it wasn't for those goddamn Jews."

In Washington, where Ernest Kanzler served on the War Production Board, officials viewed the stream of departures of top Ford executives with alarm. Their concerns were somewhat alleviated with every jeep or Liberator that rolled off a Ford assembly line. But "Uncle Ernest," as Edsel's children affectionately called Kanzler, had a more intimate knowledge of the interior rot at the Ford Motor Company. With the expulsion of capable top executives and the continued deterioration of Henry, the improbable ascendancy of Bennett to the top of a very chaotic heap was a distinct possibility. Should that happen, Eleanor Ford—who along with her two oldest sons, Henry II and Benson, had inherited Edsel's minority stake in the company—seemed ready to make good on her threat to sell their stock, thus bringing the "outsiders" who were long anathema to Henry into the corporate fold. Characteristically blunt, Eleanor had already accused her father-in-law of killing her husband, a charge with which her children agreed.

The four kids were now young adults. Josephine, known as "Dodie" to her friends, was a new bride, having married industrial designer Walter Buhl Ford in early 1943 in a low-key ceremony at Gaukler Pointe. There were no expectations of Josephine, who would give birth to two sons and two daughters over the next seven years, of entering the family business. Eighteen-year-old William had followed his brothers into Hotchkiss, an exclusive prep school in Connecticut, then entered Yale, where he began naval cadet training. An outstanding skier and tennis player (he was talented enough to be invited to try out for the Junior Davis Cup team) and the number one cadet in his class, Billy was surprisingly competitive and slightly arrogant. He hoped to be assigned to the Pacific theater but would wind up stationed in New York instead. There was no doubt that Edsel and Eleanor's "pet" (who would go on to earn an engineering degree after the war) had a future in the company, but whatever his ultimate role, in 1943 his time was still years off.

The story was different with Benson and Henry II. Benson, a long-faced young man with an eye problem, had left Princeton after two lackluster years to join the company. He married Edith McNaughton in 1941 and, despite his disability, enlisted in the army as a private. The gesture pleased his father, who had endured so much grief during the last war for his controversial draft deferment. Edsel, in fact, became livid when Bennett, acting on his own, pulled a few strings to get Benson assigned a cushy desk job at Selfridge Field, an air base located north of Detroit.

As the oldest boy, Henry II had grown up expecting to be groomed to someday succeed his father as the head of the company. Now family members were trying to position him to replace his grandfather. Little in his past suggested he was up to the task. Large, fleshy, and slope-shouldered, the Flivver King's grandson was an indifferent student at Yale, where one of his nicknames was "T," as in Model T. This was preferable to his adolescent moniker of "lard ass," given him by his occasional playmate, little John Dahlinger, who resented his bullying ways. "I was flunking engineering, so I switched," Henry said of his days at Yale. "Then I flunked sociology, too." He was denied his diploma when a professor discovered the term paper required for graduation had been purchased; the damning proof was the receipt he had forgotten to remove before turning in the assignment. In 1938 he was named to Ford's board of directors.

In the summer of 1940, Henry married Anne McDonnell, a member of a large, refined Irish Catholic family who split their time between a three-floor, twenty-nine-room mansion on upper Fifth Avenue in New York and a fifty-room "cottage" in Southampton. At the McDonnells' insistence, Henry converted to Catholicism as a precondition to marriage. The conversion galled his grandfather, who already had a visceral dislike of the McDonnells because they made their money on Wall Street. Nonetheless, at the "Wedding of the Year"—held on Long Island and presided over by Monsignor Fulton J. Sheen—the patriarch of the Ford clan behaved himself, showing off his considerable dance moves to the 1,000 Social Register guests. After honeymooning in Hawaii and the Canadian Rockies, the newlyweds returned to the Georgian home Edsel had bought for them in Grosse Pointe. Edsel's first-born also received 25,000 shares of Ford stock.

That summer, Henry and Benson started their apprenticeship by working at various departments at the Rouge. Henry had a disarming charm, his blue-eyed insouciance drawing in even unblinking hard cases such as Bennett. Unlike the passive Benson, Henry also had a surprising toughness. Both would come in handy when Henry, who joined the naval reserves a few months before Pearl Harbor, returned to Dearborn after Edsel's passing to reclaim the Ford birthright.

∽o∾

It was principally FDR's high regard for Edsel that kept the government from nationalizing the vital but chaotic company to ensure an uninter- rupted supply of jeeps, tanks, troop carriers, trucks, generators, aircraft engines, gliders, and bombers rolling out of its factories. In the months following Edsel's death, Kanzler worked in concert with Eleanor to save the imperiled family dynasty. Using his connections, and citing the critical importance of keeping one of the country's major defense contractors operating smoothly, Kanzler was able to convince Secretary of the Navy Frank Knox to grant Henry II, then an ensign based at the Great Lakes training center outside Chicago, an early discharge.

Henry, like his similarly pampered brothers, had found the democ- ratization of the military refreshing and had conflicted feelings about leaving "this man's navy." But on July 26, 1943, he received a letter from Knox, officially closing out his twenty-seven-month military career and offering the opinion that "the services you will render as a private indi- vidual will surpass any work you could possibly do in your present sit- uation." It was an extraordinary letter for a young officer to receive, and for the rest of his life he kept it framed and hanging on the wall inside his bathroom. "The navy taught me a lot about how to get along with people," he would one day explain. "It teaches discipline. It teaches you how to read a clock, which a lot of people never learn— and how to take orders and accept them, whether you believe them or not. There has to be a certain amount of that in life, too."

Three weeks later, young Henry reported to the Rouge to begin work for "Old Henry," as the newspapers starting calling the senior Ford to differentiate him from his twenty-five-year-old grandson. With no official title or duties, young Henry said later, "I just moseyed around on my own, visited the plants, talked with fellows—trying to find out how things operated." Henry II decided it was in his best interest to stay cordial with Bennett, whose spies reported every con- versation and movement. Knowing that he was viewed as an interloper

Henry Ford II at ease among Rouge foundry workers, 1945.

by even his own grandfather, who suspected a growing movement to get him to give up the reins to his company, Henry began to gather around him a small group of advisers and supporters. These included sales manager Jack Davis, an old friend of Edsel's, who had been exiled to the West Coast after crossing Bennett a few years earlier; production aide Mead Bricker, a husky, no-nonsense type who refused to be cowed by Bennett or Sorenson; and John S. Bugas, a former FBI agent who switched loyalties as the battle for succession heated up.

Bugas, tall, lanky, and poker-faced, had endured a hardscrabble upbringing in Wyoming, earning a law degree before joining the bureau. He first became involved with the company in the winter of 1941–42. A massive internal theft ring, tolerated if not outright instigated by Bennett as a way of rewarding stooges and cronies, was responsible for millions of dollars of missing tools, parts, and machinery. As director of the Detroit office of the FBI, Bugas was called in to investigate. He grew friendly with both Edsel and Bennett, eventually accepting a position in "industrial relations" at Ford. Because of his law enforcement background, he had a better handle than most on the extent of Bennett's nefarious connections and activities—which may have accounted for Bennett's job offer. Bugas initially saw a rough charm in the man, enjoying social visits to Bennett's Ann Arbor castle and displaying his riding skills at his horse ranch. Bennett, for his part, kept his new aide close at hand, setting him up in an office adjacent to his.

In December 1943, young Henry was elected to a vice-presidency. The following April he was named executive vice-president, the last rung before the presidency. His apple-cheeked forthrightness impressed nearly every person he crossed paths with, from grizzled factory hands to veteran journalists. "Everybody likes twenty-six-year-old Henry Ford II," observed one business publication. "The unanimity in praise of his modesty, earnestness and simple human likeability is almost alarming." He won over a group of Detroit reporters by interrupting an informal question-and-answer session with a simple query. "Now I want to ask you a question," he said. "Where's the men's room?"

If Henry II was theoretically the number two man in the company, nobody could tell it by the monthly board meetings. These meetings "were the funniest thing in the world," recalled Bennett, with "no purpose other than to comply with the law." With no director daring enough to demonstrate any initiative, the board basically rubber-stamped whatever Ford wanted. Henry II later said stockholder meetings "took place in my grandfather's head." On those occasions when Ford actually showed up, he typically went around and shook hands with everybody, then said to Bennett, "Come on, Harry, let's get the hell out of here. We'll probably change everything they do, anyway." One piece of business left unchanged was the granting of a formal salary to Henry's constant companion. Bennett, long accustomed to periodically drawing on the "kitty" in Liebold's safe, now was to receive $75,000 a year. How much he continued to make on the side was anybody's guess—and nobody's business.

As Henry II continued to familiarize himself with all aspects of the business, he was stunned to find the company had become as decrepit and idiosyncratic as Old Henry himself. The carmaker, which had not posted a profit since 1931, was losing millions of dollars a month because of waste and mismanagement. He came across one department still making Tri-Motor propellers, though the plane had been out of production for years, and he discovered the terribly undermanned accounting department actually stacked and weighed all invoices for merchandise costing under ten dollars. There was no materials scheduling, no cost controls, no engineering of any consequence. Key personnel in all departments had either been driven away or defected to more stable workplaces. Those that remained were afraid to speak out.

Promising executives avoided the Dearborn carmaker like the plague, preferring to cast their lot with other companies. Morale was lower than the keels of the lake carriers hauling iron ore to the Rouge.

In the spring of 1944, as the world awaited the much anticipated D-Day invasion of France, major skirmishes broke out in Dearborn. To his dismay and disgust, Henry II learned of the existence of a codicil to his grandfather's will that Bennett had secretly drawn up after Edsel's death. According to its terms, the service chief was to become the secretary of a board that would run the Ford Motor Company for ten years after Old Henry's death. The board was loaded with Bennett loyalists but included none of Edsel's children.

Young Henry was in despair. He told his allies he was thinking of throwing in the towel. He would sell his stock and try to convince dealers all over the country to get out, too. "This thing killed my father, but I'll be damned if I'm going to let it kill me," he declared. "I'm going to get out before it does." Bugas settled him down, then went to see Bennett.

Bugas and Bennett had already had their falling-out. One evening Bugas and his wife had gone out for a sociable evening; too tired to drive home, they decided to take a room for the night. The next day Bennett confronted Bugas: What had he been doing shacking up with a red-haired woman at a downtown hotel? Bugas was flabbergasted— and then understood that he was being tailed by Bennett's spies. After an angry exchange, Bugas returned later to find that his office had been moved into the washroom, a flimsy partition separating his desk from the toilet.

With this history behind them, Bugas approached Bennett. The service chief didn't want to talk about the codicil. Finally, he told Bugas to come back the next morning.

Bennett needed time to make up his own mind about the legality of the instrument he had coerced the old man into signing. In retrospect, it would not have withstood a legal challenge, though that wasn't clear to Bugas and Henry II at the time. For starters, the witnesses to the codicil had signed it out of the presence of Ford. That alone made it invalid. Moreover, Henry had carried the document around for several months and used it as a sort of jot book; the cryptic messages and biblical sayings he had pulled out of his faltering mind and scribbled all over the codicil hardly suggested a person competent enough to understand the implications of what he had put his name to.

When Bugas returned the following day, Bennett flashed a devilish smile, crumpled the codicil, then set it on fire. "Take this to Henry," he said, theatrically shoveling the ashes into an envelope.

To Bugas's great surprise, Bennett had put a match to his best chance of taking over the company. Young Henry was emboldened. For perhaps the first time, he felt truly confident that a third generation of Fords, not the founder's "personal man," would control the destiny of the family business.

It took more than a year of behind-the-scenes cajoling by Clara Ford and a final ultimatum by Eleanor Ford to bring the issue to a climax. Turn the company over to her son, Edsel's widow demanded in a closed-door showdown with her father-in-law at Fair Lane, or she would sell all of her stock. With that, all ties with his grandchildren would end. Henry, who appears to have suffered another stroke sometime in the middle of 1945 (medical records were later destroyed and memories are fuzzy), was by now a sick, weary eighty-two-year-old man incapable of mounting a sustained defense. The pressure exerted by the Ford women was too much. He said he would step aside.

But young Henry, called to Fair Lane by his grandparents, did not automatically accept the offer. Bugas had already counseled him not to agree to the presidency unless he was given a free hand in making over the moribund company. First and foremost, that meant clearing the house of men whose allegiance remained with Bennett. Ford fumed and then, with Clara fixing him with a hard stare, agreed.

Henry II was still soaking in the ramifications of the news when Bennett called him. For the better part of two years Bennett had gone through the charade of "discussing" young Henry's concerns with Ford, always returning with "I've been to see your grandfather and he wants. . . ." Any doubts Henry may have had that Bennett had ever even met with the senior Ford on these occasions were dispelled by the service chief's smarmy phone call: "Henry, I've got wonderful news. I've talked your grandfather into making you president of the company!"

Bennett's unctiousness gave way to bitterness at the September 21, 1945, board meeting that made the transition of power official. Henry Ford's letter of resignation was just starting to be read aloud when Bennett, clearly agitated by his lost bid for power, bolted the room, snarling "Congratulations!" to Henry II on his way out. After the meeting he told the new president of the Ford Motor Company, "You're taking over a billion-dollar organization you haven't contributed a thing to."

Bugas was handed the task of going to Bennett's office and informing him his services were no longer needed. There are varying accounts of what happened, usually involving the presence of at least one firearm. The most sensational had Bennett calling Bugas a "son of a bitch" and pulling a .45 out of a desk drawer, whereupon the ex-FBI man produced his own .38 revolver and, in his best Gary Cooper style, coolly said, "Don't make the mistake of pulling the trigger, because I'll kill you. I won't miss. I'll put one right through your heart, Harry."

"As soon as I turned around I expected to get shot in the back," Bugas would tell friends when recounting the episode. "The minute I turned the door handle I figured I had the bastard whipped."

Bennett would always insist this kind of *High Noon* showdown was a figment of Bugas's imagination. Bugas was "a liar and a crook," he later declared. "As a policeman, he'd make a good plant gateman." Bennett accused Jack Carlysle, a hard-nosed crime reporter for the *Detroit News* and Bugas's friend, of helping to spread the fictional close-out of his thirty-year Ford career. According to Bennett, if Bugas had dared pull out a pistol, he would have wrestled it away and punched him to the ground. Others, familiar with what Bugas's wife admiringly called his "cowboy morality," thought such a melodramatic confrontation perfectly fit their man.

Whatever the details, the effect was the same. The moment Bugas turned on his heel, a feudal empire run for years on caprice, conspiracy, and coercion literally turned to ash, as Bennett spent the next few hours burning files in a wastebasket. The following day the little man in the basement left for California. As promised by Henry II, he was kept on the payroll for the next year and a half, then pensioned off at $424 a month for the rest of his life.

Young Henry went to see Old Henry at Fair Lane to tell him firsthand of Bennett's firing. He was apprehensive. He expected an explosion, but his grandfather had a surprisingly listless response to the news.

"Well," he said, "I guess Harry is back where he started from."

∽○∾

On the last day of his life, Henry Ford had oatmeal for breakfast, pronounced it the best he'd ever had—"Please fix some more for my breakfast tomorrow," he asked—and then spent an early spring day visiting familiar haunts: the Engineering Laboratory, Greenfield Village, the Administration Building, the Rouge. Afterward he had his driver take him to the Catholic cemetery adjacent to St. Alphonsus Church in Dearborn, where he shuffled through the damp grass in his slippered feet. He took in the names and dates of departed friends and wistfully told stories among the markers and tombstones. That he would soon be joining them obviously was on his mind, for his next stop was the family burial grounds at Joy and Greenfield roads, where his mother and father lay.

"Well," he said, looking around, "this is where they're going to bury me when I die. In among the rest of my folks."

It was April 7, 1947. The day before, Easter Sunday, Henry and Clara had returned from their annual trip to Georgia to find heavy rains had overflowed the banks of the Rouge River, knocking out all power and telephone service at Fair Lane. Workers in the flooded powerhouse were able to get electricity restored long enough for Henry to listen to his favorite radio programs that evening before the steam engines conked out again. The Fords were informed that nothing more could be done until the following day. They understood. Gas lamps and candles would have to provide illumination throughout the darkened estate and wood fires, warmth. At nine o'clock Henry and Clara went to bed. Before turning in, Henry asked for a glass of milk.

A couple of hours later, Clara anxiously awakened the maid, Rosa Buhler. "I think Mr. Ford is very sick," she said.

Buhler hurried through the darkened house to tell the chauffeur to find a phone to call the doctor. When she returned to the Fords' bedroom, she found Henry in bed, pale and breathing harshly. He had suffered a cerebral hemorrhage. "Henry," Clara said over and over as she caressed his forehead, "*please* speak to me." The women propped him up with pillows, and his head plopped against Clara's shoulder. He looked "just like a tired child," the maid remembered. He tried to fold his hands, as if to pray. Clara, numbed and disoriented, got up to dress before the doctor arrived, then was called back.

"I think Mr. Ford is leaving us," said Buhler, who felt his pulse and put an ear to his chest, listening for a heartbeat.

It was twenty minutes to midnight when Henry Ford—a man whose life and legend had been predicated on the harnessing of power—left the world in the same candlelit fashion he had entered it nearly eighty-four years earlier. Later, the only items found inside the tycoon's suit pockets were a comb, a pocket knife, and a mouth harp.*

The world, caught up in the chaos of rebuilding and realigning after years of total war, nonetheless decelerated to note Ford's passing. From every corner, from Pittsburgh and Des Moines to Paris and Moscow, the obituaries were almost uniformly positive—not always the case when a famous public figure involved in great controversies dies. In this instance, however, it was impossible to ignore the universal impact of the tinkerer whose Model T had slayed distance and opened unprecedented social and economic vistas. Never mind his battles with organized labor, stockholders, Jewry, or even his own son; most ordinary people felt the Flivver King had touched them and their lives in a simple, positive, and elemental way. "No other man ever so changed the face of the world in his lifetime as did Henry Ford," eulogized the *Detroit News*. "His memorial is the face of America as he left it. In no other one lifetime has that face been so completely transformed. No other individual, while he lived, so radically affected the lives of so many."

More than 100,000 people filed past his bier at Greenfield Village, moving along at the brisk rate of 5,000 per hour. Waiting in line, Don Lochbiler overheard scores of familiar stories about the puttylike figure at rest inside the $15,000 bronze casket.

> It was remembered how, at a congress of his sales managers, he listened patiently while the men suggested changes to increase sales. Ford heard them out for two hours without saying a word. Then he yawned, stood up and stretched.
>
> "Gentlemen, as far as I can see there is only one trouble with the Ford car," he said. "We can't make them fast enough."
>
> Other stories concerned a contrasting side of his nature, his reverence for all life. There was the Saturday when he told Dahlinger, on a tour of the Ford farm acreage: "The wheat is ready to cut. Better get into those fields next week."
>
> On Monday morning, a caravan of agricultural vehicles headed out to the wheat fields. Just before work began, however, the wire-wheeled Ford coupe known all over Dearborn as "the chief's" drove up.

---

* The U.S. government placed a value of $466 million on the Ford Motor Company for tax purposes upon its founder's death. Henry's $80 million estate included $26.5 million in a personal bank account and $20 "due from the sale of hay" from a Ford farm.

"Better hold up a few days," Ford told Dahlinger.

"But the crop's just right and we're ready to go," answered the farm superintendent.

"I know," said Ford. "But I took a walk here yesterday and saw a lot of meadowlarks. The young ones are still in the nests. Wait until the fledglings will be able to fly away and not get hurt."

On the day of the funeral, April 10, some 30,000 hushed mourners stood in the cold drizzle outside St. Paul's Cathedral on Woodward Avenue. All government offices were closed. Detroit City Hall, draped in black, had a heroic three-story-high portrait of its greatest citizen hanging in front. When the service began at 2:30 P.M., church bells throughout the city rang for a full minute. Motorists, pedestrians, and workers stopped in respect. Afterward, the industrialist's remains were taken in a Packard hearse to the small Ford cemetery at Joy and Greenfield. The seemingly endless cortege slowly wound its way through the slick streets, past the thousands of onlookers on sidewalks holding umbrellas and soggy newspapers. A freshly dug grave, next to those of his parents, awaited in open-mouthed silence for the lowering of the casket. As the late afternoon sun struggled to pierce the marbled overcast, Henry Ford returned to the clayey soil his immigrant father had first traipsed over exactly one hundred years earlier.

# 23

~~o~~

## *Rearview Mirror*

# The Last Years
# of the Flivver King

*John McIntyre, a Scottish immigrant, worked a quarter-century operating the powerhouse on the Fair Lane estate, a position that made him privy to the daily lives of Henry and Clara Ford.*

Edsel and his father seemed to be very great pals. Whenever I saw them around, they appeared to be real friendly. I never saw them argue or anything like that. When Edsel Ford was ill, that was when I saw Mr. Ford drop back himself. After Edsel died, I met Mr. Ford on the path going up into the kitchen, and I wasn't six inches from him; he walked right past me and looked down at the cement. He didn't even see me. It just seemed to me that his mind was on the boy, and he was gone. When the boy left, it just seemed to take something out of him.

Many years earlier, I dug a basement for Mr. Ford and put all the drains in over there in what they called the old plumber shop on the Fair Lane estate. He used to come down there every morning between 7:30 and 8. He'd come back at lunch time and also before we would go home. He seemed to be very interested in this old plumber shop. There was a kitchen in it, a cooking stove and a refrigerator. Mr. Ford used to speak to me quite a bit down there. I used to say, "Oh, the mosquitoes are awful, Mr. Ford!"

He'd say, "Keep working; you'll chase them away."

From there I went to the Fair Lane estate powerhouse. They had heard that I had quite a bit experience with steam boilers and they needed a man over there to operate the powerhouse. That was the beginning of 1932 I started there. My duties were to see that enough heat went up into the house and to take care of the six refrigeration systems. There was one in the kitchen, pantry, flower room, cold storage room for fur coats and also one for the jams, jellies and potatoes.

I had very few calls from the house complaining about the heat or refrigeration. Mr. and Mrs. Ford left that to me. In the later years they were quite fussy about the heat; they liked a lot of heat.

Mrs. Ford was very careful of a dollar, more so than Mr. Ford; he didn't care about money very much. Mrs. Ford didn't make any waste of any kind. Mrs. Ford had a maid, head butler, second butler, and she had a cook and a laundress on five-day employment. She had the colored fellow by the name of John Williams as houseman. It was rather a small staff to run such a large house. There was an awful lot of furniture stored down in the basement which caused a lot of the dirt.

Mr. Ford didn't take any active part in the running of the boilers and the operations down there. He would come down and look around. Of course, if he saw anything that should be fixed, he drew our attention to it. One day in particular I was cleaning up the front door and the windows in the summertime. Someone had come into the powerhouse and put a greasy hand on the wall.

Mr. Ford said, "The door is looking pretty good, Scottie, but," he says, "come here, come here. See that? A clean sponge would just take that right off." He didn't like dirt anywhere, and he wouldn't stand for any dirt or filth around the powerhouse.

Mr. Ford would come around the powerhouse but he would stay away from the greenhouse. The greenhouse was Mrs. Ford's.

Mr. Ford's cars were kept in the garage. He always had two cars in the garage, and sometimes he would drive them around his estate. Mrs. Ford had an electric car; she was still running that car up until '28 or '29, somewhere along there. We had a charger to charge the battery for her. She liked that electric car because it was easy to run. It was just a straight handle on it, just turn the switch, and it goes.

Mr. Ford spent a lot of his time up at the experimental laboratory. There was no one allowed in there while he was there. I don't know what kind of experimenting Mr. Ford was carrying on in the experimental room, but he had soybeans, oats, wheat, barley and corn up there, all in bottles. He would keep an open bottle of whiskey, wine and one of gin. He had been mixing these at nights. He would mix the alcohol with the different farm products he had in stock. He didn't have soil up there where he was growing these, just the seed and the alcohol.

The first thing in the morning before Mrs. Ford would come down, he would take his bicycle and he would ride to the back gate and turn around and ride to the front gate, which is a distance of two miles. He left the bicycle on the porch and went inside to have his breakfast. When he was feeling well, that was his routine every morning.

I met Mr. Ford every morning between 7:00 and 7:30 when I was coming into work. He always walked to the powerhouse, unless it was an awful stormy morning. He was a great runner. I never in my life saw a man who could run as fast and run fifty yards as what Mr. Ford could do. He was in his seventies then.

Mr. Ford was a very healthy man. He was never subject to headaches or colds, to my knowledge. He challenged me in a foot race one time when I met him up on the road, and I told him I thought I was a little bit too heavy to run. He says, "Oh, you just think you are. You're going to age too fast, Mac," he says. I didn't take the challenge because I know he could outrun me.

Mr. Ford didn't like the lack of activity. I met him one Sunday afternoon on the road, and he had a big sharp axe over his shoulder. He says, "Hello there, Scottie, what do you think of my key?"

I said, "Key, what are you talking about?"

He says, "Don't you see my key? That's a key."

I said, "I thought it was an axe."

He said, "You can chop wood with it. Some of these people around here are locking up these doors in these outhouses; they think they're smart, but when I get this key around here, I'll go back and tell them, 'You better go over and get a new door over in there,' after using my key to get into the outhouse."

I've seen Mr. Ford in his overalls. He would put his axe over his shoulder and hike through the woods. I have seen him chopping on trees, and he could swing an axe too. He always had it good and sharp. I think when it got dull he just bought a new one; he just kept them in stock all the time. Sometimes there would be as high as six axes there, and he would use the whole six.

Mr. Ford would change his mood from day to day. You could tell when he was mad about something. He seemed to walk faster, and his hands would go. I would spot that and stay clear of him. Mr. Ford had a very quick temper. Anything that was done without his knowledge made him angry. He was very quick. We were very careful to keep him informed of what we were doing.

If Mr. Ford wanted something done one way and I wanted it done another way, I couldn't argue with him. You would do it the way he wanted it, and that is all there was to it.

I was told something by a man who was a builder. He worked for Mr. Ford at the Rouge. He was a good man, a superintendent. Mr. Ford met him out at one of his plants, and he told him how he wanted a chimney stack built. He said, "Now, that is the way I want that stack built. Will you do that for me?"

The builder said, "Oh yeah!"

The stack was built. Mr. Ford called this fellow over and he said, "Is that the way I told you I wanted this stack built?"

He said, "We couldn't build it your way, Mr. Ford."

Mr. Ford said, "You couldn't?"

"No."

Mr. Ford said, "You report back to the Rouge in the morning."

The stack was built the way he wanted it. The other one was ripped right down.

Mr. Ford liked to talk to people who were just two-by-fours like myself. He would pick out special people that he liked. You never could tell what it was that he liked about them.

Mr. Ford never gave me his background. He was more interested in personal matters, on how you were brought up and what line of work you were working at in the early days. He talked very simply, just common two-by-four talk.

He used to tell stories once in a while. He liked a good joke. One night I was in there, and he came down to the boiler room and we were talking back and forth. I said, "Well, Mr. Ford, I will have to start feeding the boilers for the men coming in at midnight."

He left me, and I never paid any more attention and I started to clean my fires. I had sixty pounds of steam on; it gets pretty hot, you know. I got the fire all cleaned up and the clinkers and I looked up at the gauge, and she is dropping, dropping, until finally the damn thing came down to only fifteen pounds of steam.

I had the drafts wide open and a big fire on, and the water was getting down in the glass. I was getting kind of worried. I run around back and forth and finally I heard a little noise in the vent shop. I went in and looked up at the ceiling and I saw that a big six-inch valve was open. The steam was flying through the relief valve right up into the open space, and I was losing all the steam. The old son-of-a-gun had opened the valve! I never saw him for four or five weeks after that. That was just *one* of the little jokes he played! He said once, "I gave Scottie a little bit of fun this night."

He used to play tricks in the house sometimes, too. There was one time I remember. Mrs. Ford was a great one to pick up the newspaper in the morning. Mr. Ford was always down first in the morning. He got hold of an old paper that was six or seven years old, and the top headline in big black letters was "Jerry Buckley Murdered." He put it on top of the fresh daily paper. Mrs. Ford came down and had her breakfast. She picked up the paper and went into the sun parlor.

She said, "My goodness, Henry, Jerry Buckley is murdered."

He says, "Oh, Clara, that was a long time ago."

She says, "No, it is right here on today's paper, Henry. My goodness, do you think I can't read?"

During these times when he took a notion to come to the power-house, you had to watch him because he was liable to do anything.

Mr. Ford must have been nervous and restless because he had a great deal of responsibility. Sometimes I would see a light on in his bedroom and I would know that he had gotten up. He would some-times take a walk down to the powerhouse. Sometimes at five o'clock in the morning if he couldn't go to sleep he would take a walk down. It was perfectly natural for a man with the amount of responsibilities he had.

As a rule, Mr. Ford had a routine he followed every day. During the week I think his main rule was to get over to the Dearborn plant, after riding his bicycle and so forth. After that he had a schedule for getting around. If he had an appointment for the Rouge or with Mr. Dahlinger, he made that appointment. For years I know Mr. Ford was away be-tween eight and nine o'clock on a Saturday morning. He would go to these small plants outside. They had one at Saline, Macon and Nankin Mills.

On Sundays, Mr. Ford would come down around the powerhouse in the morning. Mrs. Ford always liked to look through her Sunday papers. They always took a rest, in their later years, an hour or two in the afternoon. They used to walk quite a bit out on the lawn after

Clara arranges flowers at Fair Lane in 1939.

supper. Of course, the mosquitoes would start to bite and they wouldn't get too far. They generally spent their Sundays together. He would sometimes drive Mrs. Ford around himself.

The gate people would let anybody they knew in the gate. Anybody they had any doubt about, they would call the house and get in touch with the butler to ask if this certain person could come in. If the butler had any doubts about it, he would go and see Mrs. Ford. If she said, "Yes, let them in," okay; and if she said, "No, I don't know anything about them," well, the gateman would just tell them they couldn't come in. I didn't talk to Mrs. Ford very much—that is, unless she called. If she had any work for you to do in the house, she would call you and ask you how much longer it was going to take you to do it. She didn't like strangers in the house; she wanted you to do your work and get out.

Mr. Ford was a man who didn't care for company at any time. He would much rather be out among the two-by-fours. I am talking from personal experience because he used to come down and talk with us on a Sunday. If he had something to do, I have known him to leave the company and the house and go down through the swimming pool and to the garage and get into the car and beat it. It was just something he had to do and he didn't want to bring it up with them, and he just left.

Mr. Ford had quite a number of radios around the house. Mrs. Ford liked the radio. They had one in the dining room. She had one up in her bedroom, one in the sun parlor, and there was one in the library where she used to get the broadcast of the children from Greenfield Village. They had the telephone rigged up some way so that they could hear the Victrola over the telephone.

I know Mr. Ford didn't like liquor. He kept it upstairs in his experimental room. He never served it to his guests in the home. The wines that were kept down in the basement at the residence were just used for special occasions. Anything that was kept in stock was in small bottles. They used it in cooking and such things.

When the grandchildren were young, the Edsel Fords used to come over on weekends. They came practically every weekend in the summertime. They stayed Friday night, Saturday night and went back on Sunday night. Mr. Ford had a great time taking his grandchildren into the powerhouse and showing them around. He used to use the swimming pool quite a lot, too. Both Mr. and Mrs. Ford would go in swimming with the children. The pool wasn't filled, just enough for the children.

Mr. Ford was sick before he left for the South in '45. I always thought it would have been better if he had stayed at home. The war was on, and they drove him down in the Lincoln. He was a sick man, and that wasn't good for him at all. It was a long trip for a man of his age.

It was about three months before he left for the South that I noticed that he was failing. He had been slowly getting worse since the time that Edsel had died.

When he came back from Georgia, he just recognized me sometimes. I remember the time, oh, maybe six months before he died; Mrs. Ford was taking him for a walk around the grounds. I was fixing the two radiators for the swimming pool, and they came in from the English garden way. The door was open, and I was working right there. He didn't even know me. He just looked at me and never even smiled. Mrs. Ford asked me what was the matter, and I told her two of the radiators wouldn't shut off and I said, "I have to change the valves, Mrs. Ford."

She said, "I suppose these things have to be done."

Mr. Ford never spoke, never said a word.

Towards the end of Mr. Ford's life he didn't like to take baths. He stayed away from them as much as he could.

I can tell you something about the last day of Mr. Ford's life. On that Tuesday night we had a couple of motors from the Rouge plant, and I saw when I went down that they wouldn't take the load. They were smoking pretty bad, and I thought it would be nice if I would go up and warn the butler, Mr. Thompson, that if anything should go wrong again, they would be in darkness that night. He went in and saw Mr. Ford, and Mr. Ford rose from the living room and he came into the hallway and shook hands with me.

He said, "Hello there, Scottie. Are you having trouble?" He was more like himself that night than I had seen him in eighteen months.

I said, "Well, I just came up to warn Mr. Thompson here that I was afraid we weren't going to hold the lights for you tonight. I thought maybe if you or Mrs. Ford woke up in the middle of the night and found the lights were out, it would be nice for me to come and tell you ahead of time."

He said, "That's all right, Scottie," and he tapped me on the shoulder. "That's all right. I know you will all stick by me; you've always done it for years. I never worry about these things. You fellows are pretty good." He looked at Thompson and he said, "Don't pay any attention to them. Just leave them alone, and they will be all right."

That was at ten minutes to 9. My motors blew up at 9:25, but they were already in bed by that time. I waited until a quarter to 12 and then I went home. I was just one hour in bed when they come and woke me up. I was in a dead sleep. There was nothing anyone could do, that no human being could do. There just wasn't enough power for any electricity at all. When the generator set is out of commission, you just can't get no lights at all.

That is one thing I can really say: Mr. Ford was really nice and sensible in his talk, and he was dead two hours after that.

Mrs. Ford took his death pretty hard. After Mr. Ford died, I kept out of her way as much as I possibly could. If I had anything to do, if I had to fix something in the basement or the lights, I tried to make sure she was in some other room when I was doing it.

I spoke to Mrs. Ford a day or two before she died. The maid called me up to see about giving the drainpipe a little adjustment. Mrs. Ford called me to the main stairway and she said, "Well, Mac, we're giving you more trouble."

I said, "Well, that's what Ford Motor Company is paying me for."

She kind of smiled and said, "Well, I suppose so."

Henry Ford, front-page news for decades, went out in a blaze of boldfaced headlines when he died on April 7, 1947.

I said, "How are you feeling, Mrs. Ford?"

She said, "Well, I'm awful tired, Mac. It is nice and comfortable here."

I said, "Well, you just stay there. As long as the nurse wants you to stay there, just stay in there and rest yourself."

When I came back out, she said, "Well, did you get it all fixed up, Mac?"

I said, "Yes, everything is okay now."

She said, "Thanks ever so much."

That is the last time I ever spoke to Mrs. Ford. She was taken to the hospital two or three days after that. She died there.

*Postscript*

# Ford after Ford

C lara Ford, having grown frail and melancholic after Henry left, died in a hospital bed on September 20, 1950, following a brief illness. The passing of the eighty-three-year-old matriarch had no effect on the Ford Motor Company's direction, for it had already been left to a third generation of Fords—Edsel's three sons—to guide it into the postwar world.

They inherited a mess. "At Ford's today," *Newsweek* observed in 1947, "the name of Harry Bennett is a convenient peg on which to hang the blame for everything that ever went wrong." But there was plenty of blame to pass around, David Halberstam would write in *The Reckoning*, beginning with the company's founder:

> By fighting the unions so intransigently, Ford . . . had ensured that when the unions finally won power they would be as strong as the companies themselves, and that there would be a carryover of distrust and hatred which would make them—even in the postwar years when the unions became a junior partner—an adversarial, distrustful junior partner. There were other, more concrete, burdens as well. Because he had been locked in the past and had frozen his technology, the company was on the verge of bankruptcy. Worse, he had done something that was truly cruel and, in a family company, professionally ruinous—he had destroyed his own heir, one who was, in Detroit's phrase, a damn good car man. There was no doubt in the minds of the ablest Ford men of that day, and of their competitors at GM, that if the old man had stepped aside, Edsel Ford would have improved the company tremendously. But he never got the chance.

He was crushed, and a whole generation of good men were forced out, which put a heavy weight on the succeeding generation.

Of the three brothers, Benson and William proved to be relative lightweights when compared to Henry II, who emerged as the kind of "industrialist-statesman" that a modern corporation required. After firing more than a thousand holdovers from Bennett's regime, many of them personally, and selling off most of his grandfather's nonautomotive holdings—rubber plantations, timberlands, village industries, and the like—Henry set about trying to remake the company in the image of General Motors. He hired Ernest Breech, a candidate for the top spot at GM, as executive vice-president. Breech helped Henry direct the work of a group of former U.S. Army Air Force officers nicknamed the "Whiz Kids." During the war the ten bright executives had created a management information system for the general staff; now they promised to do the same for the Ford Motor Company. The Kids decentralized what had been a corporate autocracy, establishing separate accounting systems for individual operations and coining the phrase "profit center" in the process. The results were phenomenal. The company made a modest $2,000 profit in 1946—its first in fifteen years—and then saw that figure explode to $258 million in 1950.

Henry II displayed the kind of humanism still lacking in most giant corporations. "He rarely does anything without asking himself, 'What would father have done?'" observed public opinion pollster Elmo Roper. Henry, who would become a great supporter of civil rights causes, was eager to apply his college coursework in "human engineering" to Ford workers. In its historic 1947 agreement with the union, the company became the first carmaker to provide employees a pension. "You got a little bit of human dignity," said one veteran of the assembly line. In 1956, the rank and file even got a chance to invest in the company as the Ford Foundation decided to diversify its immense wealth by splitting its shares and going public. It was the greatest initial stock offering in history, with more than 350,000 ordinary Americans paying $64.50 a share for the right to own a piece of the company that had given the world the Model T, the V-8, and—unfortunately for dividend statements and Edsel Ford's memory—the Edsel.

The Edsel was announced as a whole new line of medium-priced cars that would fall between the Mercury and the Lincoln. An estimated $250 million worth of engineering and design work went into the heavily hyped final product. Ford's ad agency considered more than 6,000 names, including "Mongoose," "Utopian Turtletop," "Zip," "Zoom," and "Dorf" ("Ford" spelled backward) before settling on "Edsel." "It fails somewhat of the resonance, gaiety, and zest we are seeking," admitted an executive in the new Edsel Division. "But it has a personal dignity and meaning to many of us here."

The vehicle came out in September 1957, with the company confidently predicting sales of 250,000 that first year. Instead, a bad economy, poor marketing, and an unappealing design doomed it. Critics hated the unusual vertical grille, which comics said looked like a Buick sucking a lemon. The "Teletouch" automatic transmission, operated by push buttons in the steering-wheel hub, also struck many potential car buyers as too strange for their taste. Much to the dismay of Eleanor and her children, the Edsel became synonymous with "flop" and "loser." It immediately became the punch line of gags by Jackie Gleason, Carol Burnett, and other comics. The ridicule hasn't lost much steam in the forty-plus years since production was halted in November 1959 after only 110,000 of them were sold. The Edsel was parodied in *Mad* magazine and inspired a political button ("Ford is an Edsel") during Gerald R. Ford's 1976 presidential campaign. Most recently, during the 2000 Republican primary syndicated columnist George Will wondered whether George W. Bush's presidential designs would "go the way of the Edsel" or whether he could "prove that he is not, like that car, a product designed in disregard of changing market forces." The following year, headline writers took note of William Clay Ford's front-office overhaul of the Detroit Lions (he has been sole owner of the National Football League team since 1964) by proclaiming: "Ford Tired of an Edsel." The Edsel remains one of the most spectacular corporate failures in history, ranking right up there with the New Coke of the 1980s, and wound up costing the Ford Motor Company an estimated $350 million.

"I had a long talk with my dad one time about why Ford Motor Company chose to use the name," said Edsel Ford II, Henry II's only son. "There were lots of other names looked at originally for the car. The marketing guys just kept coming back and saying, 'We want to honor your father . . . we think it's a good idea . . . the name researched very well . . .' and so forth and so on. So they literally wore my father down and he finally acquiesced. And the rest is history."

~o~

The second half of the Ford Motor Company's history is in many respects as rollicking as the first. But a close examination of such topics as the introductions of the Thunderbird, Fairlane, Mustang, Escort, and Taurus, the careers of executives such as Robert McNamara, Lee Iacocca, and Jacques Nasser, and the public relations disasters surrounding the Pinto and Explorer safety recalls, falls beyond the scope of this book. We can, however, look at how the other principal characters in the Henry and Edsel saga left the stage to a new cast.

Edsel's widow, Eleanor, continued her work as a patron of the arts and as a noted civic leader. Eleanor died in 1976 at the age of eighty, outliving her sister, Josephine Kanzler, who drowned in the family pool in 1954, and her brother-in-law, Ernie Kanzler, who died in 1969. Eleanor left behind an estate of nearly $90 million, some of which is used to preserve the Edsel and Eleanor Ford House, one of the few surviving homes of Detroit's auto barons.

The Edsel Fords' only daughter, Josephine, who turned eighty during the company's centennial year, lives a secluded life in Grosse Pointe Farms. Like her parents, she is a quiet but extremely generous patron of the arts, donating millions of dollars to the Detroit Institute of Arts and another favorite cause, the nearby Center for Creative Studies.

William Clay, two years younger than Josephine, also shuns the spotlight. After graduating from Yale (where he captained the tennis and soccer teams), he married Martha Parke Firestone, the granddaughter of Henry Ford's camping partner, tire magnate Harvey Firestone. Appointed a director in 1948, the youngest of Edsel and Eleanor's children inherited his father's styling sensibilities, supervising the design and development of the Lincoln Continental Mark II, the successor to the original Continental. He was chairman of the design committee from its inception in 1957 until his retirement as vice-chairman of the company in 1989. Unfortunately, he also inherited his great-grandfather William Ford's intemperance. He battled alcoholism for years, finally drying out for good in his early forties. By then his career path had been stalled by his drinking, by Henry II's domination, and by his own lack of drive. The author of seven holes-in-one still sits on the board of directors, serving on the board's finance and governance committees. Like his sister Josephine, he remains involved in a variety of charitable activities.

Harry Bennett in the witness chair at the Kefauver hearings in Detroit,
February 9, 1951.

"Best of the Ford boys," Harry Bennett once said of Benson Ford,
who headed the Mercury division from 1948 to 1956 before being
shifted into the less demanding position of dealer relations. "He was a
good guy, the kind who would get drunk once in a while." Unfortunately, the glad-handing Benson would die an alcoholic in 1978. He
was only fifty-nine when he suffered a fatal heart attack while boating
on the Cheyboygan River.

Outside of testifying in 1951 before the Kefauver Commission
investigating organized crime, Bennett never returned to Detroit. Characteristically, he prepared for the hearing by digging up as much dirt
on Senator Estes Kefauver as he could. "He never knew how much I
had on him, but it would have embarrassed him," he gloated years
later. Bennett lived out West until his death in a nursing home in 1979.
In his final years he took to painting his shoes silver to compensate for
his failing eyesight.

John Bugas, whom Henry appointed head of Ford International
despite his lack of automotive qualifications (and then later reluctantly
fired for that reason), became a millionaire through his stock options.
He retired from Ford in 1968 and lived out his days on his Wyoming
ranch. Henry and Bugas shared a deep bond, the two often reminiscing

about their collaborative battle to oust Bennett in the forties. "Those were the days. We might have been killed," said Bugas, who died in 1982.

The company had several different presidents beginning in the 1960s, but Henry II stayed in control as chairman. Before he stepped down in 1980, he made clear that the appointment of top management did not automatically mean a Ford would run the company. "There are no crown princes in the Ford Motor Company and there is no privileged route to the top," he said at the stockholders' meeting where he announced his retirement. In appointing his successor, Henry passed over his brother William, who he regarded as "a professional dilettante," and named Phil Caldwell as chairman and Donald Peterson as president—the first non-Fords to head the firm in three-quarters of a century. "Hank the Deuce" was determined that biographers and historians would never delve into his and his father's lives as deeply as they had his grandfather's. During the 1950s he had most of Edsel's personal papers destroyed; before leaving the company he shredded all but a handful of his own. He died at Henry Ford Hospital on September 29, 1987, succumbing to the heart problems that had caused him too late to reprioritize his life. Practically every obituary used the word "saved" in describing his legacy. Although his well-publicized love affairs and brushes with the law—not to mention the beard he had grown late in his career—had given Henry an almost renegade image, in truth he had sacrificed much to salvage the institution bearing his family's name.

"You have to realize that when my father took over Ford Motor Company there was almost nothing there," said Edsel II. "His vision was to take it and put it back together again. What he did, in my opinion, is legendary. It goes down in the annals of business history."

Edsel II, born in 1948, is an affable type who graduated from Babson Institute of Business Administration and said, on joining the company in 1974, "I hope someday to run the company. But if I can't, I can't." He was named chief operating officer of Ford Credit in 1991 and voted a company vice-president two years later. He abruptly left the company in 1998 to devote more time to outside business and charitable interests. But he maintains an office on the eleventh floor of the twelve-story "Glass House" on Michigan Avenue in Dearborn—Ford's world headquarters since 1956—where he serves as a consultant on issues involving dealers. There are several reasons why Henry II's only son was never really groomed to succeed his father, perhaps none as important than the fact that the Deuce wanted him to actually live a life. Are you *sure* you'd want the job? he'd ask Edsel time and again.

"My father really did believe he was married to Ford Motor Company because there really wasn't much else in his life other than the company," continued Edsel. "And that was all right. Even as children, we understood that. He didn't try to hide anything. He always said, 'You are going to have to get used to my lifestyle and that is: I go to work every Monday through Friday and on the weekends I work.' I remember briefcases stuffed full of things that he brought home over the weekends. He would sit and go through all those papers.

"Did I miss out? Sure, obviously. But then again, when we were together, when we did things together as father and son, we did them extremely concentrated. When I had him, I had him alone. I had him for three or four days and it was very close. I always think of Thanksgiving. From a very early age we always went to the football game at Briggs Stadium, and then we would cross over to Canada and go duck hunting. I could never shoot as well as he could. He was a great shot."

It's been a topsy-turvy ride for the Dearborn carmaker since the reign of Henry II. The company posted record sales and profits in the late 1980s, thanks to the introduction of the Taurus/Sable. Denigrated as "flying potatoes" by Lee Iacocca (Henry's heir apparent, whom he had fired because his empire-building had reminded him too much of Harry Bennett), the vehicles' aerodynamic shape influenced the way the entire industry designed their cars. And every U.S. carmaker got fat at the turn of the new century, principally on the sales of sport utility vehicles. But Ford lost $5.5 billion in 2001 due to the Firestone tire debacle that had consumers calling the Explorer the "Exploder." Quality problems contributed to the company's ever-shrinking share of the total vehicle market: a slide from 26 percent in 1995 to 21.4 percent. With the company seemingly disintegrating under chief executive officer Jacques Nasser, an abrasive Australian who had developed fractious relationships with suppliers, dealers, and top managers, the board ousted him in October 2001. They replaced him with Bill Ford Jr., the son of William Clay Ford and the cousin of Edsel Ford II.

A forty-five-year-old hockey dad who had fled Grosse Pointe for the university town of Ann Arbor, Bill Ford was thrust into a position he never necessarily wanted. Although he had already spent twenty-

An unfortunate legacy: the 1958 Edsel.

three years in a variety of positions with the company, and was chairman of Ford Switzerland before becoming chairman of Ford Motor, the bright-eyed Princeton grad never held a single top operating or finance job. Now he was the CEO of the world's second largest industrial company (after GM), with 350,000 employees and revenues in the $145 billion range. "Despite his intellect and talent," said *Fortune*, "a lot of people believe he wouldn't be in the job if his name wasn't inside the blue oval." Three months later, at the 2002 North American International Auto Show in Detroit, the fourth-generation Ford delivered a grim turnaround plan. Over the next five years the company would eliminate 35,000 jobs, shut five plants, discontinue four models, and cut $9 billion in costs. Although investors backed off and company shares fell to their lowest levels in more than a decade, he was able to come back to the same venue one year later and show that the company had exceeded nearly all of its commitments in the first twelve months of its turnaround. More problems face the Dearborn carmaker as the comeback continues: self-immolating price wars, serious in-roads by lower-cost foreign carmakers, and an uncertain international economy because of the ongoing threats of war and terrorism. Meanwhile, Ford's daring acquisitions of several European nameplates (Jaguar, Volvo, Aston Martin, and Land Rover) when times were flush have yet to bear fruit. Morale, both on the shop floor and inside the Glass House, is flagging. Even the beginning of the company's gala five-day centennial celebration, the unofficial kickoff to Ford's second century, was met with a daylong downpour in Dearborn. To Bill Ford, the clearing skies that followed were more portentious than the rain. The company was on track to deliver annual profits in the $7 billion range by mid-decade, he said. In any event, he told a reporter, if he dwelled on the negatives "I'd be in a padded room somewhere."

Edsel Ford II feels for his cousin. Carrying around a name found on hundreds of millions of nameplates over the last century can be a burden—and a responsibility. "I think the family is very serious about our name and what it means. And how we must make sure we don't damage it. It is very interesting because I think we—as a family tree—we've had a few strays, like everyone else. But they all come back."

Comeback, coming back—it's all of a piece with Old Henry's belief in the strength of dynastic continuity. As his great-grandson steers the Ford Motor Company to the starting line of its second hundred years, the Flivver King and his Tin Lizzie continue to loom large in the rearview mirror. When the inevitable polls at the end of the millennium came out, an international panel of 133 automotive experts declared the Model T "the car of the century" and *Fortune* named its creator the "businessman of the century." Henry Ford "didn't invent the automobile, but he invented the automobile business," the magazine correctly stated. "As for his larger legacy, well, just look around you."

Looking around the Motor City today, one finds the symbols of Henry's and Edsel's corporate, public, and private sides exist much as they did during their lifetimes: at the Rouge, currently undergoing a $2 billion makeover; at Fair Lane, now the centerpiece of the Dearborn campus of the University of Michigan; in the courtyard of the Detroit Institute of Arts, where Diego Rivera's auto workers are cloaked in unaccustomed dignity; and at the house at Gaukler Pointe, where the fireplace inside Edsel's study has not been lit since his death. If one believes in reincarnation, as Henry Ford so desperately did, everything is in place for a tireless tinkerer and his loyal son to return home.

# Notes

Abbreviations used in notes

BHC    Burton Historical Collection, Detroit Public Library
*DFP*   *Detroit Free Press*
*DJ*    *Detroit Journal*
*DN*    *Detroit News*
*DSN*   *Detroit Saturday Night*
*DT*    *Detroit Times*
FA     Archives of Henry Ford Museum & Greenfield Village, Dearborn, Michigan
*NYT*   *New York Times*
WRA    Walter Reuther Archives of Labor History and Urban Affairs, Wayne State University, Detroit

## 1. Farmboy, Tinkerer

"When we had mechanical toys": Margaret Ford Ruddiman, "Memories of My Brother, Henry Ford," *Michigan History*, Sept. 1953; "Detroit will resolve": Richard Bak, *Detroit Across Three Centuries* (Chelsea, Mich.: Sleeping Bear Press, 2001), p. 39; "William Ford was a churchwarden": Sidney Olson, *Young Henry Ford: A Picture History of the First Forty Years*, reprint (Detroit, Mich.: Wayne State University Press, 1997), p. 13; "The first thing that I remember": ibid., p. 14; HF's overall impression: ibid., p. 15; "Shame cuts more deeply"/"Life will give you": ibid., p. 18; "of that rarest type"/"I remember distinctly": Peter Collier and David Horowitz, *The Fords: An American Epic* (New York: Summit Books, 1987), p. 20; "She taught us": Olson, p. 17; "It is not necessary"/"You see that home": Collier and Horowitz, p. 22; "Every clock": Olson, p. 20; "Father was quick": Ruddiman; "I had seen": Henry Ford (with Samuel Crowther), *My Life and Work* (Garden City, N.Y.: Doubleday, 1923), p. 22; "I learned then": Collier and Horowitz, p. 24; "They put Henry"/"manufactured everything": Reminiscences of Frederick Strauss, FA, acc. 65, p. 3; "Stick in your toenails": Robert Lacey, *Ford: The Men and the Machine* (Boston: Little, Brown, 1986), p. 24; "I have an idea"/"At the end of that first day": Olson, p. 33; "The problem that fascinated him": ibid., p. 35; "Dear Clara": FA, acc. 1, box 1; "had quite a few beaux": Lacey, p. 28; "I remember going home": Elizabeth Breuer, "Henry Ford and the Believer," *Ladies' Home Journal*, Sept. 1923; "Cutting the timber": Olson, p. 45; "How we roared": ibid., p. 47; "It almost broke her heart": ibid., p. 49; "I didn't run": Reminiscences of David O'Donnell, FA, acc. 65, p. 5; Edsel's name: Reminiscences of Clarence Davis and Esther Davis, FA, acc. 65, p. 69.

## 2. The Horse Is Gone

"There is something uncanny": *NYT,* Jan. 3, 1899; "literally carpeted": Clay McShane, *Down the Asphalt Path: The Automobile and the American City* (New York: Columbia University Press, 1994), p. 51; "Before this": Olson, p. 57; "The engine is a vertical one": Frank Donovan, *Wheels for a Nation* (New York: Thomas Y. Crowell, 1965), p. 41; "Henry had all kinds of time": Olson, p. 60; "Henry is making something": Allan Nevins and Frank Ernest Hill, *Ford: The Times, the Man, the Company* (New York: Charles Scribner's Sons, 1954), p. 156; "It was raining": Samuel Marquis, *Henry Ford: An Interpretation* (Boston: Little, Brown, 1923), p. 26; "The wheels on one side": Lacey, p. 44; "Father may have resented": Ruddiman; "Young man": Nevins and Hill, *Ford: The Times,* p. 167; "Well, you won't be seeing": Olson, p. 91; "He was a tall, genteel man": Reminiscences of Irving Bacon, FA, acc. 65, pp. 2–4; "I never saw": Donovan, p. 55; "was almost never alone": Olson, p. 58; "The design of the motor": ibid., p. 98; "If they ask for me": Strauss Reminiscences, p. 53; "I'll never insure": Donovan, p. 81.

## 3. Rearview Mirror:
## Ford the "Automobileer" in 1900

"She's ready": *Detroit News-Tribune,* Feb. 4, 1900; Horse vs. auto: Olson, p. 119.

## 4. Who Can't Afford a Fordmobile?

"We must make the cars": Olson, p. 179; Clara's diary entries/"We are keeping house": FA, acc. 1, box 21; "When I was a tiny child": Olson, p. 149; "Until I discovered this theory": *DT,* Aug. 26, 1928; "That chicken was hit": David L. Lewis, "Harry Bennett, Henry Ford's Tough Guy, Breaks 30 Years of Silence and Tells His Side of the Story," *DFP Magazine,* Jan. 20 and 27, 1974; "Henry had been covering": Olson, p. 146; "Henry has worked": ibid., p. 147; "The roar of those cylinders": Ford, p. 50; "Well, this chariot": Louise B. Clancy and Florence Davies, *The Believer: The Life Story of Mrs. Henry Ford* (New York: Coward-McCann, 1960), p. 60.

## 5. Hunka Tin

"It was skyscraper high": David L. Cohn, *Combustion on Wheels* (New York: Houghton Mifflin, 1943), p. 143; "The ice seemed": Ford, pp. 57–58; "I will build": Olson, p. 186; "Bloomsburg was": Reminiscences of C. C. Housenick, FA, acc. 65, pp. 6–7; "Because of the peculiar nature": E. B. White, *The Second Tree from the Corner: Time Past, Time Future* (New York: Harper & Brothers, 1954), pp. 36–37; "Hunka Tin": David L. Lewis, *The Public Image of Henry Ford* (Detroit, Mich.: Wayne State University Press, 1976), p. 95; "The Little Ford": "The Songs They Sang About Fords," *Ford Times,* June 1978; "I am afraid": Bak, p. 79; "I wish my father": Collier and Horowitz, p. 48.

## 6. The Five-Dollar Day

"We believe in making": *DJ,* Jan. 5, 1914; "I think Edsel": Reminiscences of Frederick Searle, FA, acc. 65, p. 38; "Tell him he can have it": Harry Barnard, *Independent Man: The Life of Senator James Couzens* (New York: Charles Scribner's Sons, 1958), p. 45;

"automobiles will be going": Norman Beasley and George W. Stark, *Made in Detroit* (New York: G. P. Putnam's Sons, 1957), p. 216; Couzens statement: *DJ*, Jan. 5, 1914; "It is this element": *DN*, Jan. 6, 1914; "I felt that Mr. Ford": Joyce Shaw Peterson, *American Automobile Workers 1900–1933* (Albany: State University of New York Press, 1987), p. 58; "one of great importance": *DJ*, Jan. 5, 1914; "Give him a better job": Collier and Horowitz, p. 67; "We began with": Carol Gelderman, *Henry Ford: The Wayward Capitalist* (New York: Dial, 1981), p. 87; "It must not be imagined": Thomas V. DiBacco, *Made in the U.S.A.: The History of American Business* (New York: Harper & Row, 1987), p. 176; "You wouldn't tell them": Peterson, p. 56; "Bill, I have a million dollars": William C. Richards, *The Last Billionaire: Henry Ford* (New York: Charles Scribner's Sons, 1948), p. 203.

## 7. Rearview Mirror:
## The Crystal Palace in 1914

"My father hated his job": Frank Marquart, *An Auto Worker's Journal: The UAW from Crusade to One-Party Union* (University Park: Pennsylvania State University Press, 1975), pp. 5–9; "Of course there was order": Julian Street, "Detroit the Dynamic," *Collier's*, July 4, 1914, in Melvin G. Holli, ed., *Detroit* [Documentary History of American Cities] (New York: New Viewpoints/Franklin Watts, 1976), pp. 134–135.

## 8. War on Several Fronts

"Events were moving": Collier and Horowitz, p. 84; "Forty years ago": *New York Sun*, Jan. 11, 1914, Cited in Rudolph Alvarado and Sonya Alvarado, *Drawing Conclusions on Henry Ford: A Biographical History through Cartoons* (Ann Arbor: University of Michigan Press, 2001), pp. 34–35; "I do not consider the machines": Collier and Horowitz, p. 70; "New York wants war": Robert Conot, *American Odyssey: A Unique History of America Told Through the Life of a Great City* (New York: William Morrow, 1974), p. 181; "We're going to stop the war": Oswald Garrison Villard, *Fighting Years* (New York: Harcourt, Brace, 1939), p. 304; "worse than ineffable folly": quoted in *DFP*, Nov. 27, 1915; "Guess I had better go back": Collier and Horowitz, p. 76; "I was bothered": *NYT*, Jan. 1, 1916; "I don't consider the Ford Peace Ship": Reminiscences of Irving Caesar, FA, acc. 65, p. 22; "I've had enough": Barnard, p. 99; "You cannot publish this": ibid., p. 100; "I might as well": Caroline Latham and David Agresta, *Dodge Dynasty: The Car and the Family That Rocked Detroit* (New York: Harcourt Brace Jovanovich, 1989), pp. 121–122; "There had been considerable talk": ibid., pp. 133–134; "Did you ever before": *DN*, Nov. 4, 1916; Dodge trial testimony: Collier and Horowitz, p. 83; "Where a corporation": Latham and Agresta, p. 139; "After the war": Allan Nevins and Frank Ernest Hill, *Ford: Expansion and Challenge, 1915–1933* (New York: Charles Scribner's Sons, 1957), p. 70; "You call Washington": ibid., p. 143; "Mr. Ford, we are living": ibid., p. 118; "while I am willing": *DN*, Nov. 4, 1918; "unalterably opposed": Harold Studley Gray, *Character "Bad": The Story of a Conscientious Objector*, ed. Kenneth Irving Brown (New York: Harper & Bros., 1934), p. 138; "Young Ford should take": *DSN*, April 13, 1918; "I want no stay-at-home appointment": Patricia Barbara Smith, "In the Wings Was Edsel: A Portrait of the Mysterious Prince," *DFP Magazine*, Oct. 17, 1965; "it took more courage": Nevins and Hill, *Ford: Expansion and Challenge*, p. 78. "The failure of Mr. Ford's son": *DSN*, Oct. 26, 1918; "If Ford allows": *Chicago Tribune*, June 23, 1916; *Tribune* transcripts: Gelderman, pp. 177–179; "History is more or less bunk":

*Chicago Tribune,* May 25, 1916; "slight boyish figure": Collier and Horowitz, p. 88; "They forced us to open": Gelderman, p. 186; "Now the mystery": *Nation,* July 26, 1919; "We sort of like": Lewis, *Public Image,* p. 107.

## 9. Joy Ride

"After the name of HF": Charles E. Sorenson (with Samuel T. Williamson), *My Forty Years with Ford* (New York: W. W. Norton, 1956), p. 27; "to devote my time": Nevins and Hill, *Ford: Expansion and Challenge,* p. 106; "Ford Motor Company has no mortgage": ibid., p. 107; "Of course, there will be no need": *NYT,* July 12, 1919; "HF has reached": Lewis, *Public Image,* p. 111; "A great business": Nevins and Hill, *Ford: Expansion and Challenge,* p. 525; "It would go beyond": Neil Baldwin, *Henry Ford and the Jews: The Mass Production of Hate* (New York: Public Affairs, 2001), p. 194; "We have to recognize": James J. Flink, *The Automobile Age* (Cambridge, Mass.: MIT Press, 1988), p. 114; "This is my business": Norman Beasley, *Knudsen: A Biography* (New York: Whittlesey House, 1947), p. 109; "To my mind": Ford, pp. 91–92; "The old group of executives": Marquis, p. 155; "an industrial fascist": *NYT,* Jan. 8, 1928; "I knew they were all after me": Gelderman, p. 362; "Part of Sorenson's great value": Harry Bennett (as told to Paul Marcus), *We Never Called Him Henry* (New York: Fawcett Books, 1951), pp. 28–29; "He openly tried to foster": ibid., p. 31; "Even among the smallest": Reminiscences of Emil Zoerlein, FA, acc. 65, pp. 66–67; "more people have heard of him": Flink, p. 112; "You know, Henry": Reynold M. Wik, *Henry Ford and Grass-Roots America* (Ann Arbor: University of Michigan Press, 1972), p. 1; "How can a man over sixty": *NYT,* Nov. 1, 1923; "We hope Ford will get": *DN,* Dec. 12, 1921; "Mr. Ford has enough": Clancy and Davies, p. 159; "Hereafter, I am going to see": Nevins and Hill, *Ford: The Times,* p. 586; "He has lived all his life": Sarah T. Bushnell, *The Truth About Henry Ford* (Chicago: Reilly & Lee, 1922), p. 158; "He was not of the profligate type": Bacon Reminiscences, p. 54; "I'm in a peculiar position": Marquis, p. 8; "Make a picture": Bacon Reminiscences, p. 163; "He liked to jump": Davis Reminiscences, p. 59; "If a black cat": Bennett, p. 18; "Gee, Mr. Ford": John Cote Dahlinger and Frances Spatz Leighton, *The Secret Life of Henry Ford* (Indianapolis: Bobbs-Merrill, 1978), p. 46.

## 10. Farewell, Lizzie

"Henry's Made a Lady": "Songs They Sang About Fords"; "The Ford company has always tried": *DN,* March 25, 1922; "I have never been able": undated [1930?] *Detroit Motor News* clipping, Edsel B. Ford file, BHC; "never had a valet": Reminiscences of A. J. Lepine, FA, acc. 65, p. 88; "A feature of his travels": ibid., p. 93; "You ought to be": Nevins and Hill, *Ford: Expansion and Challenge,* p. 62; "God damn it, we are way behind": Gelderman, p. 257; "Sorenson's job": Reminiscences of Harold Hicks, FA, acc. 65, p. 174; "What's over there?": Henry Dominguez, *Edsel Ford and E. T. Gregorie: The Remarkable Design Team and Their Classic Fords of the 1930s and 1940s* (Warrendale, Pa.: Society of Automotive Engineers, 1999), p. 38; "Ford had perhaps": Warren I. Susman, *Culture as History: The Transformation of American Society in the Twentieth Century* (New York: Pantheon, 1985), pp. 139–140. "The only thing wrong": Collier and Horowitz, p. 123; "Poor Lizzie": "Songs They Sang About Fords"; "Father made": Gelderman, p. 255; "We've got a pretty good man": Nevins and Hill, *Ford: Expansion and Challenge,* p. 447; "There stands the car": Garet Garrett, *Henry Ford: The Wild Wheel* (New York: Pantheon, 1952), p. 65; "The New Ford": Alvarado and Alvarado, p. 166; "I was sick":

Dominguez, p. 44; "I have drove Fords": Lewis, *Public Image*, p. 207; "Why Hicks, women don't": Hicks Reminiscences, p. 170; "But, since the drift": Lacey, p. 187.

## 11. *Chronicle of the Neglected Truth*

"Since HF Apologized": Lewis, *Public Image*, p. 147; "I know who started": Gelderman, p. 219; "comes to put its shoulder": Baldwin, p. 79; "Mr. Ford was prejudiced": Lewis, "Harry Bennett, HF's Tough Guy"; "Jewish supremacy in the theatre": Henry Ford, *The International Jew: The World's Foremost Problem*, ed. G. F. Green, reprint (London: n.p., 1948), pp. 145–146; "I am sure": Nevins and Hill, *Ford: Expansion and Challenge*, p. 312; "door to the Ford mind": Baldwin, pp. 95–96; "Everything that was being done": ibid., p. 103; "there had been": Ford, p. 250; "What's wrong, Dr. Franklin?": Collier and Horowitz, p. 104; "Few thinking men": Baldwin, p. 132; "Let's be reasonable": interviews with Bill Kahn and Rosalie Kahn Butzel; HF's apology: Baldwin, pp. 238–240; "The booklets undoubtedly influenced": Lewis, *Public Image*, p. 143; "He made some remarks": Zoerlein Reminiscences, pp. 64–65. "I don't know": Reminiscences of Ernest Liebold, FA, acc. 65, p. 1384.

## 12. *The Little Man in the Basement*

"We Nominate": undated [1935?] *Detroit Athletic Club News* clipping, Harry H. Bennett file, BHC; "There was a lot of drinking": interview with Mark Beltaire; "Do you really want": Bennett, p. 122; "I became his most intimate companion": ibid., p. 5; "I'd always wished": ibid., p. 14; "As often as not": ibid., p. 37; "a profound morbid interest": ibid., p. 65; "It was a dictaphone": George Cantor, "The Ford-Bennett Days: Fear Ruled the Rouge," *DFP Magazine,* March 19, 1972; "I fought too much": Lewis, "Harry Bennett, HF's Tough Guy"; "Harry, never try to outguess me": Bennett, p. 17; "They were all rotten": interview with Al Bardelli; "Everybody was just scared": Reminiscences of Albert Smith, FA, acc. 65, pp. 49–50; "submerged his own interests": Reminiscences of Stanley Ruddiman, FA, acc. 65, pp. 30–31. "He had a way": Hicks Reminiscences, pp. 172–174.

## 13. *Rearview Mirror: The Crown Prince at Work and at Play*

"Shortly after I started to work": Reminiscences of A. A. Backus, FA, acc. 65, pp. 3–18, with minor amendations.

## 14. *Airships and Time Machines*

"The next time": Timothy J. O'Callaghan, *The Aviation Legacy of Henry & Edsel Ford* (Ann Arbor: Proctor Publications, 2000), p. 24; "Well, this is for": Reminiscences of William Stout, FA, acc. 65, p. 108; "I am interested": *Cleveland Plain Dealer,* May 28, 1927, cited in O'Callaghan, p. 190; "Ford wouldent leave": O'Callaghan, p. 79; "The whole thing": ibid., p. 102; HF's interest "more important": Stout Reminiscences, p. 99; Sorenson's influence: ibid., pp. 108–109; "If only Mr. Ford": Walter Karp, "Henry Ford's Village," in *A Sense of History: The Best Writing from the Pages of American Heritage*

(New York: American Heritage/Houghton Mifflin, 1985), p. 664; "Villages which had once": Frederick Lewis Allen, *Only Yesterday: An Informal History of the 1920s* (New York: Harper and Row, 1931), p. 136; "It was a relief for him": Harold K. Skramstad Jr. and Jeanine Head, *An Illustrated History of Henry Ford Museum and Greenfield Village* (Rochester, Mich.: Avon, 1990), p. 5; "When I went to": Lacey, pp. 245–246; "Edison's straight-shot privy": Robert Conot, *A Streak of Luck: The Life and Legend of Thomas Alva Edison* (New York: Seaview, 1979), p. 443; "But, here is Mr. Edison again": Skramstad and Head, pp. 18, 20; "As to HF": Conot, *A Streak of Luck*, p. 445.

## 15. An Invitation to Organize

"The idea that Ford is adored": Edmund Wilson, "Detroit Motors," in Edmund Wilson, *The American Earthquake: A Chronicle of the Roaring Twenties, the Great Depression, and the Dawn of the New Deal*, reprint (New York: Da Capo, 1996), p. 239; "I have never confronted": Helen Hall, "When Detroit's Out of Gear," *Survey*, April 1, 1930, in Holli, p. 170; "People don't realize": interview with Doug Fraser; "It's a good thing": *NYT*, Sept. 7, 1930; "These are really good times": "Interview, Model 1931," *Outlook and Independent*, March 25, 1931, cited in Lewis, *Public Image*, p. 233; "immunity to social ambitions": Wilson, p. 235; "Ford hates the New York bankers": Cantor, "Ford-Bennett Days"; "The blacklist in Detroit": Richard Frankensteen oral history, WRA, p. 31; "We used to drive our men": Peterson, pp. 55–56; "It used to be a saying": Martin Jensen oral history, WRA, p. 6; "You Gotta Fight That Line": Victor G. Reuther, *The Brothers Reuther and the Story of the UAW* (Boston: Houghton Mifflin, 1976), pp. 198–199; "He would walk into a department": Jensen oral history, p. 9; "There were a number of jobs": ibid., p. 6; "I didn't have $25": *DN*, Feb. 13, 1990; "The ordeal that I hated most": John Zaremba oral history, WRA, p. 5; "It's worse than the army": Wilson, pp. 219–220; "working conditions were dehumanizing": interview with Paul Boatin; "I knew there was something wrong": Frankensteen oral history, pp. 4–5.

## 16. Bullets and Frescoes

"Edsel resented me": Lewis, "Harry Bennett, HF's Tough Guy"; "One day they were setting": Steve Babson et al., *Working Detroit: The Making of a Union Town* (New York: Adama, 1984), pp. 57–58; "They were the only game": William H. Hackett, "Working for Ford During the '30s: Glad to Have a Job But Scared to Go to Work," *Vista*, March 1978; "The marchers were heterogeneous": *DFP*, March 8, 1932; "Who are the leaders here": Bennett, p. 93; "I would guess": Babson et al., p. 59; "Dearborn pavements": Sidney Fine, *Frank Murphy: The Detroit Years* (Ann Arbor: University of Michigan Press, 1975), p. 404; "The newspaper stories": Bennett, p. 94; "They had a mutual interest": interview with Linda Downs; "I have found": Laura Rose Ashlee, "Diego Rivera, Edsel Ford and Detroit Industry," *Michigan History*, May/June 1994; "Rivera knew": Boatin interview; "I had the feeling": interview with Lucienne Bloch; "He was far above the rest": Joe McCarthy, "The Ford Family," *Holiday*, June 1957; "Diego Rivera's method": Stephen Pope Dimitroff, *Apprentice to Diego Rivera in Detroit and Fresco Workshops Manual* (n.p., pp. 19–20; "Diego was a glutton for work": ibid., p. 27; "The machines look": Bloch interview; "Rivera successfully captured": Ashlee; "Senor Rivera has perpetrated": Don Lochbiler, *Detroit's Coming of Age, 1873 to 1973* (Detroit, Mich.: Wayne State University Press, 1973), p. 300; "I admire Mr. Rivera's spirit": Ashlee; "fused together": Diego Rivera, *My Art, My Life* (Secaucus, N.J.: Citadel, 1960), p. 197.

## 17. A Matter of Style

"So gradually has Edsel": Glenn F. Jenkins, "The Rise of Edsel Ford," *DSN*, July 11, 1936; "Edsel Ford's involvement": Lacey, p. 330; "You don't take": Bacon Reminiscences, p. 223; "Let them fail": Barnard, p. 229; "He had his own way"/"All the Ford executives": Dominguez, p. 51; "That's the Edsel Ford": interview with Edsel Ford II; "bitterly sarcastic": Hicks Reminiscences, p. 48.

## 18. The Overpass

"That one incident": Frankensteen oral history, p. 69; "I have never bargained": *The Rise of Organized Labor: Worker Security and Employer Rights* (Middletown, Conn.: Xerox Educational Publications, 1977), p. 50; "They were called 'gallopini'": Boatin interview; "I've picked someone": Sorenson, p. 260; "workers had been promised": Reuther, p. 149; "The next thing I knew": Robert Kanter oral history, WRA, pp. 21–22; "There were ten photographers": ibid., p. 24; "affair was deliberately provoked": *Rise of Organized Labor,* p. 48; "Technical trespass has never": ibid., p. 51; "What made Bennett": Harry Ross oral history, WRA, p. 65; "If there was anyone": ibid, p. 38; "The hurtful thing": Allan Nevins and Frank Ernest Hill, *Ford: Decline and Rebirth, 1933–1962* (New York: Charles Scribner's Sons, 1962), p. 234; "It is pathetic": Ross oral history, p. 64.

## 19. Rearview Mirror: Battling "Fordism" in 1937

"I remember one day": This chapter is based on the author's interviews and correspondence with Bill May and an untitled manuscript written by May in 1986.

## 20. A New Social Order

"The day they walked": Nick DiGaetano oral history, WRA, p. 61; "I didn't wear a mask": *DN*, Feb. 13, 1990; "All wars, labor unions": Lacey, p. 372; "They'll have an awful fight": *Rise of Organized Labor,* p. 51; "I'd come home so tired": Bardelli interview; "It still had his initials": interview with Bruce Simpson; "It was Lovett's responsibility": Ford R. Bryan, *Henry's Lieutenants* (Detroit, Mich.: Wayne State University Press, 1993), p. 185; "Say Fred": Ford R. Bryan, *Beyond the Model T: The Other Ventures of Henry Ford,* rev. ed. (Detroit, Mich.: Wayne State University Press, 1997), p. 86; "Now the music": Lewis, *Public Image,* p. 328; "We called the strike": Studs Terkel, *Hard Times* (New York: Avon, 1971), p. 167; "He told me to arm": Bennett, p. 136; "Well, you've got a plant": ibid., p. 137; "Mr. Ford gave in": ibid., p. 136; "perhaps the greatest"/ "I'm not going to sign": Sorenson, p. 268; "Who is this man": ibid., p. 256; "it was our conjecture": Frankensteen oral history, p. 69; "We have decided": Nevins and Hill, *Ford: Decline and Rebirth,* p. 166; "It was a little tough": Terkel, p. 169; "Don't ever discredit": Sorenson, p. 271.

## 21. You Know How Father Is

"You're lucky to have"/"Edsel is over there": *DFP,* May 27, 1943; "You can live as long": Bennett, p. 164; "Aren't you president?": Collier and Horowitz, p. 179; "a sort of Grand

Canyon": Charles A. Lindbergh, *The Wartime Journals of Charles Lindbergh* (New York: Harcourt Brace Jovanovich, 1970), p. 613; "roar of the machinery": Alan Clive, *State of War: Michigan in World War II* (Ann Arbor: University of Michigan Press, 1979), p. 30; "I'm making fine progress": Bacon Reminiscences, p. 175; "Stop this talk": Sorenson, p. 256; "For two cents": Collier and Horowitz, p. 184; "Oh, we had some experiences": Lindbergh, p. 615; "became quite a sick man": Lepine Reminiscences, pp. 63–64. "Grandfather is responsible": Sorenson, p. 321; "When word was flashed": *DN*, May 26, 1943; "I knew that Edsel": Bennett, p. 166; "In his official capacities": *DFP*, May 27, 1943; "In retrospect, Edsel emerges": Lewis, *Public Image*, p. 367; "it was very strange": interview with Ford R. Bryan; "Well, Harry": Bennett, p. 165.

## 22. Running on Empty

"One time Mr. Ford": Reminiscences of Joseph Zaroski, FA, acc. 65, p. 23; "I'm pretty sure": Reminiscences of Rufus Wilson, FA, acc. 65, p. 34; "I wouldn't know where I was going": Gelderman, p. 364; "Joe, we've got to go back": Collier and Horowitz, p. 197; "The whole official structure": Dominguez, p. 279; "By the time I knew Mr. Ford": Cantor, "Ford-Bennett Days"; "Your daddy should be home": interviews with George Ebling Jr. and Virginia Ebling; "I was flunking engineering": Booton Herndon, *Ford: An Unconventional Biography of the Men and Their Times* (New York: Weybright and Talley, 1969), p. 60; "The navy taught me": Walter Hayes, *Henry: A Life of Henry Ford II* (New York: Grove Weidenfeld, 1990), pp. 12–13. "were the funniest thing"/ "Come on, Harry": Bennett, p. 167; "Everybody likes": "Ford Heritage," *Fortune*, June 1944; "Now I want to ask you": Lewis, *Public Image*, p. 400; "This thing killed my father": Robert Couglan, "Co-Captains in Ford's Battle for Supremacy," *Life*, Feb. 28, 1955; "Henry, I've got wonderful news": Collier and Horowitz, p. 208; "You're taking over": Herndon, p. 67; "Don't make the mistake": Collier and Horowitz, p. 209; "As soon as I turned around": interview with Dominick Vettraino; "liar and a crook": Lewis, "Harry Bennett, HF's Tough Guy"; "Well, I guess Harry": Herndon, p. 187; "Well, this is where": Lewis, *Public Image*, p. 473; "I think Mr. Ford": Reminiscences of Rosa Buhler, FA, acc. 65, p. 17; "No other man": *DN*, April 9, 1947; "It was remembered how": Don Lochbiler, *Detroit's Coming of Age, 1873 to 1973* (Detroit, Mich.: The Detroit News/Wayne State University Press, 1973) p. 379.

## 23. Rearview Mirror: The Last Years of the Flivver King

"Edsel and his father": Reminiscences of John McIntyre, FA, acc. 65, pp. 2–34, with minor amendations.

## Postscript: Ford after Ford

"At Ford's today": Lewis, "Harry Bennett, HF's Tough Guy"; "By fighting the unions": David Halberstam, *The Reckoning* (New York: William Morrow, 1986), pp. 164–165. "He rarely does anything": Patricia Barbara Smith, "Henry Ford and Son: Love and Tension in the Epic Struggle," *DFP Magazine*, Oct. 24, 1965; "It fails somewhat": Lewis, *Public Image*, p. 368; "I hope someday": *DFP*, Jan. 10, 1974; "I had a long talk": Edsel

Ford II interview; "Best of the Ford boys"/"He never knew how much": Lewis, "Harry Bennett, HF's Tough Guy"; "Those were the days": Collier and Horowitz, p. 432; "There are no crown princes": ibid., p. 418; "You have to realize": Edsel Ford II interview; "Despite his intellect": "CEOs Under Fire: Can Ford Save Ford?" *Fortune,* Nov. 18, 2002; "padded room": *DFP,* June 12, 2003; "I think the family": Edsel Ford II interview; "didn't invent the automobile": "The Businessman of the Century," *Fortune,* Nov. 22, 1999.

# Selected Bibliography

Allen, Frederick Lewis. *Only Yesterday: An Informal History of the 1920's.* New York: Harper and Row, 1931.

Alvarado, Rudolph, and Sonya Alvarado. *Drawing Conclusions on Henry Ford: A Biographical History through Cartoons.* Ann Arbor: University of Michigan Press, 2001.

Babson, Steve, Ron Alpern, Dave Elsila, and John Revitte. *Working Detroit: The Making of a Union Town.* New York: Adama, 1984.

Baldwin, Neil. *Henry Ford and the Jews: The Mass Production of Hate.* New York: Public Affairs, 2001.

Barnard, Harry. *Independent Man: The Life of Senator James Couzens.* New York: Charles Scribner's Sons, 1958.

Baskin, Alex. "Ford Hunger March." *Labor History,* summer 1972.

Beasley, Norman. *Knudsen: A Biography.* New York: McGraw-Hill, 1947.

Bennett, Harry (as told to Paul Marcus). *We Never Called Him Henry.* New York: Fawcett, 1951.

Bonsall, Thomas E. "Edsel: The Forgotten Ford." *Automobile Quarterly* 29, no. 3 (1991).

Bridenstine, James A. *Edsel and Eleanor Ford House.* Woodlawn, Md.: Wolk Press, 1988.

Bryan, Ford R. *Henry's Lieutenants.* Detroit: Wayne State University Press, 1993.

Bryan, Ford R. *Beyond the Model T: The Other Ventures of Henry Ford.* Revised ed. Detroit: Wayne State University Press, 1997.

Bryan, Ford R. *Clara: Mrs. Henry Ford.* Dearborn, Mich.: Ford Books/Wayne State University Press, 2001.

Clancy, Louise B., and Florence Davies. *The Believer: The Life Story of Mrs. Henry Ford.* New York: Coward-McCann, 1960.

Cohn, David L. *Combustion on Wheels.* New York: Houghton Mifflin, 1943.

Collier, Peter, and David Horowitz. *The Fords: An American Epic.* New York: Summit Books, 1987.

Conot, Robert. *American Odyssey: A Unique History of America Told through the Life of a Great City.* New York: William Morrow, 1974.

Dahlinger, John Cote, and Frances Spatz Leighton. *The Secret Life of Henry Ford.* Indianapolis: Bobbs-Merrill, 1978.

Dominguez, Henry. *Edsel Ford and E. T. Gregorie: The Remarkable Design Team and Their Classic Fords of the 1930s and 1940s.* Warrendale, Pa.: Society of Automotive Engineers, 1999.

Downs, Linda, and Mary Jane Jacob. *The Rouge: The Image of Industry in the Art of Charles Sheeler and Diego Rivera.* Detroit, Mich.: Detroit Institute of Arts, 1978.

Ferry, W. Hawkins. *The Legacy of Albert Kahn.* Detroit, Mich.: Wayne State University Press, 1970.

Fine, Sidney. *The Automobile Under the Blue Eagle.* Ann Arbor: University of Michigan Press, 1963.

Fine, Sidney. *Frank Murphy: The Detroit Years.* Ann Arbor: University of Michigan Press, 1975.

Flink, James J. *The Automobile Age.* Cambridge, Mass.: MIT Press, 1988.

Ford, Henry (with Samuel Crowther). *My Life and Work.* Garden City, N.Y.: Doubleday, 1923.

Garrett, Garet. *Henry Ford: The Wild Wheel.* New York: Pantheon, 1952.

Gelderman, Carol. *Henry Ford: The Wayward Capitalist.* New York: Dial, 1981.

Greenleaf, William. *From These Beginnings: The Early Philanthropics of Henry and Edsel Ford, 1911–1936.* Detroit, Mich.: Wayne State University Press, 1964.

Greenleaf, William. *Monopoly on Wheels: Henry Ford and the Selden Automobile Patent.* Detroit, Mich.: Wayne State University Press, 1967.

Halberstam, David. *The Reckoning.* New York: William Morrow, 1986.

Hayes, Walter. *Henry: A Life of Henry Ford II.* New York: Grove Weidenfeld, 1990.

Herndon, Booton. *Ford: An Unconventional Biography of the Men and Their Times.* New York: Weybright and Talley, 1969.

Hershey, Burnet. *The Odyssey of Henry Ford and the Great Peace Ship.* New York: Taplinger, 1967.

Jardim, Anne. *The First Henry Ford: A Study in Personality and Business Leadership.* Cambridge, Mass.: MIT Press, 1970.

Karp, Walter. "Henry Ford's Village." In *A Sense of History: The Best Writing from the Pages of American Heritage.* New York: American Heritage Press/ Houghton Mifflin, 1985.

Kimes, Beverly Rae. *The Cars That Henry Ford Built.* Princeton, N.J.: Princeton Publishing, 1978.

Kraft, Barbara S. *The Peace Ship: Henry Ford's Pacifist Adventure in the First World War.* New York: Macmillan, 1978.

Lacey, Robert. *Ford: The Men and the Machine.* Boston: Little, Brown, 1986.

Lasky, Victor. *Never Complain, Never Explain: The Story of Henry Ford II.* New York: Richard Marek, 1981.

Latham, Caroline, and David Agresta. *Dodge Dynasty: The Car and the Family That Rocked Detroit.* New York: Harcourt Brace Jovanovich, 1989.

Lee, Albert. *Henry Ford and the Jews.* New York: Stein and Day, 1980.

Leonard, Jonathan Norton. *The Tragedy of Henry Ford.* New York: G. P. Putnam's Sons, 1932.

Lewis, David L. "Harry Bennett, Henry Ford's Tough Guy, Breaks 30 Years of Silence and Tells His Side of the Story." *Detroit Free Press Magazine,* January 20 and 27, 1974.

Lewis, David L. *The Public Image of Henry Ford: An American Folk Hero and His Company.* Detroit, Mich.: Wayne State University Press, 1976.

Lichtenstein, Nelson. *The Most Dangerous Man in Detroit: Walter Reuther and the Fate of American Labor.* New York: Basic Books, 1995.

Marquis, Samuel. *Henry Ford: An Interpretation.* Boston: Little, Brown, 1923.

McShane, Clay. *Down the Asphalt Path: The Automobile and the American City.* New York: Columbia University Press, 1994.

Meyer, Stephen, III. *The Five Dollar Day: Labor Management and Social Control in the Ford Motor Company, 1908–1921.* Albany: State University of New York Press, 1981.

Nevins, Allan, and Frank Ernest Hill. *Ford: The Times, the Man, the Company.* New York: Charles Scribner's Sons, 1954.

Nevins, Allan, and Frank Ernest Hill. *Ford: Expansion and Challenge, 1915–1933.* New York: Charles Scribner's Sons, 1957.

Nevins, Allan, and Frank Ernest Hill. *Ford: Decline and Rebirth, 1933–1962.* New York: Charles Scribner's Sons, 1962.

O'Callaghan, Timothy J. *The Aviation Legacy of Henry and Edsel Ford.* Ann Arbor: Proctor, 2000.

Olson, Sidney. *Young Henry Ford: A Picture History of the First Forty Years.* Reprint. Detroit: Wayne State University Press, 1997.

Peterson, Joyce Shaw. *American Automobile Workers, 1900–1933.* Albany: State University of New York Press, 1987.

Reuther, Victor G. *The Brothers Reuther and the Story of the UAW.* Boston: Houghton Mifflin, 1976.

Richards, William C. *The Last Billionaire: Henry Ford.* New York: Charles Scribner's Sons, 1948.

Rivera, Diego. *My Art, My Life.* Secaucus, N.J.: Citadel, 1960.

Ruddiman, Margaret Ford. "Memories of My Brother, Henry Ford." *Michigan History,* Sept. 1953.

Simonds, William A. *Henry Ford: His Life, His Work, His Genius.* Indianapolis: Bobbs-Merrill, 1943.

Skramstad, Harold K., Jr., and Jeanine Head. *An Illustrated History of Henry Ford Museum and Greenfield Village.* Rochester, Mich.: Avon, 1990.

Smith, Patricia Barbara. "In the Wings Was Edsel: A Portrait of the Mysterious Prince." *Detroit Free Press Magazine,* Oct. 17, 1965.

Smith, Patricia Barbara. "Henry Ford and Son: Love and Tension in the Epic Struggle." *Detroit Free Press Magazine,* Oct. 24, 1965.

Sorenson, Charles E. (with Samuel T. Williamson). *My Forty Years with Ford.* New York: W. W. Norton, 1956.

Stern, Philip Van Doren. *Tin Lizzie: The Story of the Fabulous Model T Ford.* New York: Simon & Schuster, 1955.

Sterne, Margaret. *The Passionate Eye: The Life of William R. Valentiner.* Detroit, Mich.: Wayne State University Press, 1980.

Twork, Eva O'Neal. *Henry Ford and Benjamin B. Lovett: The Dancing Billionaire and the Dancing Master.* Detroit, Mich.: Harlo Press, 1982.

Warnock, C. Gayle. *The Edsel Affair.* Paradise Valley, Ariz.: Pro West, 1980.

Wik, Reynold M. *Henry Ford and Grass-Roots America.* Ann Arbor: University of Michigan Press, 1972.

Wilson, Edmund. "Detroit Motors." In Edmund Wilson, *The American Earthquake: A Chronicle of the Roaring Twenties, the Great Depression, and the Dawn of the New Deal.* Reprint. New York: Da Capo, 1996.

Wolfe, Bertram D. *Diego Rivera—His Life and Times.* New York: Knopf, 1939.

Woodford, Frank B., and Arthur M. Woodford. *All Our Yesterdays: A Brief History of Detroit.* Detroit, Mich.: Wayne State University Press, 1969.

# *Picture Credits*

Page 6, collections of Henry Ford Museum & Greenfield Village; page 10, Burton Historical Collection; page 11, collections of Henry Ford Museum & Greenfield Village Burton Historical Collection; page 15, collections of Henry Ford Museum & Greenfield Village; page 16, author's collection; page 24, collections of Henry Ford Museum & Greenfield Village; page 26, collections of Henry Ford Museum & Greenfield Village; page 27, author's collection; page 33, author's collection; page 36, collections of Henry Ford Museum & Greenfield Village; page 40, author's collection; page 46, collections of Henry Ford Museum & Greenfield Village; page 49, collections of Henry Ford Museum & Greenfield Village; page 53, collections of Henry Ford Museum & Greenfield Village; page 56, author's collection; page 58, author's collection; page 60, collections of Henry Ford Museum & Greenfield Village; page 61, author's collection; page 62, author's collection; page 70, author's collection; page 74, collections of Henry Ford Museum & Greenfield Village; page 76, author's collection; page 77, Burton Historical Collection; page 80, author's collection; page 91, collections of Henry Ford Museum & Greenfield Village; page 92, author's collection; page 94, collections of Henry Ford Museum & Greenfield Village; page 98, from *Drawing Conclusions on Henry Ford*; page 104, collections of Henry Ford Museum & Greenfield Village; page 109, collections of Henry Ford Museum & Greenfield Village; page 111, collections of Henry Ford Museum & Greenfield Village; page 119, Burton Historical Collection; page 123, collections of Henry Ford Museum & Greenfield Village; page 128, Balthazar Korab; page 132, collections of Henry Ford Museum & Greenfield Village; page 133, author's collection; page 136, from *Drawing Conclusions on Henry Ford*; page 138, collections of Henry Ford Museum & Greenfield Village; page 140, author's collection; page 145, collections of Henry Ford Museum & Greenfield Village; page 146, collections of Henry Ford Museum & Greenfield Village; page 148, Albert Kahn Associates; page 155, archives of Labor and Urban Affairs;<None> page 159, Burton Historical Collection; page 167, collections of Henry Ford Museum & Greenfield Village; page 169, author's collection; page 175, archives of Labor and Urban Affairs; page 176, Burton Historical Collection; page 177, collections of Henry Ford Museum & Greenfield Village; page 179, collections of Henry Ford Museum & Greenfield Village; page 183, collections of Henry Ford Museum & Greenfield Village; page 186, collections of Henry Ford Museum & Greenfield Village; page 198, Burton Historical Collection; page 203, Detroit Free Press; page 204, Detroit Institute of Arts; page 206, Albert Kahn Associates; page 208, Detroit Institute of Arts; page 213, collections of Henry Ford Museum & Greenfield Village; page 216, author's collection; page 219, Detroit Institute of Arts; page 223, Burton Historical Collection; page 225, archives of Labor and Urban Affairs;

page 226, archives of Labor and Urban Affairs; page 227, archives of Labor and Urban Affairs; page 232, author's collection; page 233, archives of Labor and Urban Affairs; page 243, collections of Henry Ford Museum & Greenfield Village; page 246, archives of Labor and Urban Affairs; page 247, archives of Labor and Urban Affairs; page 253, author's collection; page 256, Burton Historical Collection; page 259, collections of Henry Ford Museum & Greenfield Village; page 267, collections of Henry Ford Museum & Greenfield Village; page 280, collections of Henry Ford Museum & Greenfield Village; page 283, collections of Henry Ford Museum & Greenfield Village; page 288, Burton Historical Collection; page 291, author's collection.

# *Index*